THE LOOSE SCREW

THE LOOSE SCREW

JIM DAWKINS

APEX PUBLISHING LTD

First published in 2005, Reprinted and Updated in 2006, 2007 and 2008 by
Apex Publishing Ltd
PO Box 7086, Clacton on Sea, Essex, CO15 5WN, England

www.apexpublishing.co.uk

British Library Cataloguing-in-Publication Data
A catalogue record for this book
is available from the British Library

ISBN 1-904444-61-X   978-1-904444-61-9

Typeset in 10pt Clarity Serif SF

Production Manager: Chris Cowlin

Cover Design: Andrew Macey

Printed and bound in Great Britain

CONTENTS

ACKNOWLEDGMENTS

There are a great many people who have helped me over the years while compiling the contents of this book. I am sure that I have bent the ears of many that are close to me with my enthusiasm while writing it - none more so than my partner Natasha, who has put up with the last six years of research and rewrites. She was of course there when, disgusted with the constant aggressive and violent acts of brutality and vindictiveness that I witnessed on a daily basis being carried out by a certain element of power-crazy prison officers against prisoners, I felt I had no choice but to turn my back on what I found to be a corrupt and out-of-control Prison Service. She has also seen the bouts of stress and depression I suffered as a result of the time I spent as part of that institution and therefore agreed that it was important for me to make my findings public so that others, who would otherwise be ignorant that such behaviour is encouraged and condoned by senior management in the Prison Service, could read about it. It has not been easy for her to put up with me, but she has always supported me and for that I thank you and love you very much.

I would also like to thank some men who have become very good friends to me and have offered me their support and wisdom while writing this book: firstly, my pal Charlie Bronson, who has been a great supporter and firm friend of mine for the last 12 years - Chaz, hang in there mate and I will see you for that pint in no time; Joey Pyle, who has become a good pal and by whom I have been privileged to have been made welcome - a true legend in the London underworld; Dave Courtney, who has been invaluable in sharing with me his experience of writing books and with whom I have shared many funny moments reminiscing about the time we were both at Belmarsh Prison; Tel Currie, who apart from being a very successful boxing promoter is also a very talented writer with a number of highly recommended titles to his name and a staunch and loyal friend to all that have earned his trust - thank you Tel for all your support to me and Charlie and Ronnie Biggs, and indeed all the others that you put yourself out to help in times of need - you are a true gentleman; Roy Shaw, with whom I have enjoyed many good times listening to his often hilarious and sometimes sad accounts of the time he spent in 18 different prisons, including Broadmoor special hospital, and who has kindly provided me with a glowing review; and Andy Jones, owner of the 'crime through time' museum at Little Dean jail Gloucestershire, who has been kind enough to display some of my uniforms and memorabilia in his collection. Special thanks must also go to Lorna Smith and the other members of the Prison Chat UK website team, who have all been very kind with their reviews and a great help in spreading the word about my the book - you are all doing a great job, so keep up the good work girls. Finally, I would like to thank all the other 'chaps' who have welcomed me into their trust and I know have all offered me their support, and everyone that has written reviews after reading the first edition of the book - they have played a very important role in boosting my confidence in writing this second edition.

FOREWORD BY DAVE COURTNEY OBE

Hello people, it's Dave Courtney OBE here. Please let me tell you about my pal Jim Dawkins. I have known him for some ten years and he was always known as a very fair bloke, even when he was on the other side of the fence, and seeing as though I met him while on remand in the special category A unit at HMP Belmarsh and he was one of the screws locking me up I would say that was the other side of the fence wouldn't you, ha, ha, ha!

Anyway, he became a very good pal of Charlie Bronson, Joe Pyle, and a good few of the other chaps and is known in Civvy Street, and has completed his first book and it is a fucking eye opening and very educational read as it looks at the situation of being in prison from the other side. Jim has more than done enough with the content of this book and the very disturbing documentary he has made with me, an ex-policeman and woman, an ex-traffic warden, barrister and magistrate and of course his good self as "The Loose Screw" to let me know the whose side of the fence he is on. I wish him well with this book. We all know that he is not going to be on the top of any of the authorities Christmas card list and for that Jim I think you are a brave man and I salute you.

It is so important that this book is on the crime shelf, on a scale of one to ten I would give it – 10! It dot-coms all the other chaps books and what they say. Once someone like Jim writes a book it is very enlightening to say the least about the goings-on of a prison officer, it makes all our stories more believable and true. I personally have grabbed hold of Jim Dawkins, especially as there is a chapter about me in this book and now drag him around everywhere I go verifying all my stories and so have all the other chaps. Where we might not all get on with some of the other boys that have wrote books we all get on with Mr Dawkins because he verifies everything we are saying so read this book or fucking else... dot com.

FOREWORD BY CHARLES BRONSON

I first came across Jim in the Max Secure unit at Belmarsh back in 1993. I was, at the time, flying around the jails like a lunatic with a rocket up his arse. Jim was one of those guys that stood out from the rest. It's very difficult to explain it, but some people just stick out; they're not the same as the rest. It's the same in any walk of life; some are just special. It's no secret what I think of the system and the muppets that work in it - hell, I've put enough of them on their arses - but when I come across a genuine guy, the guy gets respect off me no matter what he does for a living. My motto has always been: somebody has got to lock my door and if they do it right and don't annoy me who am I to slag them off. Fuck with me and it's war.

Jim treated me decent. Some days he would come in with a black eye or a tooth smashed out - he liked a battle. Still, what squaddie don't? Jim was just Jim, a man of the world, a fighter, and I liked the guy. He gave me a dictionary, which I've still got today. It's falling to bits, but I've still got it coz I do love a dictionary. It's only a small one, but it's perfect for me - a small thing to most, but massive to me - and I never forget such things. Jim was once on duty as the escort assigned to take me to another jail. Them days I travelled naked and wrapped up in a body belt. On that journey he snapped off my radio aerial. At the time I was fuming, but it was an accident. When we arrived at Bristol jail I was put straight into the strongbox and they took me out of the belt. I shook Jim's hand and told the rest to fuck off - the Bristol screws I never spoke to at all. I shat on the floor and covered the box with it - that's how I am.

If they was all like Jim I'd never be in jail today. I've now spent 26 years caged up, 23 years of that in Solitary. I've been at war for all this time. But I take my hat off to guys like Jim and, believe me, there are few like him. So when I do get to meet one, I won't take liberties. I wish him luck with his book as I believe he has a great story to tell, and it took bottle to do what he did. Lots would love to do it, but they've not got the bottle. They are dreamers; they only know one way: yes sir, no sir, three bags full of shit sir. Shall I kiss your ass now sir or later sir? They are grassing one another up just to climb the ladder. How can you respect such treachery? You can't. Jim saw all this and said, "I'm off". Now he tells it how it is for you all to see. That's what I call bottle. Yes, it's shocking, but it's about time somebody told the truth about our jails. Jim's a great guy, and a friend to me. He's earned respect. I admire a true fighter.

Dedicated to the loving memory of my
grandparents and my Uncle Clive.

*"Power tends to corrupt
and absolute power
corrupts absolutely"*
- Lord Acton, 1834-1902

INTRODUCTION

"You are fucking mad you are, Jim," Charlie Bronson said to me one afternoon while we were playing scrabble on the exercise yard in HMP Belmarsh's Category A segregation unit. "That's rich coming from you," I replied to the only man I know who has come out of Broadmoor with a certificate to say he has been certified sane. Many of you may agree with Charlie and think that I, a prison officer, must be missing a few marbles to be playing scrabble on my own with Charlie Bronson in the heat of a summer's afternoon. If you do, all I can say is that you obviously do not know Charlie as I have come to know him over the years. Hopefully when you have finished this book you will understand a little more about the man behind the myth.

That particular afternoon I was dressed in a grey prison-issue vest, a pair of blue prison-issue pyjama bottoms cut down to my knees and a pair of black plastic prison boots, so I may have looked a bit odd for a prison officer. When we first went out on the yard after I had agreed to help Charlie with a bit of training, I had forgotten to inform the control room of our plans. Consequently, when they saw me through the camera running around the yard with Charlie running closely behind me they raised the alarm and sent the mufti squad in as they thought Charlie had escaped and was trying to chase a nonce to give him a slap. Cheeky bastards - what were they trying to say?!

Of course, not every prison officer was privileged enough to play scrabble with Charlie, not least because most don't take the time to get to know him and build up the mutual trust and respect we have developed for each other. It took a couple of weeks for us to begin to trust one another, as I had only heard terrible rumours about him. Charlie, on the other hand, had only experienced mistrust by the Prison Service and had suffered terribly at the hands of some of my then colleagues, as you will read later. Over the first weeks after our initial meeting we swapped stories - some

1

funny, some not - of our different experiences, and in doing so we formed an unusual friendship that has remained to this day.

It was Charlie who provided the main inspiration for this book and encouraged me to empty my head into the pages you are about to read. "It's going to blow them all away, Jim. It will be a number one bestseller," he would constantly tell me. "It's never been done before, Jim. No one else has got the minerals to speak out about the prison system, Go for gold." So I did, and with those words ringing in my ears I sat down in front of my ancient computer and began tapping away with both index fingers. I am no typist and the fact that half my life's memories have been drowned in cheap lager over the years has meant it has taken almost six years to bring you the finished article. I have focused on Charlie predominantly in this Introduction, as he has been such a big influence while writing this book, but please don't think that the book is solely about Charlie.

There are, of course, numerous other stories featured that relate to my experiences so far as well as to umpteen other prison-related incidents that do not involve Charlie but are drawn from every area I have worked in within the three prisons in which I was employed. I have devoted a complete chapter, for example, to a man who was once just as feared as Charlie, both in the prison system and indeed outside, but who since leaving the service I have been privileged to call my friend - Dave Courtney OBE. Dave has been a great influence and a great help to me while writing this book, and I have also had the pleasure of being made welcome at his home and sharing some very funny times since appearing in the many shows he performs all over the country and attending numerous book-signing and charity events with him. So I am sure that any readers that have experienced prison life, or indeed have friends, family or loved ones who have spent or are still spending time at her Majesty's pleasure, will be able to relate to what I am saying. I only hope that by writing these memoirs it may shame the bad element that is still rife in our prisons and encourage those prison officers who do wish to carry out their duties professionally to have the courage to stand up to those who don't. I know it is hard, and I have been guilty myself, as you will read later, of not being strong enough at times to make such a stand, but I have learnt my lessons and made my decisions and remember the words of a wise old man: "The strongest man you will ever meet is the man who has the courage to admit his own weaknesses".

Although I initially intended to write solely about my prison experiences, I found it easier to start at the beginning and surprised myself at the variety of memories I unlocked along the way. I have not described all my exploits or had chance to mention everyone I have met in my life, and I have also abbreviated or changed the names of some of those to whom I have referred in order to protect their privacy. It has never been my intention to embarrass or offend any particular individual, so I do apologize if I have. I wanted to write the book just as it came out of my head, and all you read are my own personal views and opinions of my experiences as I remember them, with no outside influences.

I have not had the benefit of a ghost writer and have had the entire book published with nothing changed from my original manuscript, apart from a few spelling mistakes, but I hope this will only add to the realism of its contents, and indeed many of the reviews I have received to date reflect on the openness and honesty that are so apparent in the pages within. This was my intention - to give you my true views and opinions and highlight my flaws and mistakes, thereby giving a totally frank account of what I have witnessed, warts and all. I am sure that certain people will not agree with some of my opinions, and others, particularly the elements involved in some of the cowardly acts of bullying and mindless, unprofessional violence within the prison system, who will no doubt cross me off their Christmas card list, but as the old saying goes: " The truth hurts".

I hope you will warm to the humour within these pages, but I also know you will be shocked by the accounts, all of which are true, relating to the behaviour of certain prison staff that I have witnessed. As Charlie predicts, it is extremely unlikely that a book like this will ever be seen again, as it is just not the done thing for prison officers to write about what goes on within our prison walls. So read on, and I hope you enjoy reading it as much as I have enjoyed writing it.

1
"OUR GANG'S BIGGER THAN THEIR GANG"

My shirt was soaked with sweat and clung uncomfortably to my aching body under my heavy black fire-protective riot overalls. My head was pulsating painfully and felt as though it had swollen to twice its normal size and was about to explode from the tight confines of my riot helmet. I wearily surveyed the wreckage, which had until about two hours earlier been the contents of spur three on the high-security Category A unit at London's notorious Belmarsh Prison, through the visor of my helmet. Not that I could see much, as my vision was almost totally obscured by the moisture that had collected on it from my erratic breathing, and it was still in the down position as I could not muster the energy or the motivation even to raise it up. There seemed little point, as there was nothing worth looking at through the Perspex glass that screened me from the scene of destruction on the spur. I had originally left my helmet on to muffle the sounds of protests being shouted from the now full segregation unit, but even they had ceased, as the prisoners who now occupied the strip cells within were probably as fatigued as I felt following the battle we had just fought. They knew the drill only too well and would by now have realised that their shouts would be to no avail as no one would go to answer them for hours yet. It was standard practice just to leave them to tire themselves out in a cooling-off process and they would by now be huddled in the corner of their bare cells, naked apart from the canvas strip suit they would have found on the floor of the cell, disoriented and licking the wounds that most would have received during their transit from the spur to the segregation unit.

Everything seemed eerily quiet after the din of the events of the past few hours: the calm after the storm. Such eruptions happen to often in our prison, usually due to poor management of a situation that has evolved from a petty matter that could so easily have been dealt with in a professional manner in order to avoid the type of destruction I now surveyed, as well as possible injury to both staff and inmates. As I sat alone in the spur observation office desperately trying to reset my breathing to a rate of normality (I had chosen not to join the others in their ego-boosting victory celebrations in the officers' mess), I thought back to the events of the day that had resulted in this latest unnecessary confrontation.

The day had begun in exactly the same way as every other Saturday had done when I was on duty. I had dragged myself out of bed at 0600 hours with a serious lack of motivation as I looked forward to another ten-hour shift on spur three, and prolonged the journey from home to Thamesmead for as long as possible, eventually arriving at the prison car park at 0715 hours. I passed through the main gate and the mandatory search area before picking up my keys and trudging through the depressing surroundings of the main prison towards the high-security unit. Once there, I passed through the two electronically operated gates and yet another search area, and with my body in autopilot I went upstairs to the tearoom to grab a cup to take with me to my place of duty.

By just after 0800 hours, I and my colleague had unlocked the twelve inmates on the spur, passed out the breakfast meals and taken, from those that had them, various applications or requests, such as booking phone calls, arranging to change bedding or simply handling mail to be posted out via the Cat A censor's office. This was typical of the Saturday morning routine on the unit and, looking around at the inmates going about their usual business, there was no indication that this would be any different to any other day. The rest of the morning dragged past slowly, interrupted only by the comings and goings of a couple of inmates who had visits, numerous breaks to visit the tea room and the odd walk round the spur to chat to some of the guys.

My partner for the day was a fella called Stu, a Yorkshire man, who was about fifty-odd years old but looked about ninety and had the personality to match that of a grumpy old silverback gorilla. I think he only knew two words of dialect, which he used to answer me when I asked him if he wanted a cup of tea: "two sugars" - that's all I heard him speak all day.

5

Consequently, I welcomed the arrival of the lunchtime meal at twelve, as it meant after serving it the inmates would be locked up for an hour and I could get off the spur for a break myself.

All too soon I was back unlocking the lads for the afternoon period, which would follow much the same routine as the morning, or so I hoped. At approximately 1400 hours, two visits officers arrived to collect the prisoners for the afternoon visiting session. That particular afternoon three inmates were collected: two of the IRA inmates on remand for the Warrington bombing; and Gary Nelson, a large Jamaican inmate accused of killing PC Dunne. With our numbers reduced to nine, the afternoon passed peacefully with most of the inmates spending the following couple of hours writing letters, reading or watching the Saturday afternoon sport on television.

About an hour and a half had passed when the three inmates on visits returned, and I could tell by the expressions on the escorting officers' faces that all had not gone well. Nelson went straight to his cell and slammed the door against its frame, but the bolt was in the open position so it could not close fully, and the two IRA men both headed straight for Dingus's cell. I knew something was wrong, but decided to sit back and hope that it was just a case of a bad visit and they would sort it out among themselves rather than risk antagonizing them further by following them into the cell and demanding to know what had happened.

I did not have to wait long for answers. Within a few minutes of the inmates returning, Dingus, the highest-ranking IRA man on the spur at the time and a man with whom I had actually been able to build up a fairly good working relationship, approached me at the desk. No sooner had the words, "The boys are not happy, I think it best if you get off the spur for a while", left his lips, one of the Warrington lot who had been on visits came charging out of a cell wielding a plastic chair above his head. He made straight for the CCTV camera mounted on the far wall of the spur and, using the chair, began smashing at it. At the same time, Nelson and the other IRA man came out and began to dismantle the pool table and throw the TV off its table onto the floor. I looked around for some support, just in time to see Stu's hulking frame squeezing out of the second door leading off the spur, but not before he had locked the first one behind him, leaving me alone and locked in with a spur full of very irate prisoners. I spun round again to look into the observation office and saw to my horror that the officer in there was facing the other way on the phone, apparently unaware of what was happening. Luckily for me, Dingus was still by my side and he ushered me towards the door of the spur, shielding me for just enough time to allow me to fumble with my keys and escape into the sterile area between the two doors that led off the spur. I froze there for a moment, in the safety of the locked passage, to let my panic and fear subside a little and take stock of what had just happened. All my training had suddenly gone out of the window, as is so often the case when you finally become involved in a real-life situation. My colleague had deserted me and my observation officer was clearly not observing me, and I am convinced that, had I not been the man I was and taken the time to build a good working relationship with most of the lads on the spur, I would not have stood a chance of getting out of there without sustaining very serious injury or worse.

The warbling sound of the alarm bell ringing snapped me out of my frozen state. The observation officer had obviously finally heard the commotion and raised the alarm. I glanced back through the door and felt relieved I had got out when I did, as by this time the other inmates had joined the fray and were systematically destroying all the furniture and fittings on the spur. The noise was incredible as it now echoed around the confined space of the upstairs of the unit.

I made my way downstairs to the unit's main office and just as I got there a dozen or so officers were steaming through the door into the unit from other parts of the prison. Most of this initial wave responding to the alarm bell comprised officers from the prison's so-called 'elite' security department. These men and women were responsible for all the prison's planned cell searches and 'takeouts' of prisoners and were always among the first to turn up during an incident, eager to 'get stuck in'. In reality, they were a pain in the arse, causing untold disruption and daily instigating most of the confrontations that occurred throughout the prison with their over-the-top actions.

The worst offender of all was their principal officer, who was in charge of the security team. He really loved himself and thought he was a law unto himself. He had a well-expressed hatred for prisoners and loved every aspect of the job. He had, in fact, failed to get into the police force before opting for the Prison Service, and consequently rode a large white motorbike modified with fluorescent green flashes, so when kitted out in his Prison Service uniform he looked like a police biker. In fact there was a story going around that he had pulled up alongside a car that had overtaken him and flashed his Prison Service ID card at the occupants, only to be met in return with a metropolitan police warrant card produced by the plain-clothes officers in the car. I heard that as a result he had been done for imitating a police officer, but I am not sure how much of that story is true or how much was made up by the countless people that despised the man.

Anyway, within ten minutes or so the remaining three spurs of the unit had been secured and all civilian staff and visitors had been escorted out and corralled in the main area by the unit office to await instructions from the unit governor. By now the inmates on spur three had had enough time to organise themselves into a fairly good defensive position by barricading the entrance onto the spur with the pieces of broken furniture, which had been entwined with any leftover parts of the metal beds that they had not armed themselves with. The noise coming from upstairs was deafening as they relentlessly beat the cell doors and perspex glass window to the spur office with their various tools. As news spread fast across the prison 'internet', prisoners located on other spurs in the unit and even on the house blocks in the main prison began to shout encouragement to the twelve renegades.

Eventually the order came for all control and restraint level two or riot-trained staff on duty to get their riot kit out of the locker room and once dressed meet back in the unit's tea room. I had just completed my riot training a few weeks earlier, so I rather reluctantly followed the thirty-or-so-strong contingent to the room where we kept our stores. As I struggled into my overalls and strapped on my plastic shin and knee protectors, I could hear the excited nervousness among the others as they spoke about "payback" and the chance to "get stuck into the cons". I just wanted to find out what could have happened to cause this problem in the first place, on what should have been an uneventful and routine Saturday.

Once dressed and kitted out with our PR24 nightsticks and full-length riot shields, we filed back into the unit and crammed into the tearoom to await the briefing by the security PO. He entered the room, also kitted out in riot gear, and with a menacing grin on his face stood up on one of the chairs to deliver his game plan.

"Gentlemen, ladies, we have got a situation that most of you are aware began about forty-five minutes ago when three inmates from spur three returned from visits. It appears that they became involved in an argument with an officer on visits regarding one of the visitors wanting to hand over a writing pad and some envelopes."

I couldn't believe what I was hearing: all this was due to the fact that an officer could not be bothered to take responsibility for signing in a notepad and some envelopes from a visitor who had come all the way from Northern Ireland. And it got worse: the officer in question, it was rumoured, had smuggled in a hand- held television set for Gary Nelson the previous week via one of his visitors for a sum of money. Apparently, on hearing the commotion over the notepad, Nelson had approached the officer and made his views known about how petty the matter was. The officer, however, took this as a threat to expose his own little smuggling enterprise and so erupted into his own threats towards the inmates in front of the visitors.

This had obviously not only upset the inmates but also their visitors, and it was probably only the fact that one of the inmates had an elderly visitor that it did not kick off there and then. This was typical of how one officer's guilt and/or laziness in not wanting to put himself out for five minutes could magnify into such a major incident, and one that could have huge knock-on effects for all involved. My thoughts were interrupted as the PO's voice changed tone.

"So that is the situation. The duty governor has handed complete control of the incident to me, so we have a golden opportunity now to hit them hard and fast without some do-gooder looking over our shoulder. We are going in there to take back my spur, and I want to hear screams of pain. Let's show them whose nick this is. I know there are some big names in there, but just you remember this: OUT THERE THEY MAY BE MR BIG, BUT IN HERE OUR GANG IS BIGGER THAN THEIR GANG, SO LET'S DO IT."

It could have been a speech from a Hollywood war movie. I just thought: what have I let myself get involved with here? With our illustrious leader's words still ringing in our ears, we filed out and lined up outside the door to spur three, which had been covered by a medical-green curtained screen brought up from the visits search room. As we waited for the order to go, I could smell burning from the spur. The inmates had obviously set fire to their bedding in an attempt to make some kind of smoke screen. I tightened my grip around the handles of my shield and felt a nervous anticipation wash over me. I had been in similar situations before in my army days, but this time I did not trust those who were lined up beside me either to watch my back or to act in a totally professional manner.

The volume of noise suddenly increased tenfold and the acrid smell of burning foam filled my nostrils as the door to the spur was opened and we were off. No time for thinking now, just switch into auto-mode, look after number one and focus on what is in front of the scratched plastic I held firm before me. Two by two we squeezed ourselves and our shields through the narrow doorway into the smoke-filled spur. As soon as each pair was through, all we could do was stand our ground while the remainder of the teams joined us. Through the thick smoke I could make out an effective-looking barricade immediately to my front and caught a brief glimpse of one or two inmates with pieces of torn sheet wrapped around their mouths to offer them some sort of protection from the smoke screen they had created. Then the noise broke through the smoke: the shouts and the banging of handmade weapons, which connected with such force on my shield that it took all my strength to stand my ground, and vibrated up my arms as they absorbed the impact.

It seemed as if I was standing there for hours, but in reality it was probably only minutes, before the order to push forward reached me. By now the smoke from the burning mattresses had almost filled the spur. I could feel it burning the back of my throat, and my vision was seriously impaired due to constant watering of my eyes caused by the acrid smoke, which stung each time I blinked hard in an attempt to improve my field of view. Blindly we shuffled forward, our lead leg firmly against the base of our shields as we tried to force our way through the makeshift but nevertheless effective barricade to our front. Each step sapped more and more energy from my already tired and aching body, and sweat now poured down my back and forehead to add to the irritation the smoke was causing to my stinging eyes.

Inch by precious inch we edged forward through the smoke and din of the constant barrage of objects that were being hurled at our shield line. Finally a breakthrough: we managed to break away enough of the barricade to advance through it and re-establish our shield line on the other side. My chest was heaving and my lungs were burning, through a combination of sheer exhaustion and the smoke that I breathed in with every desperate gasp for air. I could feel the tension rising within the ranks and knew that, as soon as we could get amongst the prisoners, anger and bitterness would take over from professionalism and many of the officers behind our shields would unleash this anger on the inmates before them. With this in mind, I remember thinking how Dingus had helped me get off the spur and thought I now owed it to him to try to offer him some protection from the imminent wrath of the staff. As the time for the order to break into our separate teams and target individual inmates neared, I squinted into the smog before me, trying desperately to catch a glimpse of Dingus.

Most of the inmates had gathered together in the rear-left of the spur and I spotted Dingus in amongst them just seconds before the order to break ranks was shouted down the line. With a last surge of my remaining energy reserves, I ran forward at half pace. I could feel the two officers who made up my team tugging at the sleeves of my overalls as they tried to remain tight in behind the protection of my shield. I was physically exhausted, but knew I could not give up now. The shield and the two officers I was effectively dragging behind me only served to sap my strength further, but I had to keep going that last few feet. I had to reach Dingus before another team.

Two inmates appeared before me and threw what I assumed was a mop bucket of boiling water from the boiler directly at my shield. For a moment the sheer impact stopped my advance in its tracks and stunned me as my aching forearms once again absorbed the blow. I recovered and smashed my shield through the gap between the two men, knocking them to either side of me. There was no time to worry about what they would do; I just had to hope that another team would deal with them before they could launch a counterattack on the exposed rear of my team. I now had Dingus right in front of my shield and needed just one final effort to pin him against the back wall of the spur and remove him from the game, or more importantly from the reach of other teams.

As I prepared myself for the final lunge forward, I felt a shattering blow to the side of my helmet, which in my exhausted state caused me to lose my balance and I felt myself falling to the floor. I landed heavily onto the handles of my own shield, which made contact painfully with my ribcage, knocking what wind I had left out of my lungs and leaving me desperately panting for air. The two members of my team became caught in my downward motion and followed me to the floor, landing on top of me and pinning me to the ground. In these last desperate minutes of this confrontation our situation was very serious. We were dangerously exposed, not only to the inmates, who would have loved a chance to stick a last boot into a downed officer, but also to the forward momentum of our own remaining teams, who were themselves advancing for the final assault.

With a determined energy that you can only muster in such desperate situations, I kicked and thrashed my body like a man possessed until I managed to scramble back to my feet. Disoriented in the smoke and dazed through exhaustion and the blow to my head, I felt around blindly for my shield. After those few minutes of chaos in which I had been temporarily immobilized, and by the time I had retrieved the shield and regained my bearings enough to re-engage in the job at hand, I could see through the misted visor that I was too late. The inmates had all been restrained and screams of pain and shouts of protest now replaced the din of battle. I had been too late to restrain Dingus, as I saw with some sadness that he was lying face down under a group of four or five black overalls.

I staggered over to the small window at the back of the spur, stepping over groups of officers and inmates along the way. When I got there, I pushed open the two small barred windows as fully as they would reach and stuck my face out of one. With nausea washing over me due to smoke inhalation and sheer exhaustion, I sucked desperately at the clean air outside the window. More staff streamed onto the spur as word spread that the situation was under control, and someone was going round with a fire extinguisher to douse the smouldering mattresses, but all they succeeded in doing was to create more thick smoke to fill the air.

As the smoke gradually dispersed, I saw twelve mounds of bodies. Black overalls were now laced with white shirts as some fresh staff took over from the original riot teams. From the bottom of each of these mounds, shouts of pain and protest could be heard, as the restraining officers applied far greater force than was necessary to the wrist and leg locks of the immobilized inmates beneath them. The parts of the floor that were not occupied by mounds of bodies were littered with the debris of broken furniture and electrical appliances, together with water from the broken toilets. The walls were charred black from the smouldering mattresses. The place was a mess: so much damage over a notepad and a few envelopes.

For a few minutes nothing moved. Everyone took the opportunity to try to catch their breath before the next phase of the operation, which would involve moving the inmates off the spur and down the stairs and relocating them in the segregation unit.

Then the security PO took position in the middle of the spur and, with a sadistic grin on his face, shouted, "I can't hear much pain being inflicted."

No sooner had the words left his lips than the spur erupted with ear-piercing screams of pain, as the officers heeded his words and tightened their hold on their prisoners' wrists and legs.

"That's better. Now we have got your attention we will be moving you to the segregation unit one at a time. I hope this has been a lesson to you not to fuck about in my jail."

What a fucking hero, I thought to myself.

Each of the twelve inmates was then in turn dragged up from the floor and, still bent over double with an officer on each arm and one pushing his head down almost between his knees, he began the painful, slow walk to the segregation unit. The PO accompanied each move personally and kept the tension going with shouts to encourage the escorting staff to tweak the wrist locks a bit if the inmate fell quiet for a moment. One particular inmate, who tried to protest to the PO that he thought his wrist was fractured, was twice led headlong into one of the doors leading off the spur with such force that the perspex in the door shook with the vibration.

Once in the strip cells of the seg unit, the inmates were subjected to a brutal disrobing of their clothes, which were literally torn from them, and then they were left, many of them bleeding and complaining of injury, lying naked on the bare concrete floor of the cell. To relocate all twelve inmates took approximately forty-five minutes in total, and I watched in disbelief as they were manhandled down the stairs and at the ferocity and venomous way in which the staff took pleasure in causing as much pain as possible in order to look good in front of this bearded wanker of a security PO.

Once all the inmates had been relocated, the staff involved all started slapping each other on the back, with mutual congratulations on a job well done. The stories then started about who did what to what slag, etc., and it was suggested that we all go over to the mess for a celebratory drink. However, I kept a low profile, as I didn't want to be part of such an egotistical group of idiots. As far as I could tell, a corrupt officer had started this whole incident and it was made worse by a sadistic PO. I could not understand the mentality of people that seemed to enjoy inflicting pain on someone who had been immobilized. All I saw was an abuse of power, but then again I had seen a lot of that during my time in the Prison Service.

Once the triumphant troops had left for the mess and the shouts of protest had faded from the segregation unit, I sat alone and wondered what gave me such a different outlook to the vast majority of the other staff in terms of how to deal with such situations. Unlike them, I felt no bitterness or hatred towards the inmates over the eruption - to me it was just part of the job I had signed up for. I did not blame the lads for what had just happened as, in my opinion, the whole situation had arisen as a result of poor management by staff. The three inmates initially involved in the visits incident had been quite understandably upset by the attitude of the staff, but had resisted the urge to do anything in front of their visitors. Once they returned to the spur and realized they would not get a reasonable explanation, they felt, as is quite often the case especially on a weekend when staffing levels are at a minimum, that they had to take action. The rest of the inmates may not have all agreed with them, but felt they had to support them. This is the nature of our prisons and it is no different to members of staff supporting colleagues by providing false statements.

I had only been in the job about a year and a half by this time, but I already feared that I had made a big mistake and was beginning to realize that I would never be able to act in the sort of unprofessional manner in which many officers conducted their duties on a daily basis. Each day I struggled with my conscience and inside questioned whether I was doing the right thing or not.

As I sat, now totally exhausted and alone with my thoughts, I tried to think why I was so different in my attitude, why I found it so hard just to fall in line with most of the other officers and go with the flow. I began to wonder how I had even ended up on this spur rolling around the floor with prisoners. The answers to why I possessed such a hatred of bullying or over-the-top acts of violence must lie in my past. The experiences I brought with me from past life exploits and people I have met must have

15

forged me into the person I am today. I would need to go right back to the beginning to search for the answers and unravel what and who I was and where I had come from.

2
MY CHILDHOOD

I entered this world on the twenty-ninth of October 1968 in my parents' small council house in Harlow, Essex. I was born six weeks premature, weighing in at only two pounds and measuring about thirty centimetres tall. After a stay of some two months in hospital, during which it was touch and go whether I would survive, I was finally 'released' and christened Norman James Dawkins. The name and my lack of height were to give me some problems during my childhood days. However, as my big sister Jayne grew older and was unable to offer me the protection in the playground that older brothers and sisters do, I had to learn to fight my own battles and earn my own respect from my peers.

In 1968 my father Norman (hence my name), was teaching physical education at Netswell County Primary School in Harlow. He was also a very keen footballer and played amateur games for Barkingside United and the Welsh amateur team, Wales being my family's native homeland. My mother Helen was busy bringing up my sister and me. By 1971 I, my sister and my mother had moved to my grandparents' house in Maesteg, South Wales, for a brief period while my dad carried out his training as a physical education officer in the Royal Air Force at Hendon.

Shortly afterwards we joined him in our new house at RAF Honnington and, at the ripe old age of three, I set out on my first 'tour of duty' with the British forces. They were good days; we had a nice house and my days were spent playing war games and dodging the Modplod (MOD Police) with the other servicemen's kids. We spent hours roaming around the camp watching the various aircraft coming and going. Due to my dad's commitment to the air force he spent a lot of time away so it was up to mum to oversee our upbringing in the early days.

Although I was growing up on an airfield, even at that early age my fascination was not with the air force. From the age of about four or five I wanted to join the army. This stemmed from my grandad Tommy Dare, who dazzled me with tales from the Second World War, when he served with the Welsh Regiment from Normandy to Berlin.

My early childhood memories are of spending long holidays in Wales with both sets of grandparents, and my Auntie Mari and Uncle Clive. My gran and grandad (Tommy and Lillian Dare) ran a general store and I spent hours gripped with the stories my grandad had, which were both exciting and thrilling to a young boy but also extremely modest on his behalf. In all the tales he told it was always someone else he described as the 'hero'. I later realized that he was referring to his own exploits but didn't want to brag about the true horror of war to me at such an early age.

My gran, meanwhile, always felt I was not eating enough, even though I was quite 'chunky' at the time. She was always plying me with biscuits and doughnuts from Glynn 'Doughnuts', the shop's bakery delivery man. Even today she will remind me of this and she still talks about me to Glynn when she sees him. She is now almost ninety but is still as sharp as a twenty-year-old. I remember that during a recent birthday party held for her my Auntie Mari got so drunk she was sick on my sister's patio and my gran gave her a right earful about how if she couldn't handle her drink she shouldn't bloody drink it.

My other grandparents (Mue and Pop Dawkins) lived in the small village of Caerau and I spent many summer days there at 15 George Street. Pop had been a coal miner during the war, so, despite desperately wanting to join up, he was not allowed to do so because he was doing a job that was invaluable to the war effort. Mue was employed as a nurse, which was again a profession that was in demand at that time. Pop was also, like my dad, a very good footballer and as a result has always been extremely fit even into old age.

Each morning we would be up at the crack of dawn, have some toast grilled over the coal fire, make some banana sandwiches and set of for Porthcawl, the nearest coastal resort. There we would spend all day either on the beach messing around in the rock pools or on the rides at the

Coney Beach fair. They must have been exhausted but never once did they refuse to take me, come rain or shine.

Mue sadly passed away recently following a short but courageous battle with stomach cancer. I didn't see as much of her as I should have done over the last few years, but her final words to me when I spoke to her at Christmas 1999 tore me apart. She was remembering our days at the beach and fair and what we used to get up to during those long holidays. Her parting words, the last I ever heard her say, were "Don't forget that Mue will always love you ". I broke down after that conversation. It was as if she knew she was dying, even though the family hadn't told her of the extent of her illness. I knew then that I couldn't handle seeing her in such a frail condition and will always remember her as she was before the cancer struck - a truly lovely, genuine woman to whom I owed so much early happiness.

Mue had also had to cope with nursing Pop for years, who was crippled with Alzheimer's disease. Once again it was extremely painful to see a man who had been so fit and healthy all his life struck down with such a terrible condition. All my grandparents are lovely people who never had a bad word to say about anyone, and I will certainly never forget the great start in life they all gave me with their unselfish love and devotion.

My Auntie Mari and Uncle Clive are also both lovely people who, despite having three children of their own (Iwan, Cerys and Meirion), always made room for me during the family holidays to their caravan in West Wales, and treated me just like one of their own. I will always be indebted to them for their kindness and devotion also.

My dad left the air force in 1977 and we moved to Shillabeer Walk in Chigwell, to a little house that looked like a wedge of cheese due to its unusual roof. Here he began working as the educational supervisor at Dagenham Sports Centre. My first memory of Shillabeer Walk was the street party to celebrate the Queen's Silver Jubilee. I remember feeling quite upset because my sister and me only got black and white celebration mugs when all the other kids got coloured ones. The excuse I got was that because we were new arrivals they could not get us coloured ones and we

19

were lucky to get one at all. It was here that I was first introduced to the sport of boxing, although not participating as my dad wouldn't allow it, and I wasn't to get the chance to do so until my army days.

One of the sports shops in Dagenham was run by a little old bloke with the most extraordinary nose I had seen to date. He claimed to have been a champion prize fighter in his day and ran a gym above the shop for young boxers. He tried desperately to persuade my dad to let me join, and kept giving me posters of Charlie Magri, who became my idol, for my bedroom wall. My dad, however, wouldn't give in and within the year we moved once again, this time to Eltham in southeast London. Eltham was to be a big chapter in my life. It was where I spent my teen years and began to explore my own independence for the first time.

On my first day there I strode confidently into the local park in search of some new friends, wearing my best pair of flared jeans. As I approached a small gang of kids about my age they began to fall about the floor in fits of laughter, calling me all sorts of things. I didn't have a clue what was wrong with them and thought I had stumbled across the local funny farm, until it dawned on me that they were all wearing these skintight jeans, and they were giving me grief about my flares. I ran home distraught that my first mission had been cut so embarrassingly short and promptly told my mum that I hated it here and was never going out again. They didn't have enough money to buy me new jeans, so mum got out the needle and thread and tailored the flares as much as she could so I could still get them on.

So looking like a Rod Stewart reject I was ready to venture out once again and, strangely enough, was accepted into the group with no further problems. I went to school at Wyborne Primary in New Eltham and was soon a fully fledged member of the Eltham Rude Boys. I remember once the gang and I decided to decorate my dad's shed with graffiti to do with the mods and the rude boys. We thought it was a real work of art until my dad found it and introduced us to another form of art - a good belt round the head followed by repainting the whole interior of the shed with some white emulsion.

After leaving primary school I started secondary school at Eltham Green Comprehensive. This chapter of my life was to prove to be a difficult one. As I mentioned before, my dad was a physical education teacher at a school sports centre and, as a result, he knew just about every teacher, either socially or professionally, at Eltham Green. This alone caused me a great deal of pressure. Not only did I have to worry about my every move being reported back to my dad, but I also took all the flak from the other kids for being 'that Mr Dawkins' son'. I began to experience the same feelings as every teenager, i.e. that I couldn't do anything and my parents were preventing me from making my own decisions. My dad also taught weight training at the local youth club a couple of nights a week where some of the 'hardest' boys in school went. So consequently if any of them had had a run in with my dad the night before it usually meant that I would have to end up scrapping in the playground to defend myself from a good kicking due to my dad upsetting some of these kids.

Of course most playground fights attracted huge crowds, which in turn attracted teachers, who in turn informed my dad, who in turn would have a go at me when I got home for embarrassing him in front of his colleagues, so I was pretty much in a no-win situation.

My life was about to take another turn in 1982 when somehow I managed to persuade my parents to let me join the local army cadet unit - the 93rd Royal Artillery Cadet Battery based at nearby Crown Woods School. I loved it; we did weapon training, drill, and map reading and staged mock battles in the woods behind the school. For two nights a week from seven until nine, the odd weekend and two whole weeks of camp during the summer holidays I escaped into my own little fantasy world as Lance Bombardier Jim Dawkins.

I had decided that James or Norman didn't fit in with my new 'military career' so from then on I introduced myself as Jim. It was through the army cadets that I met some good friends, some of whom were to continue to serve with me in the regular army when I joined the Royal Green Jackets. Good, loyal friends like Garry Thompson, Simon Long, Steve and Del Fairs, Roger F, and Mick T to name a few. Another good friend I made during my time with the cadets was Nikki Holland-Day. She was to introduce me to my first love and childhood sweetheart, her sister Natasha.

Natasha was about thirteen and I was almost fifteen when we met at the steps of the school playing fields and it was love at first sight. I can still picture her today in her Fila tracksuit top and grey skirt and her big Michael Jackson perm. We were so much in love but I had a problem. To me she appeared so confident and beautiful that it seemed too good to be true that she could be in love with me, and I daren't risk anything spoiling what we had together.

At this time the relationship between my parents and me was so tense that I just couldn't risk introducing Natasha to them as I thought they would ruin what we had. They were aware that I was seeing her but didn't really approve because she came from what they thought was quite a rough area of Greenwich and they believed that she was distracting me from more important things like schoolwork. The fact of the matter was that because my dad knew all the teachers at my school it was left to Natasha to skip classes at her school to come and see me.

So we continued this clandestine relationship, arranging to meet at various times and places to avoid detection by my parents. We are still together today and have a beautiful baby girl, Morgan, who at the time of writing this has just turned one. The sad fact is that if I had stood up to my parents when I should have Morgan would be a lot older now with a couple of younger brothers or sisters.

Another big influence in my life at that time was my two very good friends Garry and Simon. Both they and Natasha seemed to me to have much more understanding families than mine, and considering we were all roughly the same age they all seemed to have much more independence than I was allowed. Having experienced the type of relationship they had with their parents I began to resent my home life more and more.

I began to spend a lot of time with Simon and his family, purely because I felt that they treated me more like a young man with a mind of his own.

It was around this time that my sister got accepted into Cardiff University to study medicine and I was subjected to growing pressure to do better at school and go on to college or university like Jayne. It was something I was not interested in and the more pressure I received the harder I dug my heels in.

There was only one thing that I was interested in and that was, as soon as I could legally leave school, running away to join the army, where I could marry Natasha and we could get married quarters. I began to respect Simon's mum and dad tremendously the more time I spent with them. Simon's dad, Jim, is Irish and ran his own very successful interior design firm; in fact he still does. A lot of his business contacts were well-known 'faces' from south London. It was from Jim and his contacts that I learnt about the old south London mentality of trust, loyalty and respect, all of which I consider to be the most valuable lesson anyone can learn in life and a lesson that you will never find in any university prospectus in the world.

I never did follow my family's wishes and go to university, but I will never regret it. I always consider myself to be a graduate of the University of Life and on my travels I have learnt some invaluable lessons that I will use for the rest of my life. Through Simon and his dad I met some wonderful people - good, solid people who may have dabbled in a bit of this or that but who you could put your trust in one hundred per cent, so long as you didn't take the piss.

In later years when I was considering joining the Prison Service I turned to Jim for advice. Had he told me that he didn't approve then I would not have joined, simple as that. That was how much I respected him and I still do although I haven't seen him for a while now. His advice was, as ever, simple and honest. He said, "Jim, there are good and bad screws. It's a good job providing you always remember who you are and where you're from. If you can do the job fairly, and can overcome the temptation to join in with the bad ones, you will earn the respect of the chaps doing time and keep your self-dignity intact." This advice is something I never forgot and it cropped up regularly during my career and in fact was the main reason

I decided to leave when I did. Anyway, I am jumping the gun a bit. I will cover my career in the Prison Service in more detail later on.

The situation at home was getting worse as the time approached for me to sit my 'O' levels. My parents had convinced themselves that the reason I seemed disinterested in exams and further education was due to bad influences at Eltham Green and the fact that I was still seeing Natasha. In a last-ditch attempt to push me into doing well in my exams and going on to higher education they took me out of Eltham Green and put me into a private school in Beckenham just about ten months before I was due to sit my 'O' levels.

I don't know about you, but the last thing I would do if I knew one of my kids was not interested in further education is throw good money after bad and pay for private school fees. Not that I would not do anything for my kids if they needed it, but I would rather spend my time and money encouraging and supporting them to pursue something they enjoyed or wanted to do. In fairness I suppose they thought they were doing the right thing. At least no one can say they didn't try, and I can never blame them for my lack of academic qualifications.

The fact remained that I knew where I wanted to be and you didn't need exams to get there in those days. I have always considered myself to be a laid back sort of guy. I think a lot of that stemmed from watching how worked up my dad used to get when I didn't listen to his lectures on how I would never get anywhere in life without at least six or seven 'O' levels. I have always lived by the simple rule that life is too short to get yourself all worked up over petty things. I have had a fantastic life up to now. I have seen things and been to places I may not have had the chance to experience had I chosen to do what was expected of me.

Anyway, that's enough of Jim's philosophy on life. I am not knocking anyone who has gone through higher education, nor would I wish to discourage anyone who may be contemplating it. I am simply saying that it wasn't for me and it takes all sorts to make this world of ours go round, from brain surgeons to unemployed ex-soldiers/prison officers who wouldn't listen to their parents.

The only snag with the private school was that the boys there were worse than the ones I had left behind at Eltham Green. Needless to say, the plan didn't work and on 19 September 1985 I took my oath of allegiance to the Queen in front of Major Tozer and my mum and dad at Blackheath army careers office. I had enlisted into the finest infantry regiment in the army, the Royal Green Jackets, and was due to report just five days later at the junior soldiers' light division depot in Shrewsbury.

3
THE ARMY

I had finally done it, and after saying my goodbyes to mum and dad at Euston train station I boarded the train for Birmingham New Street to begin my new life. As the train sped through the English countryside I began to try to imagine what lay in store for me. The truth of the matter was that I didn't have a clue. Despite my lifelong obsession with the army and my experiences with the cadets, I had no idea what to expect and all of a sudden I felt strangely alone.

As I mentioned earlier, my parents didn't approve of my joining. They still thought I could achieve more but, typical of my mentality, that only added fuel to the fire of my youthful dreams. Despite waiting for this moment for years - a chance to be free of the arguing about what I should do with my life and finally achieving what I saw as my independence - I felt sadness as well as excitement. I was not even seventeen and had just left home, but I felt sad that for the past few years the constant battle I waged at home had driven a wedge between me and my family, a wedge that would never really be fully removed again.

I changed trains at Birmingham and boarded a small local line train, which was to take us on the final leg of the journey to Shrewsbury. I noticed other young men on this train who were obviously going to the same place. Some of them had already got together and were talking. I have always been a bit of a loner so I didn't join any of these newly formed cliques. I like to sit back when meeting people for the first time and make my own judgement as to whom I want to get involved with. Besides, I thought, I am going to see enough of this lot over the next twelve months. I just took the time to sit quietly on my own while I still had the opportunity. There was one guy I remember on the train who seemed to really love himself. He had a 'Joey Boswell' haircut and an expensive looking red silk shirt hanging out of his designer jeans.

Like me, he was a London recruit to the Green Jackets, but his was the only voice you could hear for the whole journey. I remember thinking he looked more like he was off to join some gay modelling firm rather than the army, and I marked him up as a non-starter. In fact he did go the distance and turned into a very good soldier eventually, after one or two of the training instructors had shown him some guidance the only way they knew how.

The train finally slowed to a stop at Shrewsbury Station and as it slowed I got a glimpse of our welcoming committee. Stood on the platform were about three or four corporals, all Green Jackets and light infantry, and as soon as we alighted from the train the chaotic shouting that was to become so much a part of everyday life for the next few weeks began.

There was a group of about thirty or so of us lined up on the platform being screamed at by a rather large black corporal from the light infantry. A handful of civilians walked past grinning at the look of despair on our faces - this was obviously a scene they were used to. Even the kid in the silk shirt had shut up and was standing there looking as pale as the rest of us. As the corporal paced up the line shouting his well-rehearsed 'welcome to the British army' speech I couldn't help but think of the similarities between this and that scene in the film *An Officer and a Gentleman* where Richard Gere arrived at the naval training base, the only difference being that there were no officers in this line-up and certainly no gentlemen.

We were split into groups and put on one of the minibuses in the car park. Mine was driven by an enormous, bearded civilian who was well-rehearsed in keeping the mood of the moment going with his comments on what we had let ourselves in for. As we passed through the gates of Sir John Moore Barracks on the Copthorne Road our driver shouted out of the window to the group of hard-nosed regimental police, "You can close the gates now we've got them." I swallowed hard.

Inside the camp the scene was chaotic. There were groups of people running everywhere, some in uniform and some in civvies. We drove past a group of uniformed lads on the parade square and the look on their faces seemed to be telling us to get out of there while we still had a chance. We debussed at the administration block and as soon as we were out we were sucked into the rollercoaster ride of signing forms, receiving injections, undergoing medicals, kit issue, the mandatory skinhead cut, and being allocated to our new platoon.

In no time at all I was lined up in the ranks of Corunna platoon awaiting the arrival of our platoon commander, Warrant Officer Class One, Wilson. Wilson arrived with the rest of the training staff and at first sight looked like the laughing cavalier with his neatly trimmed moustache immaculately waxed to a needle-sharp point at each end. The only trouble was, he wasn't laughing. He gave us his welcoming speech, which in a nutshell imparted the message, "if you fuck up, I or one of my staff will beat the shit out of you". I do admire a man who doesn't mince his words.

In turn I was 'introduced' to my new section commander Corporal 'Squid' Rumble, apparently so called due to the fact that he half strangled a recruit in his previous section and, true to his name, he liked a rumble now and again. It turned out that we couldn't have wished for better men to prepare us for our new careers. Both Wilson and Squid were highly experienced men from the Third Battalion Royal Green Jackets and both were as hard as nails.

Wilson had come up through the ranks and had almost twenty- two years of experience behind him. This is one reason why I detested those high-flying governors that I would come across later in my Prison Service days who gained promotion on merit and by kissing the right arse. It goes back to my old belief that no amount of academic qualifications can substitute experience when you are dealing with real people in real life. All Wilson and Squid were interested in was that we learned what they taught us as it could save our lives in the future. If we performed well they were happy, and if not we got the 'treatment'.

So effective were their 'methods' that we rarely made the same mistake once let alone twice. It's all changed now, of course. Instructors are not even allowed to touch recruits for fear of a parent complaining about their poor little wounded soldier being shouted at. Well, if you're that protective of your 'little Johnny' then the army is not the place for him. Recruits are not even allowed to run in boots any more in case they damage their poor little tootsies. I only hope the enemy are that sympathetic and allow them time to get their Reeboks on before they overrun their positions in future -what a load of bollocks! The army will be issuing them with furry pink leotards and teaching them ballet next. Maybe we could challenge the Iraqis to a knitting competition next time instead of going through that entire hassle of getting our uniforms dirty. Mind you, we would still thrash them at that!

For the next six weeks we went to hell and back. I don't think we walked anywhere except for three times a day on our way back from a meal at the cookhouse. Not that we had time to eat much. I think the longest meal break we got was twenty minutes on a Sunday because the dinner was bigger. We were usually so exhausted that all we could do was pour gallons of the watery but ice-cold blackcurrant juice, which accompanied every meal, down our necks.

Our days were spent weapon training, learning about infantry skills, staging mock section attacks, doing triple lessons of physical education, both gym work and 'battle PE' with logs and rifles, etc. The day usually began and ended with a section or platoon run of increasingly lengthening distances. Strangely, we began to 'look forward' to these, as it was the only time we set foot outside the camp and saw some of the local area. Our feet were a mass of blisters from the new boots that never seemed to be off our feet, and we were lucky to grab three or four hours of unbroken sleep a night. Even then we tossed and turned all night dreaming about the morning's room inspection, when all our kit, which we had spent hours preparing, would inevitably be slung out of the window. Alternatively, we lay waiting for about three o' clock in the morning when Squid and his mates would roll in from the nightclub and drag us out of bed for a bit of extra-curricular 'character' building. This usually meant that they wrecked our room and lockers and picked on a couple of us to stage a fight with.

But we took it all in our stride. Those who couldn't take it were already taking the option to leave while they still could, proving that Squid's own unique methods of 'weeding out the wankers' was working rather effectively. I do remember one particular incident, which happened while we were carrying out fire picket duty. One of the lads, 'Nobby' Clarke, a naturally funny chain-smoking Geordie, tried to save himself a few quid on batteries by wiring his radio lead to one of the old bedside lights in the fire picket accommodation. He confidently flicked the switch and immediately there was an enormous bang and a flash of white light followed by every light in the camp going out. When the flames from the bedside light really began to catch we could make out Nobby, who had been thrown clean across the room, lying shaking on the floor with his face as black as coal and his hair standing up all over his head. He looked like something out of a Tom and Jerry cartoon or some old Ealing Studio comedy.

As we attempted to fight the rapidly spreading fire, as any conscientious fire picket would, Nobby's first words were, "Ahh bollocks, man. That was a fucking good radio that. Me mam's going to kill us." Not that I wish to take anything away from Nobby's mam, but the silhouette of a far more immediate threat appeared in the doorway, in the shape of Sergeant Johns the regimental police sergeant. This man stood about four-foot-and-a-fag-end tall, but he was an expert in putting you through pain like you could never imagine.

This is what he did for the next three hours with the aid of some fire extinguishers, which we held above our heads while running on the spot with our knees up to our chests. Not to mention having to take turns in dragging an amazingly heavy old fire cart around the parade square. When he finally let us go we all felt that our lungs had fallen out, except for Nobby who was still sporting his frazzled hairdo. Nobby was amazingly fit considering he smoked about a hundred fags a day, and his first words once we were out of earshot of Johns were, "Has anyone got a tab? I could murder a smoke."

Strangely enough, we managed to muster up enough strength between us to jump all over him in appreciation for the last three hours. I think we remain to this day the only fire picket to set fire to the fire picket hut.

Finally, the first six weeks reached their climax with the staging of the 'beret' parade where those of us who had 'survived' proudly received our green berets worn by the light division in the presence of our families. I had lost so much weight that my own mum and dad walked straight passed me, after looking right at me, as I waited for them outside the accommodation block. The parade went well and I felt a proud lump in my throat as the commanding officer Captain Nicholson gave a speech about what we had been through and achieved over the last six weeks.

My mum seemed to be really enjoying it when I spotted her in the crowd. My dad, however, had positioned himself next to a group of officers, and seemed more interested in getting them to notice that he was wearing his modified air force officers' greatcoat. The parade over, we went off on a well-deserved long weekend bit of leave.

In no time at all we were back at the barracks to continue training. I had joined the bugle platoon and had to move over to their barrack room across the square from Corunna platoon. I was impressed with the flashy uniform and the fact that the bugle platoon was specially trained to fire the sustained-fire (SF) machine gun. This weapon is a general-purpose machine gun mounted on a tripod, which is capable of laying down an almost constant barrage of bullets very accurately on targets up to one thousand metres away. It was the best weapon I ever got the privilege to fire.

It was in the bugle platoon that I met another man who I came to respect a great deal. He was the platoon commander who, like Wilson, was a warrant officer class one who had worked his way up through the ranks. His name was Max Bygraves, like the singer, and he was another hard man - with a name like that you have to be. One of the first and most important lessons he taught us was that no matter how hard you think you are there is always someone harder round the corner. He also told us that the hardest men were often the quietest, as they had nothing to prove to themselves or to anyone else.

This was certainly true of 'Willie' Willoughby, one of the three training corporals in the bugle platoon. You couldn't meet a more placid-looking man, but when the shit hit the fan Willie would let loose like a Tasmanian devil. During one incident down town I witnessed about five or six coppers struggling to restrain him. His whole body used to tense up into one big mass of muscle, and once they had finally managed to cuff him and get him in their car he proceeded to try to strangle the driver with his handcuffs.

On the other side of the coin we had Corporal Chris P. There wasn't anything Chris hadn't seen, done or been involved in. In later years Max's (Bygraves) philosophy was confirmed when we discovered just exactly what Chris had done, which didn't match his account. The third member of the bugle platoon's team of corporals was a tall, skinny Geordie called, wait for it, Tom Jerry. Tom had almost completed his twenty-two years' service so, although he had a wealth of knowledge and taught us very thoroughly, he had long since lost interest in the usual army bullshit that should have accompanied his current position.

The final member of the platoon staff certainly made up for Tom's lack of love for the army - Sergeant 'Pup' Coley from the First Battalion light infantry. Pup was certifiably insane. He was what you would call 'army barmy', and if he had served during the First World War they would have probably shot him. He would even carry out rigorous inspections of his kids' rooms and uniforms every morning before sending them to school. He truly was as mad as a March hare and was prone to 'loosing it' big time with us if we didn't do something to his exacting standards or we dropped him in the shit. He was, however, a great guy, a real character, and we all owed Pup a great deal. If we were ever in trouble Pup would bail us out every time, and back us up whether he thought we were right or wrong. He may have individually beaten us almost senseless later, but that was better than being stuck in the glasshouse or in Shrewsbury Police cells.

It was at Shrewsbury that I got my chance to step into the ring for the first time. The army is very big on boxing. I don't know if they still do it now, but one of our first PE lessons was 'milling', which used to be like the old cockfights. Basically we would all sit around the ring and a PTI (physical training instructor) would throw two pairs of enormous boxing gloves into the group. Whichever pair of recruits got the gloves would step into the ring for a non-stop three minute round. It may not sound like much, but I am sure anyone reading this who has boxed will agree that three minutes is a long time, especially when the gloves are so big it is as if being hit with a sledgehammer after your second or third go in the ring. It was a good character-building exercise, as you had to give it your all whether you were up against your best mate or your worse enemy, otherwise one of the PTIs would step in to have a go at you.

The next time I stepped into the ring it was to participate in the inter-company boxing tournament after Chris had told me some bollocks about how he used to be the battalion boxing team coach. It turned out that he had about as much idea as I did and, to my horror, I found out that I was to fight 'Wallie' Walcott in my first bout. Wally was a north London youth champion before he joined the army. I had known this because he was in Corunna platoon with me.

But in army boxing you just have to go for it flat out (which is where I thought I would end up after a couple of rounds with Wallie). I did all right. I lost the bout, but I went the distance and only hit the canvas twice (the rest of the time I just grabbed the referee to stop me from falling). I even managed to put Wallie on his arse once due to a lucky punch. This performance earned me a lot of respect. Everyone could see that I was totally out of my league, but I was a scrapper and I gave him a good run for his money. However, he made a hell of a mess of my boyish good looks. I couldn't eat solids for about a week, but I had proved my worth. I couldn't help but curse my dad in the third round for not letting me join the gym in Dagenham - it might have been a different story then.

We remained at Shrewsbury Barracks until they were closed down in the summer of 1986 when we moved to the new barracks at Winchester. By this time the platoon had shrunk to some fifteen of us and as a result we had formed a good bond together. My old battle partner from Corunna platoon, Andy 'Frog' Thatcher, was still with us. I had picked Frog to be my battle partner during the first six weeks due to the fact that he was the only one in the platoon smaller than me and he would have been easier to carry if the need arose. He was a good lad, an excellent soldier and a loyal and trustworthy friend.

There were only four Green Jackets left at this stage - me, Pete Mills from Ribble Road near Preston, Rob Cook from Leicester and Alex 'Harry' Betts from Harrow. Millsy joined the Third Battalion and the last I heard he was growing some things that 'aren't cabbages' on a relative's farm in New Zealand. He was a proper nutcase. His claim to fame was being elected leader of the Ribble Road gang before having to resign the position to Stinky Paterson so he could join the army. The last time I saw Millsy was in Gibraltar. He had gone absent without leave but couldn't afford a flight home, so he spent about eight weeks living in the water tank housing on top of the guardroom. When you think about it, it was the perfect hiding place, but it was proving more difficult for his mates to smuggle food up to him and even more difficult for him to pop out when he fancied a pint down the town. He gave himself up eventually and was discharged from the army on psychiatric grounds. Both Cookie and Harry joined the Second Battalion with me. Both are now out of the army and married with kids of their own.

We continued the training at Winchester until the summer of 1987. During that time most of us turned eighteen and began to educate ourselves in the art of serious drinking as most young men of that age do. By this stage our training programme had relaxed slightly. We were still getting the run around but it was a far cry from the earlier Shrewsbury days.

This respite was short-lived, however, when we received a new platoon commander who was to get us through the 'final fling' - a three-week exercise on the harsh Brecon Beacons culminating in a twenty-six kilometre march in full battle kit, immediately followed by the notorious one-mile-long Brecon assault course. This new guy's name was 'Mad Paddy' Powell, a real hard-nosed bastard whose mere name struck fear into everyone that wasn't one of his very select friends.

The first time I met him I literally ran into him on the parade square. I had been out on the piss the night before and was late for the morning parade. To top that, I had had a bit of a tear up with a couple of civvies down the town the previous night and was sporting the black eyes of all black eyes. That was it - not only had I knocked 'Mad Paddy' over on his first day, he had heard all about the bit of trouble down the town and now had first-hand confirmation that it was one of 'his lads' that was involved.

The exercise went well. The Brecon weather was 'kind' to us - it only rained for two-and-a-half weeks out of the three. It was split into three phases: a live firing phase, where we carried out various different section and company attacks on every manner of ranges with live ammunition; an offensive phase, where we had to locate and destroy various enemy positions; and a defensive week, where we had to dig trenches and defend them from various attacks. My memories of this exercise are a permanent feeling of dampness and the constant smell of the eye watering, choking CS gas, which was used to test our knowledge of how to survive a chemical attack but which lingered on our clothing for the whole exercise. We used the SF machine gun throughout the three weeks and by the end of it I had become quite an expert. As well as my own rifle, kit and SF tripod (which alone weighed 30 pounds), I carried one of the younger recruit's, Carl Gustav's, anti-tank rocket launcher for about ten miles. This act finally earned me respect from Mad Paddy and allowed him to forget about our first meeting.

In the summer of 1987 we finally passed out on a blazing hot day at Sir John Moore Barracks, Winchester. I felt proud of the fact that we had gone through so much and come out the other end as men. We had seen our ranks shrink by over half their size. It had been tough. We'd had to learn about discipline and respect. In almost two years we'd had to prove that from snotty nosed kids we were now worthy of joining the ranks of what I consider to be the finest infantry regiment in the world and certainly part of the best fighting force in the world. The fact that we were standing on that square meant that we were.

However, our training wasn't over. We had to continue training constantly to enable us to maintain the standards set by those who wore the same uniform and cap badge that we proudly wore that day, and if you know your military history you will understand that this is no mean undertaking. I don't think anyone can fully appreciate the feeling you get on such an occasion unless you have experienced the sheer physical and mental pressure that you are put through during military basic training.

Some of the methods used by the training staff may have seemed harsh and you might think they were bully-boy tactics, but I think they were needed and none of those standing on that square held any resentment for any of the staff. The fact of the matter was that they knew that the business of being an infantry soldier was not an easy or nice one.

They had to turn us into men who could operate in any condition and act with a totally unbiased attitude and who ultimately would engage, fight and kill any enemy we were put up against. My whole outlook on life had changed. I had discipline, respect, pride in myself and honour. Another lesson I learned was that real men who have all of the last four qualities didn't brag about what they had seen, where they had been, what they had done or how many other blokes they had beaten up, because they didn't need to prove themselves to anyone.

I began to detest people who were full of themselves and spent all their time boosting their own egos by bragging about their various conquests, and I still do. The Prison Service is sadly full of this type of person and was another reason behind my decision to leave. My belief is that the ones who brag about their achievements to everyone they come across have actually achieved fuck all. The people who were really there don't want to talk about it and keep their memories where they belong - in their own heads.

Even though I feel it necessary to write this book at this time, I still have a lot of personal memories of my army days that I will not include in its pages for that reason. You don't need to know. There is nothing glorious about war or death or indeed beating another human being senseless with four or five of your mates while he is on the floor. Anyone who feels that there is and likes to brag to the world about their involvement is a wanker in my book. I've no time for bullies or insecure little men who talk about things they haven't a clue about in order to try to make themselves out to be something they're not. Anyway, I am drifting away from the plot again.

Standing on that parade square I felt a warm shiver passing through my body which was a feeling of relief, extreme pride, satisfaction and self-achievement together with a feeling of trepidation about what we could expect when we joined our respective battalions.

During our two years spent at the training depot we heard some real horror stories about life in the battalion. We had even seen some real-life battalion soldiers passing through, although we were not worthy at that stage even to look at them let alone engage in conversation with them. These were men who were already at the place we were struggling to get to. They had achieved all our hopes and dreams before we even donned the khaki uniform; they had already proved their worth. We had heard stories of brutal initiation ceremonies and nightly beatings from senior soldiers, even of mental and physical torture. So you can understand why my feeling of trepidation was justified!

Once the formalities of the passing-out parade were over, we bid each other farewell and set off on a couple of weeks' leave. It was a sad time because many of us would not see each other again for some time because we were all joining different battalions throughout the light division all over the world. Many of my friends were sent to the First Battalion light infantry and sadly some of them were to have their careers tragically cut short almost two years later when the bus in which they were returning to Omagh Barracks was blown up en route by the IRA. In a strange twist of fate, however, the bombers' success was short-lived as they were engaged and killed by an SAS team operating in that area on another assignment. It doesn't bring back the young light infantrymen that lost their lives, but it did even the score slightly. No one can ever be prepared for such loss and it is always sad to lose friends in such a cowardly way, but that was the game we were in and we just had to try to play it better than anyone else in order to survive. I always have my own private moment every Remembrance Day to remember those men and other friends I have lost over the years. I will never forget them.

The leave following my passing-out parade was one of the best I was to have. Also on leave were Garry, who had himself recently joined the Second Battalion Royal Green Jackets where I was destined; Simon, who was just about to complete his Royal Electrical Mechanical Engineers course and be posted to Germany; and Steve, himself serving with the Third Battalion Royal Green Jackets in Celle, Germany. A more loyal, trustworthy and certainly 'thirsty' gang you could not find anywhere in the world. I dread to think how much lager we drank between us in that couple of weeks. It's a wonder none of us suffered any long-term liver damage. Our nightly - and daily come to think about it - haunt in those days was a small pub with a terrible reputation in Eltham called The Castle. The Castle at that time was run by a guy called Harry Starbuck a well-known 'face' in Eltham at that time, and as a result was a favourite haunt of some of the toughest men in the area.

The pub's reputation also attracted some undesirables from elsewhere either wanting to muscle in on the pub's success or looking to settle scores with some of the customers. Harry knew that if his more than capable team of bouncers were ever 'up against it' he could count on his newly trained gang of soldiers to jump in and lend a hand, which we willingly did on a number of occasions. I remember us finding it hilarious when we did get involved in such scraps. We used to spend hours afterwards laughing about it and giving Garry grief because, despite always being in the thick of it, he always managed to come out of it without a mark on his face while the rest of us would be sporting black eyes and broken noses. It was such incidents, coupled with his own vanity, that earned Garry the title of 'Pretty Boy' Thompson.

From The Castle every Friday and Saturday night we would pile into a taxi and, providing we were not already in the casualty department of Woolwich Military Hospital, we would descend on Spooks nightclub in Woolwich. This place was something else. In its historical life it had been everything from a café to a venue for underground boxing bouts. In our day it was a club that attracted all sorts of people from pimps and drug-pushers to office parties that innocently passed through the battered green double garage doors. 'Fat' Dave the doorman, who never got out of his tatty armchair for anyone, subjected everyone to an almost indecent search. Even the Queen would have been searched while Dave remained slouched in his chair had she decided to pop in for half a lager shandy on her way home. Inside, the place was so dark that the Queen could have been dancing next to you all night and you wouldn't even have known it, and as for having a conversation, forget it. You would have to go outside or learn sign language. The only time the music would stop and the lights would go on was when a fight broke out, or someone tried to 'glass' the DJ with one of the plastic glasses that all drinks were served in. When this happened, it was like a scene from the TV show *It's a Knockout*. The DJ was situated in a box, which was up near the roof. It was his job to direct the bouncers to the trouble. All you could do was freeze and listen to the DJ shout, "Left a bit, right a bit, that's him". Then - whack! - the bouncers would dish out a crippling blow to the back of some bloke's head, only to hear the DJ shout, "Sorry, my mistake, wrong one. Left a bit, right a bit, that's him" - whack! This went on until they finally got the right man, but not before they had put about three or four blokes out of action for the night.

Trouble that started in Spooks inevitably spilled out onto the streets of Woolwich once the club shut. This was a dangerous time when you had to dodge running street battles being waged between various groups of men and women all of whom were pissed out of their tiny little minds. It was during one such night that I and Pretty Boy were slowly making progress down the mile-long queue into the only open kebab shop when we noticed Steve involved in a scrap on the other side of the street. Normally we would have rushed to his assistance, but to do this would have meant losing our valuable place in the queue and possibly risking the chance of not getting a kebab at all. So we decided to do the next best thing for our friend. Due to his current position, he was unlikely to finish messing around before the kebab shop shut, so we shouted over to Steve and asked if he wanted chilli sauce on his doner and told him not to worry, it would be our treat.

Like all good things, the leave was over quickly and I had to come back to earth with a bump when the day arrived for me to report to the Second Battalion, which was currently based at Battlesbury Barracks in sunny Warminster.

4

2ND BATTALLION ROYAL GREEN JACKETS

During the train journey to Warminster I experienced much the same feelings as I had had on that first journey to Shrewsbury. Once again my head was filled with thoughts, trying to imagine what lay in store for me, and once again I didn't have a clue. The arrival at Warminster Station and indeed at Battlesbury Barracks was less dramatic than the one I had experienced at Shrewsbury. A lone landrover driven by Rifleman Dave Presnall, a little, scruffy looking bloke with an unshaven face and tired, bloodshot eyes met Cookie, 'Harry' and myself. In the years that followed, Dave and I were to become good friends and enjoy many a drunken night out in Capel Court Country Club just outside Dover, which was owned by his mum and dad. But at this particular time we were obviously keeping him from more important things than picking up a couple of NIGS (new intake groups) from the station. He hardly said a word to us and when he did open his mouth he was just whining about the army. This whining was an art unique to soldiers in the battalion and one that we were to master ourselves in no time at all.

We arrived at the camp only to find the rest of the battalion on leave and only a skeleton rear party in residence guarding the barracks. In some ways this worked to our advantage as it gave us the opportunity to settle in and explore the local town for a few days before the boys got back. We were taken out by Jimmy Clarke, a little fat sergeants' mess worker, on our first night only because he was skint and was after a few free pints and not because he was feeling hospitable or anything.

Jimmy quickly toured us round the town's main four drinking holes, The Bath Arms, The Bell, The Anchor and The Volunteer (which the owner craftily renamed The Rifleman shortly after our arrival). After the pubs had shut he then showed us the two Chinese takeaways, one up some stairs and the other on street level, so you had a choice of venues depending on how much lager you had drunk and whether you could safely negotiate the stairs or not. Both takeaways had their own risks, however. The upstairs one was where the two Fijian brothers, both corporals in D Company, liked to fine tune their favourite sport of surfing down the stairs on the back of the nearest 'NIG' they could find, which produced some pretty nasty carpet burns on their victim (sorry 'teammate'). The 'downstairs' Chinese was on the outskirts of Green Jacket territory. It was called the 'boxing ring' due to the shape of its waiting area and the fact that there were usually some squaddies from the school of infantry in there who would risk venturing so close to Green Jacket territory in search of a good meal. The outcome of this mix would always end up in a punch-up between the two groups of squaddies. These groups would in turn be compelled to join forces in an attempt to fight off the seven or eight 'Bruce Lee' chefs who somersaulted over the counter to prevent their place being smashed up.

A few days later the rest of the platoon returned from leave. I was accepted more or less straight away due to the fact that it was halfway through the month and I was in possession of a tin of tobacco. This was a rare item so close to pay day and so, although it cost me almost a full ounce, my fears of this initial meeting, as described earlier, were dispelled. It's strange how things work in the army, and I wondered that night what the story would have been had I decided not to buy that tin at Waterloo Station three days earlier.

The platoon was full of great characters, each one adding their own unique contributions to the way in which we lived. I could fill another book just describing them all, so I will only describe a few to give you the general picture. The first guy I met was a Geordie called Pete Carr. Pete was a lunatic in his own right; he modelled himself on Bruce Lee and worshipped the Seventies. Pete was also of Indian origin, although he was unsure of his true birthday and some years later when we were going to Canada he discovered he didn't have a passport and it took a lot of time and effort on the army's behalf to get him one. How he ever got into the British army without one is beyond me. As a result of his wayward personality, Pete looked like an Indian porn star from China whenever he got dressed up for a night on the town.

Following closely behind Pete was his loyal but completely different friend 'Mac' McLeod. Mac was the sensible one; well at least he was the only one in the platoon still to have money left after the first weekend of the month. He was a fitness fanatic and spent hours in the gym and out running. He was also an excellent boxer, with many trophies under his belt including battalion champion, which was an achievement in itself considering the competition you get in a Green Jacket battalion. Yet to look at Mac he seemed the most unlikely boxing champion ever. But another lesson I had learned was never to judge a book by its cover and never underestimate anyone.

Mac once had a run-in with a giant of a man from the REME (Royal Electrical Mechanical Engineers) when he fell into Mac pissed down the town and started blaming Mac for spilling his drink. Ever calm, Mac suggested they didn't fight in the bar and get nicked by the army, but rather settled it in the ring back at the camp. That was it, the gauntlet had been thrown, and the REME lads were convinced their man would win hands down due to his size. I did warn them to go to the library and read about David and Goliath, but they just weren't having it. Anyway, the day of the bout arrived and, needless to say, Mac was all over the fat git, who didn't even get the chance to land one punch. Eventually his mates threw in the towel after Mac had made a bit of a mess of him, but once again another man had stood his ground and earned the respect of someone who was all set to kick the living daylights out of him. A man who had spent a week bragging to all and sundry about what he was going to do to this 'little prick' had to eat a bit of humble pie, when the swelling went down that is!

Then there was Kia Morgan, a wiry man from Dartford who had a mass of perfectly combed black hair and matching moustache. Kia, like most of us, did like a drink and spent most of his time pissed and slurring out his own personal views on life and the army. He was, however, a very good soldier who had the utmost pride in his regiment and staunch loyalty to his friends. You could always rely on Kia to help out if you ever got into any bother.

Finally I must introduce you to Paul 'Fred' (due to his uncanny resemblance to Fred Flintstone) Symcox, the platoon's secret weapon. What Fred seemed to lack in common sense he more than made up for in sheer size and strength. In fact Fred's appearance and apparently stupid nature hid a man who was actually very clever and had more 'O' and 'A' levels than the rest of the platoon put together. Despite being prone to the odd temper tantrum, when it was best to stay well clear, Fred, like the rest of us, was extremely loyal. He proved this on a number of occasions by bailing us out of many a scrape. I remember one night we were out and Fred was being his usual loud self - this was just Fred's normal volume but people who didn't know him would often take him the wrong way. Anyway, Fred went to the toilet and Kia and I noticed four guys who had been staring at our group all night follow him in. We thought it was a bit strange that they should all want to 'go' at the same time as Fred and decided that as Fred had had about twenty pints of bitter we should go and see if he was all right. We entered the toilets almost immediately after the four guys, but realized that Fred was in no need of assistance when we saw three of them out cold on the floor and the fourth going a strange shade of blue whilst being held in one of Fred's trademark bear hugs. We apologized to Fred for our lack of faith in him and left him to enjoy himself and finish his piss.

As I said earlier, I have obviously not mentioned all the members of the platoon. They were all great guys and it was a pleasure, if not an experience, to have had the opportunity to live and work with them. You all know who you are and if you are upset that you didn't get a mention, tough shit. I'll buy you a drink at the next reunion.

Our first duty away from Warminster was the Cardiff Tattoo, which was being held in the grounds of the city's castle. We arrived and were billeted in the university, as the students were on their summer holidays. On arrival, the porter pointed out that there was a bundle of tickets on the reception table that would allow us to gain free entry into some of the city's clubs. He invited us to take one each, but as we were the first group to arrive we told him we would take the lot and asked him to forget to mention it to the others as and when they arrived. So that was us sorted for the next couple of weeks as we divided up the tickets equally between us.

The Tattoo itself, although I am sure it was spectacular for spectators, was nothing but an interruption to our main objective whilst in this lovely capital city and that was to visit as many drinking holes as possible and sample as many different types of alcohol as we could drink. Our last performance didn't finish until about nine o'clock, but luckily we were the first to march off at the end of the big finale.

We used to get on the first bus in line to take us back to the university. Once back on campus we would run upstairs, get changed, splash on a bit of Old Spice and then commandeer another bus on its way back to pick up the stragglers from the castle to drop us off in the town centre en route. We perfected this so well that we would even beat the spectators into the Owen Glyndwr pub where we would start out from each night. We had a good time every night, but no night went by without an incident of some description.

One of the other military units that was also present was the Royal Navy Recruitment team, armed with an impressive 3D replica of one of their destroyers, which was part of their display. We passed this one night at about three o' clock in the morning and decided to dance the hornpipe on it to the *Captain Pugwash* theme tune. Impressive as it was, it was not designed for such use and halfway through our performance the whole thing collapsed from under us. It was only due to the fact that we were all so pissed that we escaped injury. We had to chuckle the next day when we went past the wreckage on our bus and saw a group of sailors looking puzzled and scratching their heads. We got one of those looks we had become only too familiar with from our boss as he put two and two together.

The Tattoo over, we returned to Warminster. The battalion's primary role at Battlesbury Barracks was to carry out its duties as the infantry demonstration battalion. For the lads in the rifle companies it was a very monotonous role. They spent hours day after day performing the same demonstrations of new infantry weapons and machines to international audiences as well as putting recently qualified young officers through various tactical scenarios to prepare them for when they would take up their new posts as platoon commanders.

My platoon's primary role at that time, however, was to carry out various ceremonial duties all over the country, such as the one we had just done in Cardiff. Although this was at times fun and it gave us the opportunity to visit many different places, it was also very tiring and at times boring due to the long hours spent on coaches and living out of suitcases. Apart from anything else, unlike the members of the Peninsula Band who accompanied us on such duties, we as buglers were primarily trained infantry soldiers and we missed being able to act as such.

It was not long, however, before our tour of duty at Warminster thankfully came to an end and we began to pack up in readiness for our move to Dover. The whole battalion was looking forward to our new posting. We were due to become part of the air-mobile force and could look forward to some real infantry work once again. We also had some good tours coming up such as Canada and for me and many of my fellow young soldiers our first emergency tour of Northern Ireland.

In August 1988 we arrived at Connaught Barracks, which is situated at the top of the hill in Dover overlooking the town's impressive castle. We took over from the Irish Rangers who were full of typically rowdy, fiery Irishmen who liked nothing better on a Friday night, or any night come to that, than a good drink followed by a good punch-up. For this reason alone, although the Green Jackets were not particularly known as the best regiment to have in residency, we were welcomed by most of the town's landlords who had previously refused entry to many of our predecessors.

The nightlife in Dover was better than Warminster purely because of its port and the mix of people who passed through it. There were three main pubs in the town's centre. The Elephant and Hind in the Market Square was where most nights would begin. Then there was The Dover Tavern, which was my favourite because it was a real 'spit and sawdust' bar and at the time was run by fat Duncan. And finally there was the slightly more up-market Britannia, which actually had a fully fitted carpet in it. As I say, we quickly settled into our new posting and as a platoon we settled into our new role, which was back in B (Support) Company where you found the battalion's Mortar, Milan and Machine Gun platoons. My old mate Garry was in Mortar platoon at that time, and as during our posting in Warminster Support Company he had been billeted in Netheravon Barracks we had not seen much of each other apart from when on leave.

It was about this time that I and Natasha had finally separated during an emotional night whilst I was on leave. We had separated a couple of times before during my training, but always got back together when we met up again later. This time, though, such reconciliation seemed unlikely as she appeared a little more definite on this occasion. I remember feeling as if I had lost part of myself as I walked from her house in Glenforth Street, Greenwich early the next morning. Despite our problems she had been a tower of strength to me, but maybe I did not give her the attention she deserved and needed at the time. I did, however, know how much I truly loved her and wonder how I would cope without her in the future. I was sad, too, that I felt I would never see the rest of her family again, as I had grown very attached to all of them.

Natasha's mum, Dorothy, or Dot as everyone knew her, was and still is a marvellous woman. She is originally from Portrush in Northern Ireland and was blessed with a great Irish sense of humour as well as that nation's well-known hospitality. I had known Dot for some six years at this stage and considered her to be like my own mother as she had virtually brought me up with her family since the age of fourteen. Also I would miss Natasha's sisters - Nikki, who I mentioned earlier, and her youngest sister Samantha, or Tiny as we called her. Tiny and I got on really well. She could only have been about eight years old when I first met her, but I used to get more letters from her than I did from Natasha sometimes, and she always looked pleased to see me when I came home on leave.

I was to see Natasha once more before I left for my first tour of Northern

Ireland when I met her in The Napier Tavern in Greenwich. She told me later that she was trying to see if we could make another go of it at that meeting, but the truth of it was that I was still hurting after our last parting and couldn't bear to go through the same feelings again. We both parted that night and hoped that the other would subsequently make the first contact. For some possibly childish, stubborn reason, neither of us did. It was to be an act I would live to regret forever and it would be some nine years later before we would see each other again.

Around November 1988 the battalion began its Northern Ireland training in preparation for the forthcoming tour to Fermanagh. I for one found this training the best thing I had done in the army to date. It was training for real to prepare us for a real-life scenario unlike the usual made up 'Russian' enemy we seemed to be fighting a constant battle with on training areas all over England.

Just before the training began, I had another pleasant surprise in the form of the arrival of my other old pals, Simon Long and Steve Fairs at Dover. Simon had been posted in from Germany to join the battalions REME detachment, and Steve had volunteered his services from the Third Battalion Royal Green Jackets to help our own battalion get up to strength for the Ireland tour. This was great - the old gang was back in business. Simon's mum, Trisha, was none too pleased when she heard that all her 'boys' were going to Ireland together and didn't stop worrying or lighting candles at her local Catholic church for us until we all returned safely.

The training itself was split into three phases. Phase one was the live firing phase during which we fired all manner of different weapons on a wide variety of different ranges at the army ranges along the beaches at Lydd and Hythe. Phase two was the urban warfare training, which comprised endlessly practising how to patrol in built-up areas and react to various incidents and threats and learning various other tasks that we would need to carry out such as setting up vehicle checkpoints and searching both people and vehicles. The final phase was to be held in the bleak Norfolk countryside where we would master the art of rural patrolling and reacting to various incidents in conditions similar to those we would encounter in Fermanagh.

For the purpose of patrolling in Northern Ireland each platoon is split into two groups, one led by the platoon sergeant and one by the platoon commander. These two groups in turn are split into four-man teams made up of a lance or full corporal and three riflemen. My team was under our new platoon sergeant, Stan Bowes, who like myself was from south London but unlike myself was an excellent boxer who actually trained the very successful battalion boxing team for a number of years. He was also a very good soldier with many years of experience and previous tours of Ireland under his belt, so as a relatively inexperienced platoon we could not have wished for a better man to lead us. My team commander for the forthcoming tour was Corporal 'Ginge' Naylor, a highly experienced and dedicated man who truly loved the army and as such was both an excellent soldier and an extremely good and loyal friend. Ginge was an inspiration to us as a relatively young and inexperienced team, and we were to learn a lot from him and he was to become one of my closest and most trusted friends.

Some years later I was devastated to receive the news that Ginge had collapsed and died in Cyprus while performing a short three-mile run while undergoing a rigorous personal training programme in preparation for his participation in selection for the SAS. I know it had been a dream of his for many years to complete selection and I found it difficult to comprehend that such a fit, experienced man could have had his life cut short in such a way. Ginge, however, would not have had it any other way. He died doing what he loved most and chasing his dream, the SAS, and his many friends knew they had lost a truly great man when he passed away. I for one will never forget his ever smiling face or his trademark laugh that got us through some very difficult times, I always have a pint 'with' him at every Green Jacket reunion.

The rest of the team consisted of a young recruit, 'Robbo' Robins, who had recently joined us from the training depot and an extremely laid-back riflemen of West Indian origin known only as 'Cyrus'. Despite our lack of experience and Cyrus's lack of interest, Ginge succeeded in moulding us into an extremely effective team and we performed very well on all the phases of the training. Cyrus was particularly thrilled when Lucozade brought out its new tropical fruit flavour and he bought this by the crate to keep his already naturally low energy levels topped up during the rather hectic and physical training programme. He was a great character and I and Ginge used to joke with him that he could get shot through the chest and not let it bother him. Robbo, on the other hand, had some problems of his own. It is a huge thing, as I mentioned before, just making that transition from the training depot to the battalion without being thrust straight into the very serious and intense training programme run by the Northern Ireland training and tactics team. He did, however, perform very well considering the huge amount of pressure he must have been under not only to take everything in but also to get accepted by his new comrades, and he turned out to be a valued member of Yankee Two Zero Bravo, our call sign for the tour.

The urban warfare phase of our training culminated in a four-day stint in 'Tin City'. This was an exact replica of Belfast, which was filled with 'Civ-Pop' (members of another regiment who act as civilians and live in Tin City for the duration of the exercise) and covered with closed circuit television, which records every move twenty-three hours a day. During our tour in 'Tin City' we were given an endless amount of different tasks and incidents to deal with on the basis that we were in a real security forces base in Belfast. Each day at 2100 hours the exercise was stopped for one hour and we all crammed into the metal hangar for a briefing on the day's events. The staff used the CCTV recordings to analyze our reactions. They kept the mood going by playing records such as Tears for Fears' *Shout* and various records by U2, as well as cleverly editing the videotapes with scenes from old news reports, old comedy films and even footage from the TV series *Spitting Image* where they felt it was necessary to highlight good or bad reactions.

The final event and the one they had been building us up to was a very realistic full-scale riot involving the whole company and real petrol bombs and rubber bullets. This was an experience I will never forget, as the smell of burning rubber and petrol and the feel of real bricks hitting you, not to mention the very real casualties taken on both sides, only added to the realism of the whole exercise.

After completing the urban phase there was time for a well-deserved weekend off, which was spent topping up on the alcohol levels that had seriously diminished over the previous couple of weeks in our usual Dover haunts. One thing that I always found amazing in all 'squaddie' towns was the vast number of civilians who ventured into the town's pubs when the battalion was away and the speed at which they quickly disappeared to wherever it was they came from on our return. However, I think that in general we, the Green Jackets, got on very well with the locals in most of the towns we served in and we certainly never gave anyone any real reason to be afraid to drink in their own town. Maybe it was just the sheer number of us that descended on the town and the way in which we lived by the rule 'we work hard so we'll play hard' that intimidated some people.

On the following Monday morning at some unearthly hour, and nursing some serious hangovers, we boarded the transport for our journey to Norfolk for the final phase of our training. Norfolk is bleak at the best of times, but we hit it at the beginning of January, and it was freezing. During the brief and rare occasions that we were not out on the training area at night, we slept in corrugated iron Nissen huts, which were left by the American air force after their stay during the Second World War. These huts were actually quite comfortable and offered protection from the rain and bitter wind that swept across the Norfolk moors.

By the time we were due to leave, we had even managed to stoke up the ancient iron stoves in the centre of each hut, despite constant objections from the resident fire officer, and these proved very effective in throwing out some welcomed heat. During the exercise we learned all the different patrolling techniques that we would need to apply to our rural environment in Fermanagh.

We also spent a lot of time practising our reactionary drills and mastering the various pieces of equipment that would detect or prevent the presence or detonation of explosive devices. The other important part of the training was mastering our helicopter drills. These were now being used on a regular basis in the Province to prevent attacks on patrols on the ground, which previously relied on landrovers to drop them off or pick them up along the border areas.

The training was hard and we had to use all our infantry skills just to try to keep reasonably warm and dry, but it was also very enjoyable as we were training for a real-life deployment. We all knew that some of us may well be killed or seriously injured during the tour. To that end, we also knew that we owed it to one another to learn as much as we could and to fine tune all our skills so that we could watch out for each other over the water. Obviously there was the usual humour and mandatory whining, or ticking as we called it, but that is what keeps you going. You will find that most soldiers moan about everything they do, but this is only their way of motivating themselves to maintain the high standards that are expected of them and that the British Army always produces when called upon to do so. If there was nothing legitimate to moan about your average British soldier would make something up. It's just been a tradition in the army since Britain formed its first fighting force to repel our country's would-be invaders. The important thing in life is that you get the job done, and I defy anyone to deny that the British forces ever do anything less.

During the period of training I saw very little of Simon and Steve as they were busy doing the same with their own respective companies. Garry, however, was obviously with me in B (Support) Company, and if anyone can moan that boy certainly can. He had recently fallen in love with a lovely girl called Sarah whom he had met in a nightclub in Margate. They are still together, although she deserves a medal as far as I'm concerned for putting up with him for so long, and are living in married quarters in Ireland at the time of writing this. Sarah was from a good family from Whitstable and was very quiet and nervous when they first met. It took her a while to adjust to her new boyfriend's mates, but I am glad to say she learned very quickly how to deal with it all and now she is very much in command in her house.

The training complete, it was time for a short period of disembarkation leave, generously given by the army before you deploy to somewhere that is classed as dangerous to your health. Short was the operative word and in just five days' time, at the beginning of February 1989, we boarded a Hercules C130 transport plane at RAF Brize Norton bound for RAF Aldergrove in Belfast.

When we left the aircraft at Aldergrove I remember thinking it was like the scene in the film *Platoon,* when Charlie Sheen's character lands in Vietnam for the first time. Obviously, and thankfully, there were no body bags on the runway and it was an awful lot colder than Vietnam. We did, however, pass a platoon of weary looking Irish Rangers, who we were to take over from and who rubbed into our staring faces the fact that they were going home.

On the runway a fragile old lady stopped each one of us and greeted us with a smile. She put her tiny arthritis-ridden hands on all of us in turn, gave us a short blessing and furnished us with a pen and a tiny diary printed onto a single sheet of pocket-sized card. The diaries had various prayers on them and the words "We the people of Ulster are proud of our security forces". Later I learned that this old lady was over seventy years old. Despite numerous threats from various terrorist groups and indeed on one occasion having had both her legs badly broken by some brave bastards, she was at the airport to welcome every flight of soldiers into her country - a truly brave, dedicated and lovely lady.

We made our way to a pair of huge twin-rotor Chinooks and filed into their bellies in two single lines. No sooner had the last man entered than their powerful engines roared to full power. We set off on a hedge-hopping low-level rollercoaster ride to the small border town of Clogher and our hilltop base, which was to be our home for the next four-and-a-half months. The tactical low-level flying was, we were told, necessary as the IRA had acquired a small shipment of surface-to-air missiles and had used them against a military helicopter shortly before our arrival. Something else that had occurred shortly before our arrival was that our new base in Clogher had been the target of an IRA mortar attack. Thankfully the attack was not accurate enough to kill or injure anybody, but it did succeed in damaging parts of the camp and, as a result, we would have to live in a temporary portacabin structure half buried underground and already infested with rats and mice.

The Chinooks landed in the field adjacent to the base and we quickly filed out and made our way to the relative safety of our new home behind its wire fence and manned lookout towers known as 'sangers'. Nothing stirs the blood more than the sight of a fully loaded and armed company of soldiers, and I remember thinking that the IRA would have one hell of a fight on their hands should they decide to have a go at us.

We soon settled into our new home and after the usual formalities of kit and ammunition issue, not to mention the briefing by Major 'Mac' McGarrigle, the company's veteran commander - all given for the benefit of the Panorama film crew who were to film us as part of their *Families At War* series - we began the monotonous routine that would be our existence for the next few months. The duties we had to carry out were to be split between the three platoons who made up B Company, which were now Clogher's residential security forces.

As well as our own local area we had a commitment to share the responsibility for the whole battalion's area together with the other three companies of Green Jackets who themselves were just arriving in their own bases around Fermanagh. We had three areas of responsibility and each platoon was to carry out six weeks on each, which was further broken down into three two-week rotas.

The three areas we had to cover were local patrols around the immediate vicinity of our base and nearby town. This included guard duty in the camp's sangers to watch for any imminent threats and give reassuring cover to other patrols as they entered and left the safety of the base, which is a particularly vulnerable time. We also undertook long-range patrols, which were carried out usually along the dangerous 'bandit' country border areas with the Irish Republic. And finally we had to man the equally dangerous (due to the remoteness of their locations and the fact that there were only eight men in each one) vehicle checkpoints, which were sited all along the border of the Irish Republic. We soon settled into this routine way of life and in no time at all, despite the fact that even that early on in the tour we all were suffering from a distinct lack of sleep, we were carrying out our tasks like veterans.

As I mentioned earlier, most of our moves, and certainly those in and around the border area, were done by helicopter. Due to the recent addition of door gunners armed with general-purpose machine guns in every helicopter, to combat the growing threat from the ground, we soon took on a Vietnam War approach to our situation. The other and far more dangerous method of transport at our disposal - when the officers had used up all of the battalion's allowance of flying hours, which were allocated on a monthly basis, going to meetings and functions in Belfast or Lisbon - was by CPV (civilian pickup vehicle). These were usually transit vans that eight or more of us would have to squeeze into the back of with full kit and weapons fully loaded. We could not see anything at all through the rear, as they were totally blacked out. Apart from the danger of ambush by armed terrorists or the new MK1 mortar designed to take out such vehicles, we ran the risk of running into illegal checkpoints manned by groups of terrorists. Such groups could have emptied a hundred rounds of ammunition into the side of us before we had had a chance to untangle ourselves and react. Personally I hated using CPVs and would rather have stayed out on patrol than have got into the back of one of these 'metal coffins'.

The remainder of the tour thankfully passed without any serious incident. We had a few near misses and plenty of false alarms. We were assured by the intelligence boys at the end of the tour that we had successfully managed to avert all the attacks that were planned against us but had to be aborted due to our professionalism and careful planning.

There are many memories of that first tour for me, but it would take years to write all the funny and not so funny incidents we were involved in. My main memories are of the cold, wet, bog-filled fields, the feeling of total loneliness and homesickness at times, and the fear that we all experienced deep down most days but we all masked well with the good old British soldier's sick sense of humour.

One of the most common ways of hiding your fear of death is to talk openly about it as if it wouldn't matter. A common phrase we said to one another was "It's a good day to die", or other such jokes like, "If you die today can I have your spare boots?" I remember going out on patrol with 'Fatboy Geordie' Tompson and as we cleared the base he turned to me and said, "Jim, if I die today you can have the rest of me Jaffa Cakes, they're under me pillow." For Geordie to leave someone his Jaffa Cakes was like leaving someone your most prized possession. This type of talk may sound a bit egotistical to some, but we were all mainly young men under twenty years old who were facing the possibility of death around every corner every day, and that was one way we coped with that prospect.

Generally, we found the majority of Irish people we came across to be very decent, friendly folk. I do not pretend to be an expert on Irish history. I did, however, do a lot of research into the background of the Irish problem and realized that both sides throughout history carried out atrocities. Like with everything I do in life, I went to Northern Ireland with a totally open mind, did my tour, treated the people I met according to how they treated me, and came home again with no bitter and twisted feelings about any side caught up in the Province's troubles.

We returned to Dover in June 1989 and embarked on a long-awaited leave to spend the fifteen hundred pounds or so that most of us had saved while being in Northern Ireland. I had two objectives during this leave. One was to have a bloody good holiday somewhere hot and the other was to make it back in one piece for Garry and Sarah's wedding in July.

The first objective was completed with a last-minute booking that I and Simon got to Kos for a week. The main thing I can remember about the holiday, for obvious reasons, was our 'apartment'. It was in such a ghetto that the bus that took us to it late at night from the airport wouldn't stop and only slowed down enough for us to jump off while the tour operator nervously pointed us in the general direction. The only other thing I remember was that we spent most of our time sheltering from the sun in Popeye's Bar drinking five-pint pitchers each with a fireman and his mate, a second-hand car dealer, both from Watford. It was a great holiday. We didn't do much sightseeing and we spent too much money, but it achieved its aim of relaxing us after our recent tour.

We just about made it back in time to join in at Garry's stag night in the Plough at Lewisham, and in one piece. That is until we were crossing the road later to get to the kebab shop and a white Triumph Dolomite nearly ran us over and we hurled a bit of abuse at the driver. The Triumph and the red Sierra behind it turned round in the road and stopped in front of us. I swear to this day that I would never have believed so many people could get into two cars. The bloke who built the Tardis for *Doctor Who* must have built them. About seven black youths got out of each car and ran towards us like a scene from *Zulu Dawn*. By this time we numbered about four or five and one of us had already been knocked down by the Sierra. We fought as gallantly as was possible with a bellyful of lager and spirits each, not to mention being seriously outnumbered, but this was one battle we were destined to lose. The only good thing was that Garry had been taken home earlier by his Uncle Kenny after he had passed out in the bar, but I can assure you it wasn't difficult to pick out the groom's mates at the wedding two days later.

On our return to Dover I began to feel increasingly restless. Many of my friends were getting married and some were leaving the army. I began to do some serious soul-searching. I was missing Natasha severely, but thought it was too late as I had heard that she was in another relationship, and I began to wonder what the army had to offer me. I began to start drinking too much, which in turn led me into various troubles with the army.

I became a regular at the colonel's office charged with everything from being absent to even assaulting the fat bandmaster. I was sent away on a driving course in Driffield, Yorkshire, only to team up with an equally troubled Irish Ranger named 'Shaggy' and after sharing a few nights in the local glasshouse we were both returned to our units in disgrace. My saviour was our new boss sergeant, 'Taffy' Smith. Taffy had himself gone through similar problems as a young rifleman serving in Hong Kong and he understood what I needed. He arranged for me to go on a period of detached duty to one of our TA (Territorial Army) battalions based in Oxford. This posting was just what I needed - six months of peace and quiet working virtually as my own boss teaching and assisting the members of the TA. I returned from Oxford a more settled young man and felt ready to rejoin my mates in the battalion and begin training with them for the forthcoming tour of Canada.

The night before we flew to Canada, however, I was arrested by the Dover Police on suspicion of criminal damage at the local nightclub, Images, and spent the night and the best part of the next day in the cells of Dover Police Station. The whole thing turned out to be a case of mistaken identity. At least that is what the CID officer in charge of the case had to conclude when my sergeant major viewed the CCTV footage from the club and vowed that it was not me who was seen throwing the dustbin through the window - honest! They released me into his care and allowed me to go to Canada albeit whilst on police bail and on the understanding that I would be on the first flight back in order to report back to the station.

Whilst in Canada, however, I received a letter saying that all charges had been dropped and my bail was therefore wiped clean. This meant that I was moved back to one of the last members of the battalion to fly back to the UK together with my mate Big 'Scouse' Barlow from the Mortar platoon. The only problem with this was that we didn't have much money left, so Scouse had the idea that we sell some kit.

The Canadian soldiers idolize the British and as a result love the British army kit. We made a small fortune in one afternoon selling our helmets for one hundred and forty dollars each and I even sold a worthless piece of camouflage face netting for sixty dollars after telling its new owner that it was only issued to members of the British SAS. It had to be done, it was survival of the fittest. Anyway, the Canadian army get paid far too much to worry about losing a few quid to a couple of British squaddie conmen.

I had been lucky enough to visit this magnificent country on two previous occasions, and had visited Quebec, Toronto and Calgary. This latest visit had been to Wainwright in Alberta to participate in a six-week battalion live-firing exercise. One of the highlights of this trip was getting to spend a week in the Jasper national park under canvas where we saw everything from bears to herds of moose effortlessly crossing white-water rivers. We even got the chance to go ice trekking up the Andromeda ice fields, a huge mountain of ice that remarkably retained its icy covering despite the intense heat of the Canadian summer. After that little expedition I realized how Scott of the Antarctic's team had found the ice so exhausting to walk over.

I do remember one funny incident whilst B Company and C Company shared the same three days R&R (rest and recuperation) in a rather nice hotel in Edmonton. I wandered into the Pizza Hut next to our hotel one night to find 'Ticking' Willie a bit worse for wear in the middle of a nasty row with three Pizza Hut employees. I didn't know what it was all about; all I cared about was that one of my mates looked in trouble and outnumbered. To cut a long story short, we sorted it and hastily made our way back to the hotel. The following morning little Graham 'Porty' Portafield asked me if he could have his England World Cup shirt back, which he had lent me to wear the night before. I obliged, of course, but as soon as Porty walked out of the hotel he got nicked for causing a disturbance the night before in the Pizza Hut. By the time they had realized they had the wrong man and had released him, I and Willie had taken the liberty of returning to the camp at Wainwright slightly earlier than planned and luckily heard no more about it.

Canada was the last big exercise we took part in, apart from a smaller version of Exercise Lionheart (a Territorial Army mobilization exercise) that we ran from Rhiendarlan Royal Air Force camp in Germany, before undertaking Northern Ireland training once again for our forthcoming two-year posting to Omagh in January 1991.

We quickly realized that Northern Ireland training had not changed a great deal over the previous year or so. The forthcoming tour was to be what they classed as a residential one, where we as a battalion would be based in Lissanelly Barracks in Omagh but could be deployed anywhere throughout Northern Ireland should the need arise. On such tours, unlike the previous one, the whole battalion including families would be going, so at least this time I would not have to put up with Garry's lovesick pining for Sarah or listen constantly to him playing his soppy love songs all day long.

Also for this tour I was to be part of a different four-man team. This time Mac the boxer, who I mentioned earlier, was our team commander, and the rest of us comprised myself (obviously), Freddie 'Mad Dog' Fryer and 'Rupert', a young trainee officer from the Army Pay Corps. None of us took to Rupert straight away, as infantrymen are naturally wary about relying on non-infantry 'soldiers', especially baby officer ones come to that. But, credit where credit's due, he performed very well in training and proved an asset to the team when we deployed on the ground in Northern Ireland. We arrived in the usual manner, but the camp at Omagh was a bit different to the last one we had stayed in.

This camp had everything within its heavily guarded perimeter - two pubs, a large NAAFI, and even a cinema The difference on this tour was that we were allowed out into certain areas of the town when off duty. I found the town of Omagh to be a lovely little town. The vast majority of people there showed us nothing but respect and kindness. I was devastated to hear of the atrocious and cowardly attack there some years later and I really felt for all involved as I thought I must have met some of those who were killed or injured.

The routine we followed was very much the same old routine we had followed in Fermanagh only this time we did slightly longer stints on each phase. Some of the areas we had to cover were slightly more dangerous than those we had been responsible for on the last tour, but the same basic principles applied.

I always laugh when I remember one incident concerning the disposal of our letters, which may have addresses of family back home on them. We were given a bollocking one day by the HQ company sergeant major, who obviously had nothing better to do than rummage through B Company's bins and had found a stack of letters that had not been placed in a burn bag. He took great pleasure in asserting his authority by ordering us to dispose of them in the proper manner. The trouble was we were running a bit late for a rendezvous with the helicopter to take us out on a seven-day patrol of the border. I told the lads that if they took my kit to the helipad and stalled the pilot I would burn the letters and dispose of them before catching them up. I found a small metal bin, lit the letters and made my way to the helipad whilst still carrying the smouldering bin. Then in the distance I saw the regimental police sergeant coming towards me. Not having the time or the patience to explain what I was doing carrying this burning bin around camp with me, I threw it into the skip outside the WRAC (Woman's Royal Army Corps) accommodation block.

I passed the police sergeant with a smile and hurried off to meet the rest of my patrol. Ten minutes later we had just got airborne above the camp when we heard some distant 'thumps' coming from the ground and seconds later the helicopter pilot announced that the camp was under a mortar attack and we had to circle the area to locate the terrorist team. The scene below us was bedlam. There were people running all over the place and diving for cover as the 'thumps' got louder and more frequent. We then noticed a large cloud of black smoke rising from the camp and feared the worst, but we had still been unable to locate the terrorist mortar-base plate position.

On closer inspection we were relieved to spot that it had only been a skip that appeared to have been hit and not an accommodation block. Then it dawned on me - like that terrible feeling you get when you slowly begin to remember the events of the night before - the skip that was on fire was the one outside the WRAC block. The burning bin I had disposed of therein had caught with the rest of the rubbish really well and the 'mortar bomb explosions' were in fact old aerosol spray cans exploding in the heat. This is something I chose to admit to only a select few for obvious reasons and thankfully I think everyone on the ground was too knackered as well as relieved, not to mention in a state of shock, to launch too much of an inquiry into what had happened. By the time we returned from our patrol the following week, the whole thing was a distant memory that will no doubt be written in to future Northern Ireland training programmes.

Despite these moments of fun, I was once again getting that old restless feeling in my water. Over the previous couple of years a lot of my old mates had left the army. We had received a lot of new younger recruits from the training depot, who, despite the training sessions that I regularly held for them in the NAAFI bar, seemed as though they could never replace my old drinking buddies. As a result of this, together with the uncertainty of the recently announced plans for cutbacks within the armed forces and foreseeing a surge of redundant soldiers hitting the job centre at the same time, I took the decision to quit while I was ahead and asked the army to release me. I had the mandatory speeches from everyone from the bottle washer in the 'Plastic Pub' to the colonel about how good a soldier I was and how I shouldn't do anything hasty that I might regret. But, true to form, I had made my decision and no one was going to talk me out of it.

So on 31 August 1991 I boarded a helicopter for my final journey to Belfast, leaving the safety of the only thing I had ever known for the previous six years, and began the first step to becoming a civilian again. It was a strange day, one I had awaited for three months since I had first made my decision, but when the day came I felt nothing of the relief I had expected. All I felt was sadness, as though in a way I was letting my mates down by leaving them in this place to face another year of danger without me.

I felt extremely anxious as to whether I had made the right decision as I didn't have a clue what Civvy Street would have to offer an ex-soldier with no training other than infantry tactics and weaponry. However, it's too late now, I thought as the helicopter rose away from what had been my life for so long and the only people I would truly trust again for a long time. In a strange way I felt like I had committed a terrible act of cowardice. Despite having served six years, I almost felt like ordering the pilot to turn back a couple of times during the twenty-minute or so flight, and I probably would have done so if I had thought he would have listened to me.

When I arrived at Belfast International Airport I ran into a couple of lads from D Company who were waiting for transport to take them to

Aldergrove (the military side of the airport). I was able to have a couple of pints of real Guinness with them before they had to go and I was left to my own thoughts for about two hours before my flight.

I always felt particularly vulnerable whilst sitting in this airport, but this time more so as I felt so totally alone and isolated. I began to think how ironic it would be if I were to be blown up or shot now after surviving two tours and with just two hours to go on this, my last. Finally I boarded the flight and within three hours or so I was stepping off the train and taking the short route I had taken many times before from Mottingham Station to my parents' house in Eltham.

5
CIVVY STREET

While I had been away my mum and dad had bought a house back in Wales and my mum, who had never really settled in London, had moved back there and got herself a job with a local health authority. My dad was still at the sports centre but was due to take early redundancy the following year. So the pressure was on because I didn't really want to spend any more time than necessary in the environment that hadn't changed a great deal since I had joined the army to get away from it in 1985.

I took the first couple of weeks off. The army had owed me a couple of weeks' wages and I felt as though I could do with the time to readjust. I was to find it would take me a lot longer than two weeks to learn to cope with the outside world again. It was something I hadn't really thought about, but I didn't have any idea how to survive in this strange outside world. For six years I had relied on the army for everything - food, clothes, accommodation, security - and now for the first time in my life I was hearing all about mortgages and how you even had to pay for your water and electricity.

This may sound stupid to some, but it is something that you take for granted in the army and I was struggling to learn how to cope, in much the same way, as I was to learn later, that long-term prisoners struggle on their eventual release. In the same way, the army had just kicked me back into the society they had just as quickly scooped me up from all those years earlier without any form of rehabilitation or resettlement course as they call it.

While I was desperate for money and guidance, my old mate Simon's dad, Jim, came to my rescue and offered me a few weeks' work labouring for his firm in the Inner Temple opposite the High Court in Fleet Street.

This was a good job and I was grateful for the opportunity, but I knew it was only temporary and I was beginning to panic about my long-term future.

In the end I was forced to take a security job with Reliance Security Services on a new development near St Catherine's Dock in East London. Initially I hated this job. After the army it seemed like a right Mickey Mouse company, although I was to learn later after joining the Prison Service just what working for a real Mickey Mouse firm was like. The job entailed seven twelve-hour days followed, after three days off, by seven twelve-hour nights from six in the morning to six at night. I am not taking anything away from security guards when I say that personally I felt that I was worth more than this but I just didn't know what at the time.

Things did look up when after about four months I was promoted to the dizzy heights of shift supervisor and was joined at the site by Harry, my old mate from two RGJ, and Louis, an ex-Green Jacket from the First Battalion who I new from my Shrewsbury days. From then on we formed our own little clique, and it wasn't long before we had the whole complex sussed out and keys for every store cupboard and kitchen on it.

They were long and boring days, but the three of us did our best to liven them up. We carried out classic boredom pranks like putting boot polish on the receivers of all the telephones in the offices in the early hours, then stood giggling as we noticed these pathetic yuppies flapping around all day with black ears, none of them noticing their own ears and each too scared to tell the others about theirs. On night shift we would rig doors to slam and send other security guards and mobile units off on wild goose chases around our site and other sites all over London. On one particularly long and boring night we even moved the entire contents of an office owned by a mobile phone company two floors up to a vacant floor. These were childish acts, I know, but it kept us going, although none of us was surprised that the company had lost the bid for the renewal of the security contract when it came up at the end of the year.

Meanwhile, the situation at home had not improved much since I had left home at fifteen. Although my dad was now away in Wales most weekends and I was working long hours, when our paths did cross it was a pretty tense atmosphere. When I initially left the army I had applied to join the Ministry of Defence Police and had sat and passed the exam at the Royal Ulster Constabulary headquarters in Enniskillen. The officer adjudicating advised me that I would definitely pass as long as I wrote all my answers in pencil. Almost a year later, after I had gone through two further interviews and a home visit and while I was waiting for a date to report to the training depot, I received a letter telling me that the Ministry was very sorry but as a result of the recent announcement of the cutbacks in the military they were cancelling all recruitment. They were therefore unable to offer me employment at this time - bastards. I had been counting on that to get me out of the dead-end security job it now looked as though I was stuck with. I really began to start panicking about what I was going to do as I knew that I would not be able to stick it out where I was for very much longer.

Out of sheer desperation I did the one thing everyone said I would do prior to leaving Omagh - I wrote to my old company commander, Major Rose, asking him if he could arrange for me to re-enlist. I was shocked and extremely hurt by the brief and very blunt reply I received a few days later, after all his reassurances the day I left. He had told me in his office that I was such an asset and he was truly sorry to lose me and if at any time I found I was struggling all I had to do was drop him a line and he would sort everything out. However, the letter he wrote was short and quite frankly rude, basically telling me that I had made my bed and I now had to lie in it and that there was no way he could arrange for my re-enlistment now or in the future. I was devastated, not so much because I had lost the hope of rejoining but because a man I had respected and given so much time and dedication to, and who not six months ago I would have protected with my own life, was now writing to me as if I no longer existed.

Although this upset me a great deal, I didn't lose any sleep over it. As my friend Charlie Bronson who I was to meet a couple of years later would say, "You've got to just take it on the chin whatever life throws at you. It's not worth crying about" - words of wisdom from a man who truly knows the meaning of getting over such obstacles that are thrown in your path in life.

So here I was, stuck in a badly paid dead-end job with all my best plans for the future shattered in the form of two letters received in the space of about one week. It was now early January 1992 and I had the added pressure of my dad's voluntary redundancy looming, due to take place in June, which would effectively render me homeless. At this time I was involved in a relationship with a girl called Jackie who lived with her parents in nearby Pratts Bottom.

Although I had and never would forget Natasha, I was scared that too much had passed since we had last seen each other. I knew I wasn't ready to handle rejection from her at that time or get my fears confirmed that she may be happily married and not want me disrupting her new life. This didn't mean that I never thought about how things would have been had we stayed together, and I tried on a number of occasions to find the courage to knock on her mum's door whenever I passed through Greenwich.

I didn't really want the relationship with Jackie to get too serious, as I was not sure what I was going to do with my life let alone get into a long-term relationship and get tied down so soon after leaving the army. However, I was in no position to argue when she suggested that we buy a house together to coincide with my dad leaving for Wales. Eventually I was swept away with the whole process of house hunting and before I knew it 'we' had bought a two-bedroom house in Sidcup. I think it would be fair to say that both of us knew from fairly early on that the relationship would not last, and after many arguments and disagreements we both finally made the decision to go our separate ways four years later in 1996.

I felt relieved that we had finally managed to free ourselves from a difficult relationship. The only thing that broke my heart was having to leave my then two-year-old daughter, Lauren, who had been born on 20 February 1994. Lauren was the only reason that the relationship had lasted as long as it had, but we both came to the responsible decision that it was not fair for her to grow up in such an atmosphere. We obviously still have to see each other regularly when Lauren comes to stay, and luckily we are able to get on well for Lauren's sake. Jackie is now in another relationship and I believe that they are both very happy, as I am.

I had solved the housing problem, so all I had to do then was solve the employment problem and get a job that would pay me enough money to pay for the new house. Every day I would catch the five o'clock train from Mottingham Station, get off at London Bridge and walk the couple of miles over the bridge to St Catherine's Dock. On the way I would buy just about every available paper in order to scan the job section during my twelve-hour shift. This bourgeois existence went on until one day I noticed some sort of cap badge taking up a whole page in the *Daily Mirror*'s job section. On further examination I read it was a national recruiting advert for prison officers and my eyes fell onto the wages quoted, which started at £16,500 a year, a rise of nearly £7,000 from what I was currently earning. It was not a job I would have considered under normal circumstances, but I was in a pretty desperate situation at the time, and on that basis I decided to apply. I thought that at the very least it would offer me the wages I needed as well as the sense of comradeship that I missed from my army days.

The first stage of selection was to sit a multiple choice test at Cleland house, and at the end of the test they read out some of the names of the candidates who were in the room and asked them to leave. After a period of about twenty minutes, during which time I had convinced myself that I had failed, one of the examiners returned and congratulated us on passing this first hurdle.

Some weeks later my old pal Harry went through the same process, and I had forewarned him of the way candidates are split after the test and assured him that if he was left in the room he had passed. On the day of Harry's test they called out the names one by one until eventually Harry was the only one left in the room. He sat back on his chair rather pleased with himself at being the only one to have passed and waited patiently, he said, for someone to come and measure him up for his uniform. About an hour went by before one of the examiners came back and asked Harry what he was still doing there. Harry told him that he was the only one to pass the exam, only to find that they had changed the format since I was there and he was in fact the only one to have failed. I could just picture that smug, satisfied look on his face slowly changing as he put his tail between his legs and left. Harry being the kind of guy he was did not let it bother him too much and after a few different jobs is now a fully trained mechanic. I sometimes wish that I had failed that test.

The second phase of selection was in the format of a formal interview in front of three senior Prison Service personnel once again at Cleland House. I remember that day well. I had been on night shift the previous evening and had gone straight to the interview after getting changed out of my security uniform. Due to the rush-hour traffic I arrived at Cleland House with very little time to spare and rushed to the lifts after getting directions from the guard on the door. I just managed to squeeze through the doors of the lift before they closed fully, and almost crashed into a middle-aged woman who was the only other passenger. Nervously I said, "Thanks, love. I've got an interview with some dinosaurs for the Prison Service upstairs and I am already running a bit late. Knowing my luck I will get some left-wing lesbian sitting on the board who will more interested in my keeping her waiting a couple of minutes than finding out what I have to offer."

As it turned out I had a few minutes to spare when I reached the designated floor and had time to gulp down a quick glass of water to moisten my dry, nervous throat. Finally I was ushered to a door and knocked and entered, then my heart stopped when I saw the 'office clerk' from the lift sitting in the middle of the two other interviewers across the large boardroom table. That, I thought, was that. Me and my mouth had caused me to fail before I had answered the first question. I did, however, have to go through the whole interview, during which the bitch from the lift gave me the grilling of my life, and took every opportunity to try to humiliate me. It felt as if I had been interrogated by the Gestapo for hours, and the strange thing is that the further I progressed in the service in later years the more people I met with similar attitudes to the Gestapo.

I returned home convinced that my misunderstanding in the lift and my own pride in not allowing myself to be spoken down to at the interview had brought an abrupt end to my selection process. On Monday morning I slipped quietly back to work and began to rehearse excuses in my head as to why I had decided the Prison Service was not for me. Some two to three weeks later I received an official looking brown envelope from the Home Office and, despite my initial urge to throw it straight in the bin, I decided to open it. I don't know why. Maybe I just wanted to see how the Civil Service broke the news that you had failed. I read the first paragraph which, to my surprise, stated that I had successfully passed the entrance requirements and had been selected to join course NR31 for officer training. I was required to turn up at HMP Wandsworth on 20 July 1992 for two weeks' initial training and further selection before going on to the Officer Training School for a nine-week course based at Newbold Revel near Rugby.

Once I had received this letter I had mixed emotions about whether or not I was doing the right thing. The money and job security sounded excellent and I would have been a fool to turn the offer down in my current situation for those two reasons alone. But I could not help thinking, even at that stage, that I was going into something that would be totally against the people and place I grew up with and in. I had always been an individual person with a non-conformist method of doing things the way I felt they should be done and when they should be done.

I turned the question over and over in my mind for days, but eventually had to realize that financially I had no other option and so decided to take the job. I did, however, remember the words of my old mentor, Jim Long, and vowed always to try to stick by them and not lose my own identity, something that would test my strength of character to the limit in the coming years.

6

THE PRISON SERVICE - WANDSWORTH

Some weeks later, once again I found myself on a train heading for the unknown with those all too familiar thoughts of nerves and excitement. On this particular journey I did not have the time to think too deeply as I only had to go to Waterloo and connect to the Wandsworth line. All in all I think the journey took about an hour and in no time at all I was getting off at Earlsfield Station near Wandsworth Common.

As I neared the centre of the common I noticed for the first time the imposing grey-black walls of one of the most feared and controversial Victorian prisons in the world at that time. Its presence looming at me in the distance sent a nervous shiver down my spine and I stared at its walls almost as if I were being hypnotically drawn into its structure. For the first time I feared what I was shortly to be introduced to inside these walls.

I climbed the steps up to the main entrance, consciously staring at the ground to avoid the intimidating stares from the line of visitors waiting to be admitted for morning visits. I felt their eyes burning into the back of my head. They knew what I was and why I was there. The same hostile greeting awaited me at the gate lodge by a fat grey-haired officer who grunted and nodded his head towards a group of similarly suited young men sat on a bench when I presented my joining letter. I was to learn quickly that to him and most other officers we were the scum of the earth, lower even than the inmates in their care. We were all now officially NEPOs (new entrant prison officers), the lowest form of life in the prison. I realized that the next two weeks were going to be extremely difficult, and we could expect very little help from the qualified staff to get us through this initial training period.

After a wait of approximately half an hour, during which our number had grown to about twenty, we were led through the inner electronic gate, through the 'Sterile Area' and into the small training room. We filed in and

My Grandad, Tommy Dare

My Gran and Grandad, Tommy & Lillian

Me and my sister, Jayne, 1969

Me at Porthcawl Beach, aged 3-4

Mum, Mue, Me, Pop, Jayne, Christmas 1977

My Grandad 'Pop', front row (centre)

Left: My sister, Mue, Me, Pop and Cousin Daniel
at my Aunt Kay & Uncle John's wedding
Above: Me as a toddler

My Gran 'Mue'

Army Cadet drill competition,
Blackhealth, 1983

The remains of my Sierra after I rolled it on the A2, May 1993

Me in Greenwich, 1996

Me and Dad, Yeading Marina, 1996

Me and my old 'Mucka' Harry, in my flat in Hayes, 1997

My Gran on her
90th birthday, 1998

Me and Harry at his wedding
to Clair, 1997

Left: Jayne, Natasha, Kath,
Baby Eve, Grandad, Mum,
Me, Iwan, Gran, Mari,
Gavin, Rowan, Cerys,
Clive and Hannah.
Grans 90th, 1998

Morgan (one day old), Lauren and Mum,
February 1999

Me doing the Y.M.C.A. To cheer up a
heavily pregnant Natasha, February 1999

Morgan's first pair of glasses,
Caella, Spain, 1999

Me and Morgan, Marmaris,
Turkey, 2003

Me and Morgan, Chatham Dockyard, 2002

Natasha, Turkey, 2003

The Family, Jamaica, 2004

Me and Lauren, Dolphin Cove, Jamaica, 2004

Morgan and Lauren, Jamaica, 2004

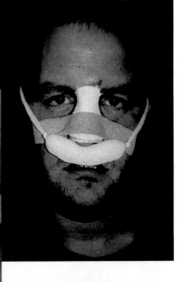

Broken nose after my lorry
fell on my head, September 2004

Morgan winning 1st prize at Leysdown
Halloween contest, October 2004

The 'Dingles' at the Giant Causeway, June 2005.
Me, Morgan, Emily, Oliver, Jessica, Sam, Dot,
Geoff, Elliott, Tasha and Nikki

Me and Morgan in Portrush,
June 2005

Left: My son Thomas, 2006
Above: Drawing by Charlie after the
birth of Thomas, 12 November 2006

Pete Carr in Hercules
en route to Canada, 1988

Me and 'Ginge' Naylor Clogher,
Fermanagh, 1989

Kia, Me and Cyrus, inside Clougher Ruc Station
moments before the Sanger was attacked by a
P.I.R.A.A.S.U. Armed with a M60 machine gun. 1989

Me and Mac in Gibraltar, 1989

The Sanger showing damage
caused by M60 rounds, 1989

took up our positions in the predetermined seats arranged around the room. Sat in front of us were three uniformed men. The first was a large man sporting two silver crowns on his epaulettes and the first cheerful looking expression I had seen since my arrival. He introduced himself as Principal Officer Freeman, who was in charge of the training school at Wandsworth. He in turn introduced the two men who flanked him. Both bore the bitter expressions on their faces that we had encountered from everyone else since our arrival. These two, Freeman informed us, were his training senior officers and they would be responsible for our training programme over the next two weeks. One was called Shepherd and the other Nutt, and I must admit that my first impressions of both of them made me draw the conclusion that we were going to have a barrel of laughs during this stage of our training.

The rest of the morning was spent with the traditional 'creeping death', where each of us took turns in standing in front of the group and giving a five-minute resume on who we were and what we had done with our lives prior to now. I could not believe after hearing everyone's story that I was in fact the only ex-forces guy in the group and the remainder came from all walks of life. To recall a few, there was Geoff, an ex-double glazing salesmen; Mickey Mc or 'Nervous Nerys' as he came to be known, who was a bit of a jack of all trades, primarily in the building profession; Mark, who had been unemployed for years but was originally a film developer; and Mick Regan, a plumber by trade who had fallen foul of the building trade recession. Mick and I were to work together later at Belmarsh with Charlie Bronson. We both held him in very high regard and the three of us were to build up a mutual respect of one another that remains to this day.

The last person I would like to mention is fat Alfie, the ex-butcher. Alfie was a real character, a proper South Londoner with all the humour and the gift of the gab. Sadly what Alfie had in character he lacked in personal fitness and enthusiasm towards this new profession and he took the option of leaving after the first week. It was a shame to lose him, as I really got on well with him as he was on my sort of wavelength.

Once we had done our 'creeping death' it was the turn of the training

71

senior officers to do theirs. Shepherd was a man of very few words, briefly mentioning his years in the Prison Service and the fact that he too had served in the army for a number of years. The only other thing he told us was that he would never work in another prison, as Wandsworth was the only place that 'did it the right way'. I was to hear this from virtually every officer I met during the following two weeks and it was not long before I was to realize what they meant.

Nutt, on the other hand, had plenty to say about himself, although he had in fact done nothing to boast about in my opinion. He told us that he was part of the accelerated promotion scheme and as a result had progressed up the ranks quicker than most. He was a university graduate who was on the fast track to becoming a governor, a grade he hoped to attain within five years of entry. I was to meet many of these high-flying yuppies in my time and never had much respect for any of them. To me they all lacked two of the most important qualities in life. In a job like the Prison Service common sense and life experience of the real world are, I believe, essential qualifications. It must have been Nutt's own insecurity that made him take great pleasure in telling us how important he was and how he had the power to sack us on the spot if we did not do what he told us when he told us. I struggled to stay awake while this pratt was giving us his fantasy life story, but I could not help noticing that by the look on some of the others faces they thought he was godlike.

Once these formalities were out of the way we were told to go for lunch and after that we would be taken into the main prison for a tour. During the hour-long lunch break we began talking to one another within the groups of five that we had been separated into. My group consisted of Mickey Mc, Geoff, Mark, Mick Regan and myself. I knew from the morning session that we were all from the same area of southeast London and were therefore all hoping to get posted to Belmarsh, a new maximum security prison near Woolwich. We all seemed to share the same reason for being there and that was job security and financial stability. Not one of us would have made the Prison Service our choice had we been able to get employment elsewhere that offered a similar package. We sat chatting for the hour, each of us trying to validate to the others the reasons we decided to choose this career, but I knew this line of conversation was in fact masking the fear of the impending tour that each of us was experiencing.

The hour came and went quicker than I would have liked and soon we were being herded into Wandsworth's infamous reception, our starting point for the afternoon.

The first thing that I remember once inside the grey walls was the unmistakable smell that hung in the stagnant air. It was a mixture of the stale sweat of hundreds of bodies and the choking stench of human waste that escaped from the slop buckets used by every inmate to relieve themselves in their cells. This stench was particularly strong at this time of day as it was one of the three times a day when the inmates got to 'slop out', i.e. empty their buckets into the drains located in the recess (toilet and washing facilities on each wing).

The thickness of the putrid air only added to the incredibly claustrophobic feeling and made my stomach wrench with an uncontrollable urge to be sick. We stood shaking in the centre of the floor and I noticed all our faces turn ashen white as we noticed five prisoners filing through the metal gate in front of us. All five were identically dressed in brown plastic shoes, blue jeans and blue-and-white striped shirts tucked into the jeans and buttoned all the way up to the neck.

As they were led past our group they all stared at us with blank expressions, but as I gazed around our group in an attempt to not look at the faces of these men, I noticed that most of us were staring back in the same way. For all of us this was our first glimpse of a real-life convict in the flesh. I could see that we all looked terrified of them, but these men were in fact 'Red Bands' - trusted prison workers who gained their positions for good behaviour. If we were terrified of these men, how would we cope when we got on the wings and met some of the prison's less conforming residents?

This silent stand-off was broken by the arrival of a huge prison officer who bellowed at us to pay attention and introduced himself as the reception principal officer. It was with this imposing figure of a man that we were to spend the next hour or so learning about the duties carried out in reception. He wasted no time in boosting his own ego by telling us that he was the most important man in the prison, a claim we were to hear repeated by many others before the two weeks were out. He also took great pleasure in telling us, in front of his audience of idolizing staff, of his hatred for NEPOs and giving us the distinct impression that we were really messing up his routine.

Our tour began at the front desk where newly arrived inmates were received for the first time. Here we were told that every inmate underwent a mini-interview and were formally booked into the prison after having their personal details checked using their own prison records. These records are called 2052s and contained within the buff-coloured cover would be details of the prisoner's movements, adjudications, offences both in and out of prison, personal details, and any other security information deemed necessary. As this was the first port of call in the prison, the officer told us that it was necessary to establish a tough attitude from the start. An example of this is Wandsworth staff's claim that every prisoner that had dared to lean or place their hands on the front desk was immediately 'dropped' by the excess staff who hang around in wait for such an opportunity. Adjudication is the process followed when an inmate is accused of breaking one of the prison's rules and regulations. It is a small court which many refer to as being a form of kangaroo court, where the inmate is placed in a room in front of a prison governor and upwards of five staff and is given the chance to defend himself against the offence he is charged with.

Over the course of my time with the Prison Service I was involved in countless adjudications, some of which I will describe later. A friend of mine, Jan Lamb, has written a book called *Guilty or Not Guilty*, which includes details of many real-life adjudications, told through the eyes of the inmates involved.

Once past the front desk the inmates are processed as rapidly as possibly through reception before being located onto one of the residential wings. This process involves strip-searching every inmate to ensure they have not attempted to hide anything on their person, and issuing them with prison-issue clothes where appropriate. Usually all inmates are then fed and locked up in holding cells to await relocation onto the wings. Depending on the prison, time and attitude of the staff on duty, the inmates will also get the chance to see a doctor or nurse to establish any course of medication they may require.

Finally 'runners' (one or two officers from each wing) arrive to escort the inmates to their respective wings. Wandsworth is made up of four normal residential wings - A, B, C and D. A further five wings make up the rest of the prison: E-Wing housed the notorious segregation unit and F-Wing the hospital. G-, H- and K-Wings were a separate area which housed all the 'beasts' (sex offenders) and prisoners who had received threats on the normal wings or who were just too weak to survive on normal location.

The four normal residential wings were separated to house different categories of prisoner. A-Wing was used at the time as an induction wing and also housed many of the prison workforce. B-Wing was used as a remand prisoners' wing, as prison rules state that remand and convicted prisoners have to be locked up separately due to the different privileges to which they are entitled. C-Wing held the prison's long-term and high-risk inmates, including those on the E-List who had attempted, or were suspected of attempting, an escape. Such prisoners were unmistakable as they wore prison denim suits with a bright yellow stripe on the back of the jacket and down each of the legs. D-Wing held the remainder of the prison workforce and other long-term residents generally in a lesser category than that found on C-Wing.

We would have to wait until our second day before we could venture into the main prison and experience the bizarre routines of the wings. With our introduction of reception complete, we had just enough time to get a brief look at the main visiting room before returning to the training room for a debrief on the first day. The main visits hall, as its name suggests, is where inmates receive visits from friends and relations. It is possibly the most volatile area of any prison. The fact that this is the only place inside the walls where prisoners can mix with people from the outside makes it extremely sensitive for both security and inmate relationships with staff.

I had been a visitor on one previous occasion when I had accompanied my old mate Simon's mum when visiting her husband, Jim, in one of the prisons on the Isle of Sheppey. On that occasion I had noticed that some, not all, staff had treated us like dirt merely because we were visiting a prisoner. This attitude towards the visitors was something I noticed immediately at Wandsworth. Don't get me wrong, I have witnessed many visitors exhibit appalling behaviour towards both staff and the inmates they have been visiting over the years, but I firmly believe that this should not affect the professionalism of prison officers employed in this area.

Wandsworth visits hall, as every other prison's, was swamped with staff for the reasons I mention above. The room was filled with small tables and chairs packed tightly together, which were surrounded by high chairs rather like the ones used by umpires at tennis games. From these raised positions the staff would stare uncomfortably at the groups of visitors on their designated tables of responsibility. If any of them saw anything suspicious they had the power to jump on the inmate and visitors concerned and terminate the visit on the spot. An inmate who found himself in such a situation could almost certainly expect a period on closed visits, where all subsequent visits would be conducted behind a glass screen. The length of time a prisoner would spend on these special visits was normally determined by the visits and security governor and based on the contents of reports compiled by officers from visits and the inmate's wing.

Of course most of the decisions regarding closed visits were legitimate and in nearly all these cases the inmates involved accepted the consequences. There were, however, cases that I know of where the inmate was placed on closed visits simply because some staff didn't like them or their visitors. In almost every visiting room I saw during my career I will always remember the tense atmosphere that hung around the room.

The staff always seemed on edge rather like I imagine the fighter pilots felt during their brief moments of rest between scrambles. Some members of staff even seemed to look forward to a disturbance as it gave them the chance to get their hands on a prisoner. This was especially so if there was a particular prisoner who was not very well liked by the staff. It was common when a prisoner in this category received a visit for as many staff from his wing who could get away from their normal duties to congregate in the visits room in the hope that he would 'perform' and they could get a piece of the action.

Another favourite pastime with many staff was to blatantly eye up certain female visitors, especially during the summer months when they may be wearing slightly more revealing clothes. This practice was not only unprofessional but also caused a lot of tension between the already fragile relationship of staff inmate and visitor. Of course, if an inmate took offence at the way in which he felt his wife, girlfriend or daughter was being stared at or talked about, he risked having his visit terminated and being placed on the closed visits list.

I was lucky enough not to be posted permanently to visits during my career, as I don't think I could have conformed to the general attitude that seemed to be required by a visits officer. I was a little too laid back to worry about upsetting a prisoner's weekly or monthly visit.

The end of our first day over, we all congregated back at the training room to meet up with Shepherd and Nutt. We had each been issued with A4 notebooks in which we were required to write up about every area we visited during the two weeks. We had to note such things as the role of each area, how many staff and inmates were housed or worked there and the location of alarm bells and firefighting equipment.

These books had to be written up daily and handed in each night to the training staff, who would mark them and return them together with their comments every morning. I left the prison gates that evening and felt tremendous relief that the day was over. I was physically and mentally exhausted, not because I had done any strenuous exercise but because my first taste of this totally different existence had been so much to take in.

On my short walk back to the station I found myself once again questioning what exactly I was getting into and whether or not I had made the right decision. Once again I answered this question by reminding myself of the financial stability the career offered. I also remembered the promise I made to Jim and myself to keep my own individuality. When I thought about the attitudes of some of the staff we had met during the day I knew then that this would be a hard promise to keep.

The following day I had arranged for Geoff to pick me up at Mottingham Station. He had also arranged to take Mickey Mc and Mick Regan, which not only eased the travelling situation but also enabled us about forty-five minutes each way to get more familiar with one another. We arrived at the prison early on the second day and took the opportunity to grab a coffee and bacon sandwich each. I think we all welcomed this chance, not only to delay the start of the day but also to attempt to quell the butterflies we were all experiencing as nervous fear of the day ahead set in.

Once again we congregated at the main gate until being ushered by our friendly gate officer through the inner gate and taking up our seats in the training room. SO Nutt, who I was really beginning to dislike, passionately delivered the first order of the day. He slammed our blue notebooks on the tables in front of us and began screaming his disgust at the quality and amount of our first day's entry. He reminded all of us, who he collectively called 'gentlemen' in his own condescending tone, of his power to sack us on the spot if we did not produce work to the standard he expected. Shepherd took no part in this show of authority and I couldn't help wondering by the look on his face whether he seemed to hold the same regard for this power crazy, young university boy that I did.

As the two weeks progressed, most of us began to hold a lot of respect for Shepherd. We all agreed that our first impression was that he was going to be the bastard of the two, but he actually proved to be one of the quietest and most helpful members of staff we met. His quiet nature, however, did not mean that he was not capable of looking after himself, and we heard one or two stories about how he dealt with people who tried to fuck him about, both staff and inmates. The main thing was that he was not a bullyboy. He obviously knew his potential and did not feel he had anything to prove by shouting his mouth off and giving people unnecessary grief.

With the morning lecture over, we left Nutt to pat himself on the back for delivering such a powerful speech. Our first port of call was C-Wing to observe the morning routine, which included the serving of breakfast, slopping out and morning applications. The scene that greeted us on C-Wing was like one from a film about Newgate Prison. The wing was reported to be the longest prison wing in the world and stretched from the circular prison centre to an arch-shaped window at the far end, which let in a small amount of light that added to the gloom. Once again the stale air was filled with the stench of human waste and sweaty bodies. There was also a tremendous amount of noise being generated from the different activities - keys and chains jangling, heavy metal cell doors banging open and shut, orders being barked by various officers, and the constant drone of voices and feet dragging along the metal landings and stairs. It was as if I had stepped back in time into an old black-and-white documentary on Communist Russia. Wherever I looked I saw rows upon rows of grey-faced men in blue striped shirts shuffling along the narrow landings, their heads and shoulders slumping as they carried their slop buckets in one hand and metal food trays in the other.

C-Wing, we discovered, could hold about three hundred and fifty inmates of whom at least half appeared to be on the landings, but I could only make out about fifteen officers. Those odds and the whole menacing scene sent a cold shiver down my spine. The whole process was being carried out with military precision, every inmate from each landing following the same route uniformly - out of the cell, along to the recess to empty their buckets, past the landing 'Wendy House' to hand in their daily applications, down one set of stairs, past the hotplate to get their breakfast, back up another set of stairs, along the landing and back into their cells. The landing officers merely moved along the landing, slamming the doors shut as soon as the last occupant was back inside.

We huddled nervously in our position next to the hotplate, where we were told to stand in order to get the best view of the whole process. Being here, though, meant that we were easy prey for every prisoner on the wing that saw the fear on our faces to intimidate us further with threatening stares and sarcastic comments.

After only about ten minutes in this position we were told to move up onto the three's landing to observe the applications process. It was up here that we were to witness our first two incidents of how brutal prison life can be. The first incident was a serious assault on an inmate carried out by his cellmate. An officer had just unlocked the cells to our left and the inmates had begun to file down the landing when I noticed in the corner of my eye someone running. I looked round in time to see an inmate bring a lump of wood crashing down on another inmate's head with such force that his head seemed to open up and he fell to the floor with dark red blood spurting from his skull. I froze, partly in disbelief, partly in shock, but mainly because I didn't know how to react and we had received strict instructions not to get involved in any incidents.

I stood there and watched as the attacker continued to rain vicious blows to the downed man's head and body in what appeared to me to be in slow motion. All the noise and other activities around me appeared to be blocked out as I seemed glued to the scene in front of me, until I heard a muffled whistle blowing in the distance followed by the sound of thunder rumbling closer and closer. My dreamlike state was broken as I was hurled to the side of the landing and was propelled into a locked cell door with a bone-crunching thump.

My eyes barely focused on a blur of white shirts that hurtled passed me at incredible speed, and launched themselves en masse on top of the two inmates. I realized that the distant thunder I had heard had been my introduction to the Wandsworth Express, the name proudly given to the response by staff to an alarm bell or whistle being blown. At that time Wandsworth officers regularly boasted about having the fastest, most effective response to alarms than any other prison throughout the Prison Service.

In minutes the wall of staff that now stood in between me and the two inmates parted and I saw two groups of three officers each holding one of the prisoners, each inmate almost bent in half, covered in blood and crying out in agony at the way their arms and wrists were being restrained.

The two groups shuffled past me and I was later informed that they were both taken to the segregation unit to await adjudication the following morning on a charge of fighting and assault.

I also discovered later that the attacker had been at Wansdworth for a good number of months without any previous trouble. He was apparently a model prisoner who kept himself to himself and appeared just to want to do his bird and go home. The victim, on the other hand, was a bit of a lad, or so he thought. He had been transferred the night before from a northern jail for a court appearance and had been put in the same cell as the other man. He had kept his new cellmate awake all night with tales of how he was a champion kick-boxer and would take no shit from anyone. He boasted about whom he had been banged up with and got on really well with - you know, the usual legends such as the Krays, Charlie Bronson and all the well-known faces. In short, he had really pissed off his new cellmate by fucking up his routine. It may sound petty to those of you who are unfamiliar with prison life, but your routine, however you decide to manage it, is the way you deal with your bird.

The easiest way for both staff and inmates to get along inside is to respect people's routines. Many prison staff, both junior and senior, have caused some very serious but totally unnecessary incidents by messing about with someone's routine.

I must admit that that incident shook me, if only by its speed and ferocity. But later that morning I was to witness another incident that left me totally confused about the morality of the career I was entering. With the wing completely fed and all the inmates, other than the workers, locked up in their cells again, there was a short time for us to grab a cup of tea and write up our blue books before having a look at the bathhouse. We were directed to the C-Wing staff tearoom, which was located in two cells that had been knocked through and kitted out with a cooker, fridge and just about everything else needed to cater for making tea, coffee and snacks.

As soon as we entered, the most enormous black man I had ever seen since the incident in Lewisham on Garry's stag night asked us for our order. We soon discovered this was Nathan, the wing's number one T-Boy, and no prizes for guessing how he got the job looking at the size of him. Despite his intimidating appearance, Nathan was a really nice bloke who was only too happy to help us out when we needed any information about who was who and where things were in the prison that we couldn't get from a less helpful member of staff.

We had received strict instructions from staff at the scene of the morning's incident not to record any details of it in our notebooks, so there was not an awful lot that we could write about. We did not even dare to talk about it amongst ourselves, as there were three wing officers in the tearoom having some breakfast, but I could tell by the expressions on the others' faces that they had also been shocked by what they had seen.

The bathhouse was located at the side of the main prison in between that and G-, H- and K-Wings where the 'beasts' were kept. It was empty of inmates when we visited, but we had the benefit of a bathhouse officer to describe the system to us. It was a simple conveyor-belt system that every prisoner had the opportunity to take only once a week at that time. The name 'bathhouse' was a little misleading, as there were actually no baths in the building. It was a long, narrow building with what must have been approximately fifty showers down each side. Each wing was allocated one day a week in which to get all its inmates showered.

At the entrance of the building there was a hatch where we were told every inmate stripped off, handed in his dirty clothes and collected a bar of soap and one tiny sachet of shampoo. They then filed into the showers and took a cubicle each. The water was turned on for three minutes only, and in that time they had to wash and rinse their hair and bodies. The officer laughed as he told us that the usual trick was to turn the water off after about two minutes and watch them coming out still covered in soap.

Once the prisoners had showered they would file through the door at the other end of the building where they would collect fresh clothes and a towel to dry themselves with. They were allowed to wrap the towels around their waists and would then be marched back to their cells to dry and change. The process was carried out on a strictly one-for-one basis, so if they didn't have a towel or any other piece of clothing to hand in at the start they wouldn't get one back. Instead, they would find themselves on report and charged with damaging prison property. Some of you reading this may think they only deserve one shower a week. I have met certain inmates that you would have to force to take one that regularly but, believe me, when you have to work there you would rather let them take as many showers as they like. It also makes everyone's life so much easier when you allow people access to a shower - think how much more relaxed you feel when you step out of the bath or shower as opposed to when you are sweaty and dirty.

The thrilling tour of the bathhouse over and our books filled in accordingly, it was time to return to C-Wing to observe the feeding of the lunchtime meal. In all prisons lunch is served at about eleven to eleven thirty in order to allow the staff to break off for their lunch officially at twelve thirty, but in practice its usually as soon as the wing is fed and secured. So as a rule the staff are a little more enthusiastic about serving lunch and dinner than breakfast. As a consequence, the staff usually try to avert any trouble that would obviously delay their own lunch break.

However, this was not the case for the two young officers on the three's landing on this occasion, who obviously thought the chance to impress some fresh-faced NEPOs was worth losing some of their lunch hour. I am, of course, referring to the second incident of the day, which I mentioned earlier. I was stood with Mickey Mc on one of the bridges that spanned across the wing when a cocky young London lad who was all of eighteen came out of his cell and said "Morning Guv" in a cheeky but harmless way to the two landing officers stood on the bridge next to us. As he went past Mickey and myself he said to us, "Don't listen to them or you will never learn how to be a good screw", and laughed on his way down the stairs. The two officers seemed to let this harmless banter really upset them and both puffed out their chests as they told us, "We will have that little fucker when he comes back". They also told us to put our notebooks away and not write anything down about what we were about to see, as we would not learn this part of the job at the training school but would pick it up when we got posted to our permanent nick. The young lad came back up the stairs carrying his dinner and a mug of tea, and was very closely followed back to his cell by the officers. At the cell they made it quite clear that the moment we heard a commotion we were to blow three times on our whistles and get back out of the way.

The inmate's cellmate was ordered out of the cell and the two officers went in and pushed the door almost closed. We could hear the young lad trying to convince them that he was only having a bit of a laugh and apologized if they'd taken offence. The officers apparently were not interested in this and within a few seconds we heard an almighty crack and a cry of pain followed by an almighty crash of furniture as it seemed to really kick off.

Mickey Mc blew his whistle and almost immediately I heard the thunderous sound of the Wandsworth Express charging towards our location. Time to get out of the way, I thought. Dozens of staff arrived at the scene and the prisoner was eventually brought out, bent over in restraint with blood pouring from what looked like a very badly broken nose, and some pretty severe bruises already beginning to appear on his face and naked torso. The two officers came out grinning, as if they had just emerged from a free brothel, and received congratulatory pats on the back from some of the other staff.

We then overheard them discussing with a senior officer which one would claim on their report that the inmate had attacked them first and therefore had to be restrained. I stood there and could not believe what I had just heard, especially as I knew how calculated the attack was. However, I was in no position to do anything about it as no one would believe me over two officers and whoever else would support the story with false statements. Over the next few years I would witness many incidents such as this one and, although I am ashamed to admit it, whilst I never physically assaulted an inmate in such a way I did provide backup stories to help cover other officers. This was not out of choice but rather through peer pressure, and it was the pressure to perpetrate such lies that contributed to my reasons for resigning from the service.

I heard later that the young lad received three days' CC, i.e. cellular confinement, solitary with no bed during the day, plus the loss of twenty-eight days' remission, not to mention the broken nose and the record of an assault on staff that would plague him for the rest of his sentence regardless of what prison he went to, and all for a bit of cheeky banter. I must stress that not all prison officers behave in such a way, but that incident was the first indication of the huge amount of pressure the majority of decent officers are constantly under to partake in such bullying or at least to help cover it up.

On the way home that night the three of us all agreed that both incidents had left a mark on us. The only one of us that tried to make out he thought it was brilliant was our driver Geoff. He was getting himself all excited when he was telling us how he had had to practise real self-control in order to stop himself from jumping in and having a go. The fact that we had seen him shit himself and dive for cover in the tearoom seemed to have slipped his mind, but we let him have his moment of glory. However, the following day Geoff would show his true colours once again when we entered the gym for our first of many physical education lessons by none other than Gary Taylor, a regular contender for Britain's strongest man and the Wandsworth gym senior officer.

After the usual briefing to start the third day, we made our way to the gym for our first lesson. Over the previous couple of days we had heard all sorts of rumours about what to expect in the gym at the hands of the sadistic Mr Taylor. Everyone seemed to look to me to help them through it, being ex-army, but I was more worried than all of them, even 'fat' Alfie who was sweating buckets at the mention of the word fitness. My experience told me that I would be expected to perform one hundred per cent better than the rest of the group purely because of my background. The fact of the matter was that I had probably done less physical activity than any of them over the past year and was dreading the prospect too.

We got changed and lined up inside the gym, each of us staring nervously at the circuit of weights and exercises already set up around the floor. Then we saw an even more daunting sight, which almost blocked out the light completely as he squeezed his huge torso through the gym office doorway. Mr Taylor had arrived and he looked even worse than the accounts we had heard about him previously. I noticed that Geoff had gone ashen white and seemed to be struggling to breathe regularly. I thought, I know this guy is big but there's no need to go over the top. Then I realized his eyes were focused beyond Mr Taylor and his terrified gaze was fixed on two inmates standing in the gym office making tea. He stuck his hand up and demanded to speak to Gary Taylor in private. This is a great start, I thought - if there's one thing I have learnt it is not to piss PTIs off before the gym lesson. Gary was not about to squeeze back into the office for anyone, so he told Geoff to say what he had to say in front of the group.

Despite his pleas and the obvious desperation in his voice, Geoff had to admit what was wrong in front of us. It turned out that one of the gym orderlies, an inmate who was about sixty years old and four-foot tall, used to be Geoff's milkman and Geoff, the man who couldn't wait to steam in yesterday, now demanded an immediate interview with the Governor as he felt he had to resign. By the time Geoff had stuttered out his request the rest of us, Gary included, were all on the floor pissing ourselves. Seeing our response, Geoff ran out of the gym and spent the next half an hour sulking in the toilets.

Obviously bumping into someone you have known on 'the out' can provide you with some problems when carrying out your official duties as a prison officer. The most obvious one, depending on the relationship you had with the prisoner before his incarceration and, of course, the way you choose to carry out your duty towards him and other inmates, is the possibility of blackmail or conditioning. By conditioning I mean that you could allow the inmate to use your old relationship or your good nature to force you into doing things for him. Such requests would usually start off small and apparently insignificant, but once you had committed yourself to carrying out their wishes you were then at risk of the threat to carry out tasks of increasing demand. If you did not draw the line and chose to carry out these tasks you could find yourself on a very slippery slope to the job centre or even a prison sentence of your own.

Because I was raised in the south London area, it was inevitable that I would meet people I knew doing time during my career. It was always something I found difficult to deal with and I will describe one or two such occasions and how I dealt with them later. I will also mention at this point that at least ninety per cent of the inmates I have dealt with over the years made comments to me about how I was 'all right' and they would have no problem buying me a drink if they saw me outside. One or two already have, and one in particular was, and is, a man for whom I have the greatest respect and it was an honour for me to be in a position to have a drink and a chat with him. Again, I will cover that in more detail later.

So, although Geoff's frantic pleas did amuse us greatly at the time, he did the right thing in raising his concerns. Only with experience would we learn to evaluate these sorts of risks ourselves and make the decision as to whether they were high enough to take further.

The gym session was nothing like as bad as we had been told to expect, and Gary turned out to be a great guy. We did a fair amount of work in the gym at Wandsworth in preparation for the C&R (control and restraint) training we would do at the college. This included a couple of very gentle jogs around the common that were about two to three miles long. It was the first of these that convinced an already unsure Alfie that enough was enough and he threw in the towel, much to the disappointment of most of us, who had grown very fond of his humour.

The remainder of our first week was spent observing the routines of the other normal residential wings. Each wing followed pretty much the same routine as the others, and all at that time ran on a twenty-three-hour bang-up. This meant that unless an inmate was employed in one of the prison work details he would only come out of the cell for one hour's exercise a day. There was no such thing as association in those days, and it would still be a few years until the staff would be forced to introduce it to many of the old London prisons.

In our final briefing of the week we were told that we had improved significantly since our arrival, but that there was still great room for improvement and we should continue to maintain the standard we were setting for our second and final week. The second week would involve visiting the more 'specialist' areas such as the segregation unit, the hospital and G-, H- and K-Wings, as well as the nerve centres of the prison, the control room and the 'centre'.

I felt relieved to leave the prison gates knowing that I had two full days before having to return. In a strange way I was beginning to enjoy learning about how the prison worked and observing the strange existence led by those inside. I had also begun to realize that the best way for me to deal with the job I was setting out to do was to be myself and use my own brand of sarcastic humour and experience of people and life. This, I concluded, would involve building up good relationships with the inmates I would be looking after wherever possible. Unfortunately, however effective this method would prove to be, I could already tell by the attitudes of some staff that it would be extremely difficult for me to build relationships with inmates without alienating myself from my colleagues. Even by the end of that first week I had noticed how some of our group had dramatically changed their outlook on the role of a prison officer in an attempt to become more accepted by the staff we were dealing with.

I did not have a lot of time to think about the past week over the weekend break, as most of my time was taken up arranging the forthcoming purchase of my new house. As a result, it seemed as if I had not been away from the place when at seven thirty on Monday morning I found myself sat in front of the cheerful face of Senior Officer Nutt once again to begin our second and final week at Wandsworth.

Although still nervous and apprehensive about what to expect, I felt much more relaxed than I had a week ago. The first area we visited that day, however, would soon herald a return to the tension and boil up a hatred the like of which I had never experienced elsewhere in all my travels. We were due to observe the routines on G-, H- and K-Wings, which housed some of the lowest creatures known to man in my eyes.

As soon as we entered the gate into the building that housed G, H and K, I noticed a very different atmosphere to that found on the normal residential wings. There was nothing like the volume of noise for a start, and the staff and inmates all shuffled about with shifty looks on their faces and the place smelt more like a hospital than a prison wing. There were a large number of hospital officers flying around with trolleys full of strange-looking liquid drugs and pills, and more than half the inmate population seemed to be inching along with the use of crutches or wheelchairs. Most of these had pathetic, sad-looking expressions on their faces as if trying to gain pity or use their disabilities as some sort of sick excuse for the disgusting crimes for which most of them had been convicted.

When we arrived, an officer offered to get us a cup of tea, but when I saw the state of the tea boy that would be making it I declined. To be truthful, I didn't trust the dirty bastard to make tea without spitting in it or worse. I hated the atmosphere that hung over this place and made my decision then that I would go to any lengths to avoid working with these people during my career. Luckily I did manage to avoid it because, for some reason that I could never work out, there were always plenty of staff who volunteered to work in these places. The only explanation I could think of for this was that looking after 'nonces' (prison slang for sex offenders) was generally thought of as easier than looking after normal prisoners. The thought of having to sit in on mandatory 'group therapy sessions' and listen to these creatures describe in great detail their crimes and blame their actions on their parents or upbringing made me feel sick in the pit of my stomach.

Some of you reading this may question my professionalism on making these comments. All I would say to you is try to imagine the worse case you have heard in the news on child pornography or rape. Then imagine having to give that person your undivided attention all day and listen to how much they enjoyed it or thought it normal, and tell me that you wouldn't feel for the victims, especially if you have children, young relatives or wives and girlfriends of your own.

After the tea break that I didn't partake in, we ventured onto the landings to watch the remainder of the wing get fed. The officer on the ground floor informed us that after every mealtime a count was carried out to ensure that all inmates were locked away. He assigned each of us a cell door and told us to go and look through the 'Judas' hole (a small flap for observation in the door) and count the inmates inside.

You may not believe me when I tell you what I saw through the flap in the cell door I had been allocated, but I swear to you that it is the truth. Inside there were three beds, and one inmate was lying quite peacefully on the top bunk bed smoking a roll-up. The bottom bunk bed was empty, but there was another inmate sitting on the single bed with his feet on the floor. I saw a third inmate kneeling in between his legs with his head bobbing up and down. It took a while for the shock to wear off and for me to realize just what I was witnessing. I am sure you have realized by now that here, as bold as brass, was an inmate giving one of his cellmates a blow job. He must have sensed my staring in disbelief because he turned to look straight at me and just grinned before returning to carry on 'doing' his cellmate. I slammed the flap shut and cursed the fact that I had no keys to get in and slap the dirty fucker. I felt physically sick and could not believe what I had just seen. To make matters worse, I thought, the third inmate was just lying there as if nothing unusual was happening. I rushed back to the officer, who had been joined by two of his colleagues, and reported what I had seen. They just laughed and told me that those two were always up to it that is why they were banged up together. I could not believe the reaction I got from these officers. The Prison Service has for years fought against various campaigns for conjugal visits between heterosexual adults, but here was clear evidence that homosexual relationships were not only going on but were also being encouraged by staff to ensure the smooth running of the wing.

I am not discriminating against homosexuals - each to their own as far as I am concerned - but how can the Prison Service deny heterosexuals some form of relationship and allow homosexuals to practise theirs so blatantly?

Our time on G, H and K could not end quickly enough for me and I valued greatly the short walk in the open between there and the main prison, as it gave me a chance to breathe in some fresh air in order to flush out the stench of the place that was suffocating me. We did not have far to go to our next port of call, just through the side gate into the main prison, which led to the prison's centre. I wandered in aimlessly with the rest of my group, still numb from what I had just witnessed, and all I remember next was hearing a voice bellow from nowhere, "Get out of my fucking centre you insignificant little bastards". I assumed someone was shouting at a group of inmates until I spotted a huge principal officer with a face as red as a beetroot charging towards us. He was still screaming obscenities at us when he reached where we were standing and eventually we realized that he was upset because we had just walked straight across the ornate brass star shape that made up the floor of the centre.

For those of you who have not had the pleasure of visiting Wandsworth in any capacity, it is strictly taboo to step on any part of the brass grill. Everyone who walks through the centre must walk around it and only in a clockwise direction. A member of staff who doesn't comply with this could expect to be severely reprimanded and get extra duties, and any prisoner who committed this most terrible crime could expect to get the 'treatment' followed by a few days down 'the block'.

It was this red-faced, potential heart attack victim's job to monitor all movement through the centre as well as dictate the order in which the wings were to be fed and ring the huge brass bell and direct the staff in case of an alarm bell on any one of the wings. It was to the centre that staff would report at the beginning of every shift during the days of central detailing, when you were not allocated a permanent place of work but were sent daily to wherever you were most needed. It was here also that the senior officer would report his wing lock-up roll and not until the centre PO was happy would he give the order for the staff to break off.

Because of this power alone, this man thought he was some kind of God and wasted no time getting us into his office where he proceeded to tell us a number of stories about himself. Just as I was about to fall asleep he even brought his stave (truncheon) crashing down on his table as he told us that he had single-handedly quelled the Wormwood Scrubs riots of 1976 with the use of his little bit of wood. Strangely enough, I was to meet about three or four people over the years that claimed to have done exactly the same thing. I was glad to hear a whistle blast during his egotistical speech, which sent him charging out of his office. Luckily it was only a false alarm, but it enabled us to escape to the safe haven of Nathan's tearoom on C-Wing in the commotion for a welcomed cup of tea and the chance to get more of his help to fill in our notebooks.

Over the next couple of days we had brief tours of the hospital wing, the workshops, the cookhouse, the control room and even the administration building. All were quite boring and uneventful, so I have no interesting memories of any of them. Equally as mind-bending was the tour of the main gate where our friendly gate officer explained his highly technical role of throwing keys to officers down a little chute when they turned up for duty.

It was on the second to last day when we got to visit the darkest hole of the prison - the notorious segregation unit, or 'the block' as it is known in prison. Wandsworth's block, as I mentioned previously, was located on E-Wing; in fact it was actually situated underneath E-Wing. The entrance was via a set of some twelve stairs, which had at the bottom a pair of blacked-out doors in front of the double metal gates. It was claimed that every inmate that was taken to the block got physically thrown down these stairs into the arms of the 'block screws', who usually 'forgot' to open the metal gates until the inmate was in a crumpled heap at the bottom.

All the officers in the block at that time were at least six-foot tall, apart from one known as 'Pitbull'. He stood at about five-foot six, but had been allowed to work there despite not reaching the usual height criterion due to his fearsome reputation as a scrapper. Granted he looked as though he could handle himself with his busted nose, shaved head and large, ugly scar down the left-hand side of his face. But then, with fifteen or so colleagues always at hand and never having to face odds of less three officers to one inmate, he should have been able to handle himself. It was Pitbull that was given the task of showing us round the block, which as usual began in the tearoom.

Pitbull was a lot quieter than most of the other staff we had come across, but he soon filled us in on the grim details of how the block worked. We were told that the real justice was dished out to prisoners that did not conform to the prison rules here in the dim depths of the jail. The block, he explained, was untouched by the prying eyes of visiting officials or clergy unless plenty of warning had been given to allow them time to avoid being caught 'educating' an inmate to the Wandsworth way. He made it clear by this that most of the inmates that were resident here received a daily dose of the treatment at the hands of the staff, and I don't mean medical treatment, although that may have been necessary afterwards. The staff here seemed convinced that this was the only way to deal with difficult prisoners, and not only appeared to have a free hand to carry out this extreme form of discipline but also seemed to have the support of the senior management.

In fact it is a practice that has been going on in almost every prison in the country and has only recently come to light after prisoners at Wormwood Scrubs made several allegations of serious assaults by staff in the segregation unit. Whilst I cannot argue with the fact that prisons need segregation units to ensure the remainder of the prison runs smoothly, I totally disagree with the actions of extreme violence, and in some cases physical and mental torture, that have been carried out on inmates in these places.

It was here that I was first to hear of Charles Bronson, the most notorious prisoner in the system according to the 'brains' behind the Prison Service. We were shown one of the two 'strong boxes', which were cells with tiny, sealed windows and concrete beds and stools. Entry to these cells was via two sets of doors, an outer set of steel double doors and an inner steel cell door. It was in one of these 'boxes' that Charlie had managed to rip the concrete stool out of the ground and use it to batter his way through the first door and almost through the second door before being overpowered by riot teams due to total exhaustion. He had been restrained in a 'body belt' at the time, which is a steel-lined, heavy leather belt with two handcuffs on each side to hold the arms tightly down by the waist, and had succeeded in freeing himself from this Victorian device before tackling the stool and doors.

From here we went out onto the exercise yard, which consisted of a small square piece of tarmac completely fenced in on all sides and, unlike the other yards we had seen, this one also had a metal caged roof. This roof, we were told, was a recent addition as some years previously Charlie had made it onto the roof of the prison by scaling the drainpipe. This feat seemed even more remarkable when we noticed that the drainpipe was cemented to the wall so you couldn't wrap your fingers round it. We were told how Charlie had clung to it despite an officer pulling at his legs and others throwing their staves at him. I began to hope I would never have to have this man under my charge.

Not all segregation units are run in such a way, and I do agree with the need to have such places in prisons. Prisoners sometimes value the time they spend in the 'seg' as it gives them a period of respite from the normal hectic world of the wings. Unfortunately, as I mentioned previously, it was not until the Scrubs affair came to light that moves were taken to monitor staff's actions towards prisoners placed in these units. I will not hide the fact that in life people piss other people off at times and there are occasions when a good old-fashioned slap is the quickest and best way to deal with certain incidents. I will also not try to hide the fact that I have given one or two prisoners and members of staff a dry slap when I felt they deserved it. But with me that was where it would end. I would always do it one on one and I would never then place a prisoner on report and make out he assaulted me. Most prisoners preferred this and would never report you. In the same way, if it ever backfired and I got the slap, which did happen occasionally, I would accept it and take no further action. This was the way I was trained in the army. If you fucked up you were usually given the option of being placed on report or accepting a clout from whomever was dealing with the situation. It was quicker and caused fewer consequences to accept the latter.

Many of you may interpret this method as a form of brutality but, believe me, compared with some methods I have seen it was often the only way. If nothing else, it prevented the inmate from falling into the hands of the

94

bullies who were always on the lookout for an excuse to practise their techniques. As I think I have mentioned before, I hate bullying. The dictionary definition of a bully is a 'hired ruffian' or 'schoolboy tyrant', in other words someone who enjoys picking on people either because they are weaker than them or they have the support of others to outnumber their victim.

Prisons are by their very nature breeding grounds for hatred and violence and occasionally in extreme cases you have to deal with violence by using violence. Prison officers are highly trained to deal with violent inmates in a controlled manner, which is very effective. However, there are sadly a number of officers who abuse this skill and use it to bully and cause the inmate as much unnecessary pain as possible.

The tour of the segregation unit signalled the end of our two weeks at Wandsworth. All that remained were some final documentation and, of course, the final briefing with the training staff for which PO Freeman returned. Surprisingly, those of us that were left received good reports and were all told that we would be welcomed back to work there permanently on completion of the nine-week residential officer training course that we were about to embark on. I had no desire to return and desperately wished I would get my posting to Belmarsh as I hoped there would be less pressure there to behave in such a macho way. We collected our travelling and joining instructions, bade our farewells and left the gates of Wandsworth for the last time, clutching under our arms our blue notebooks, which were to prove of no use in the future.

7

PRISON SERVICE COLLEGE COURSE - NR31 NEWBOLD REVEL

I had once again arranged to travel up with Geoff, Mickey Mc and Mick Regan to the college, which was located near Rugby. The mood on the way up was good and we were all in high spirits, once Geoff had finished moaning about the damage that would occur to his clapped-out Cortina's suspension due to the amount of luggage we had. We had been told that the course we were starting was the best part of the training.

The Prison Service had two main colleges at that time, one at Newbold Revel and the other in Leeds. Due to the volume of recruits that had been taken on in recent months, satellite courses were also being run at various police colleges around the country, which were on loan to the Prison Service to help cope with the additional requirements. We learned from staff at Wandsworth that there was fierce rivalry between the colleges. Members of staff who had trained at Leeds claimed to be the better officers and vice versa. It was certainly true that Leeds would have been the better venue of the two, as it was situated in the town centre and provided easy access to the acclaimed nightlife. Newbold, on the other hand, was located in a very picturesque setting in the grounds of an old stately home. There was, however, only a small bar on site and one public house, The Union Jack, within walking distance about a mile up the road. It was this lack of watering holes that I found preoccupied most of my time during the journey as opposed to what the contents of the course would entail, which seemed to be uppermost in the minds of my companions. I decided to make it my first mission to check out the options on arrival and make the best of the situation.

Our journey up the M1 took us about two and a half hours, and as we turned into the fairly well-concealed entrance of the college I caught a glimpse of The Union Jack public house. It was not a very promising sight and I could only hope that the beer tasted better than the external appearance of the pub would lead you to think. We proceeded up the long driveway over a cattle grid and soon were halted by a security barrier. After identifying ourselves by remote intercom to the security office, the barrier was lifted and we drove round to the main car park. The scene was not dissimilar to the one I remember at Copthorne Barracks all those years ago. It was, perhaps, not quite so hectic, however there were large numbers of people running around in various stages of the reporting process. We parked the car and made our way to the main entrance of the old stately home to report in with security and be told what to do next.

Eventually we discovered what rooms we had been allocated and were advised that we had approximately one hour before we had to congregate in the main lecture hall for our welcome speech and introduction. We collected our luggage and made our way to our rooms. Presumably, as we had arrived together we had been allocated rooms next to one another. At first we all thought this was great, but as the course went on Geoff was to regret having me as a neighbour. I used to knock him up every morning at about three o'clock to borrow some of his coffee and his kettle in an attempt to try to sober myself up a little before going to bed.

The rooms, all singles, were actually of a very high standard and, although not en suite, they did have a sink, which provided an excellent substitute urinal when the walk down the corridor seemed a bit too long in the wee small hours. The only disadvantage was that the doors to the rooms were on springs, which shut rather rapidly. I think we were all guilty of locking ourselves out on the way to the showers on more than one occasion. We would then have to make the humiliating walk across the courtyard, in full view of the whole college and wrapped only in a towel, to borrow the master key from security.

We made our way into the main lecture hall and took our seats for the initial briefing. I was surprised to notice how many of us there were. I guessed that there were about two hundred men and women packed into the seats overlooking the stage awaiting the opening address by the college governor, Mr Berry. My first thoughts when he appeared on stage were that we had made a mistake and were in fact at a Sinn Fein rally, because Mr Berry could have been Gerry Adams' twin brother. Maybe this was why I did not take to him then or indeed for the duration of the course. Another reason I knew I wasn't going to like this man became apparent as soon as he began speaking. He had a very arrogant manner and from the start he spoke to us as if we were all primary school children and he was the headmaster. He did welcome us with his first sentence, but then proceeded to tell us how he would not tolerate this and would not tolerate that. He warned us of the consequences of breaking any of the long list of college rules and seemed to be basing all his threats on the conduct of the last course, which seemed unfair to me considering we had not even started yet. In truth, a good majority of us did break almost every rule he described to us, which all seemed to be linked to alcohol-related antics, but no one was ever dismissed as a result.

When he had said his piece he handed over to one of his staff, who began reading out the names of recruits to assign everyone to the sections that they were to be placed in for the duration of the course. I have never been very good at meeting people for the first time and so I listened carefully, hoping that I would be placed into the same section as one of my companions from Wandsworth. Unfortunately it appeared that the staff had carefully structured the sections so that no one who had carried out the two-week initial training at the same prison was placed in the same section.

I soon discovered that I was to join F-Section, which seemed to be even more carefully put together than the rest as we were the only all-male section and mainly comprised all the ex-servicemen on the course. Maybe Berry wanted to keep all his potential rule breakers together for ease of monitoring, but as the weeks went by I think he lived to regret this decision, as he had underestimated just how much we would all pull together. One thing we all knew from our past experiences was that there is little they can do if you all stick together, and there was no way that he could sack a complete section if we all took responsibility for one of our number breaking the rules. That way it was impossible to prove who was responsible and therefore who to punish.

Once we had taken our places with our new sections, we were introduced to our section training staff. Each section had a principal officer and two senior officers who were responsible for the day-to-day training. Our principal officer was a man called Dave Oram. He was immaculately dressed with razor creases in his shirt and trousers, and his prison-issue boots were highly polished to a standard I had not seen since my army training days. His impeccable appearance, however, did not mean that he was a bullshit merchant. He was actually a very nice man who had no ideas above his station and he was always very fair and honest when dealing with us on any matter. He was almost at retirement age and, although he had served a great many years in many different prisons, he was nothing like the 'storytellers' or bully boy element we had seen at Wandsworth. He just took great pride in his personal appearance, a quality that the next instructor we met did not seem to worry too much about.

Mr Ian English was slightly overweight and his ill-fitting uniform looked as though it had never seen the hot side of an iron in its entire career. However, hat he lacked in self-pride he certainly made up for with his sense of humour, and we grew to look forward to his lessons as his tales always had us rolling about the floor in fits of laughter. He had joined the college recently from Belmarsh, although most of his career had previously been at Pentonville. This meant that I was able to learn a lot from him about the place I hoped to be posted to and quash some of the bad rumours I had heard about the place from the dedicated Wandsworth officers.

Among the many funny stories Mr English had was one about two Jamaicans who he had had on his wing at Pentonville and who were awaiting deportation. They claimed to be heavily involved with black magic and were desperately fighting deportation as they believed a terrible fate awaited them at home. Ian decided to use this fact to play one of his practical jokes and, after some research into voodoo and black magic, he came up with his plan. Before the wing was unlocked he armed himself with some salt and red ink, and on the landing outside the two inmates' cell he proceeded to mark out some form of voodoo sign with the salt and ink, which doubled up as pig's blood. When the order to unlock the wing came, the two men were about to exit the cell as normal when they spotted this sign on the floor. Ian said their feet froze, suspended above the sign, and with a chilling shriek and a deafening cry of "Lordy, Lordy, goodness gracious me!" the pair leapt back into their cell and locked themselves up. Despite his attempts to explain the joke, the pair of them were convinced they had received some sort of threat in the form of this sign and it took Ian and colleagues some three days before they could persuade the pair to come out of the cell. Although Ian had researched that salt and pig's blood were some of the materials used in black magic ceremonies, he had made up the way he had laid these materials out on the floor. He was later to discover that his design actually bore a striking resemblance to that of a genuine voodoo death sign.

Another of his stories involved a dispute he had recently had with a neighbour concerning the siting of a compost heap. Ian had lost the legal battle, but, not content with the outcome, he had set to work on a plan to reap his own vengeance. A keen fisherman, he always had an abundant supply of bait breeding in his garage, so late one night after his neighbour's lights had gone out he armed himself with a bag of maggots and proceeded to empty them through next door's letter box. The outcome cost him dearly in the small claims court, which did not listen to his plea of insanity, but Ian remained firm in his opinion that it had been worth it just to hear the reaction the following morning.

The third and final instructor in F-Section was a man from Canterbury prison named John Kirtley. At first glance he looked as if he was going to be a nasty piece of work. Like Ian's, his uniform although always clean seemed also to be allergic to irons, and he had a hard-looking face framed with a mass of wiry black hair and an equally unkempt thick black moustache. At first I got the impression he was an ex-military man, but this was not the case as he informed us that he had joined the Prison Service at the age of eighteen. In fact John was a very quiet man who, like Dave Oram, had a wealth of experience to share with us. He was very highly trained in the control and restraint technique, a form of self-defence taught to all prison officers. John was not only a riot team commander but also a fully qualified instructor. Unlike some of the staff we had encountered at Wandsworth and a few of the training staff we would meet later in the course, John knew how effective this technique was. He could not impress on us enough the need to carry it out using only the approved methods we were taught and how potentially dangerous it could be if we abused our skills and went too far when carrying them out. He told us of many occasions when staff had caused serious damage to inmates or had caused their colleagues to be placed in dangerous positions due to their being too overzealous when performing C&R. It is something that was designed to prevent injury and damage occurring to both staff and inmates during incidents, but many staff do abuse this knowledge and adapt their skills to inflict as much pain as possible to inmates.

The most common types of injury sustained are damaged or broken wrists, due to the nature of the holds used, when too much pressure is applied. At the other end of the scale there have been allegations made that some inmates have died as a result of poorly executed C&R methods by staff that were not correctly supervised or had not been sent on the annual refresher courses. Once again, it is a valuable skill to have and it is necessary due to the occasional behaviour of some inmates not only to protect yourself as an officer but also to prevent one inmate causing harm to another or even himself. Unfortunately, some staff do abuse it and there is not enough done to monitor its use correctly.

It was during this initial meeting that I learnt some really 'good' news - I had been chosen to be F-Section's representative to form a fire picket that night. Not only, as you may recall from earlier, did I have no good memories of carrying out fire picket duties, but this would certainly put paid to my plans to check out the watering holes as previously planned. It almost felt as though they knew of my love of lager and were trying to make my life difficult from the first day. Nevertheless there was nothing I could do about it and I took some comfort in the fact that the duty was a sleeping one after midnight, which meant I could return to my own room at that time. I was also assured that each of us would have to carry out this duty at some stage during the course and it was better to get it out of the way now.

After lunch in the very nice mess hall with some charming waitresses on hand to serve us, something that most of us from our backgrounds had not experienced before, we were introduced to our classroom. F-Section was housed on the top floor in the last classroom in the building and the room was laid out with the instructors' table at the front and our chairs in a semicircle around the remaining three walls.

When we arrived, the first thing we did was rearrange the names that had been placed on each chair so we were sat in the small groups we had begun to form at lunch. The first thing the instructors did when they arrived was rearrange us back into the original seating plan for the customary creeping death. As we made our way around the classroom, I discovered that there were only about five of our number that were not ex-services and we all made up a group of men from all over the country.

Our age group ranged from twenty through to fifty-eight and it was interesting to notice what a mixture of personalities there was among us. One young man, with whom I was to become good friends during the course, was 'Fitz' Fitzgerald. He was about my own age and like me had come from an army background but originated from Manchester. Fitz had a great sense of humour and between us we would keep the rest of the section amused for hours, either in the classroom or during our drunken escapades in the evening.

I masked my uneasiness at meeting people for the first time by resorting to humour, and one of the first things I did was tell everyone that I was at the wrong college and thought that I had in fact joined the Fire Brigade. This storyline was kept up for the whole of the course and earned me the nickname of Fireman Jim. I think I became so involved in this role that I even had some of the instructors believing I was slightly mad. It was similar to the way that the old prisoners of war would take bricks for walks to feign madness in order to be repatriated. I would even wear a plastic fireman's hat, which Fitz brought me back from a weekend in Blackpool, instead of my Prison Service cap - that really had them talking about me at boardroom level!

Talking of fire, once our introductions were over and we had finished our evening meal, it was time for me to report for my fire picket duty. There were six of us in total and when we reported we were broken down into three groups of two. Our duties consisted of patrolling the grounds of the college between the hours of six and midnight, with at least one of our two-man teams out at any time. Actually, 'two-man teams' is politically incorrect because we did have two ladies amongst our numbers. It was with one of these - a young girl called Sam - that I was paired off. She seemed to be a very nice young lady who told me she was twenty and originated from somewhere in Yorkshire. She was quite an attractive girl and was more than keen to chat away all night. This suited me, as I had not had much experience of working with women up to this point and was feeling a bit uncomfortable if not a little shy.

As we made our way through the wooded area of the college grounds Sam said something that would confirm to me that she did not share my shyness. She stopped by a bench, looked around her, turned to me and said in her strong Yorkshire accent, "This looks like a reet good place for a shag, don't yer think?" I could not quite believe what I had just heard and was unsure whether she was making a general comment or inviting me to help her find out if her opinion was correct. It was the sort of spontaneous invitation you would normally only read about in the pages of a dirty magazine's readers' letters section, so I have been told. I decided not to tempt fate so early on in the course and just agreed with her and then commented on the time and how we must get going.

Sam and I remained friends for the duration of the course, although despite this initial encounter we never did get intimate. She eventually got together with another member of F-Section, although some years later when our paths met again whilst out enjoying a drink she confessed to me that I had been the one she fancied and she had been disappointed that I had never returned her advances. Not wishing to make her feel unwanted again, I did make up for it later that evening and regretted not taking her up on her offer sooner. This took place during the time I was having serious doubts about my relationship with Lauren's mum. I was, however, still living there and, due to Sam's enthusiasm, I had to ensure I kept a shirt on permanently for almost two weeks until the scars had healed on my back. I later heard reports that Sam had been sacked for allegedly having an affair with an inmate at Feltham, although this was later overturned when the inmate confessed he had made it up due to a crush he'd had on her. Although offered, Sam did not resume her job after that as she probably felt she could not trust the system again. I have never heard or seen anything of her since.

Another duty we had to carry out that evening was to accompany the orderly officer when he went to ensure the peaceful closure of the college bar. This really got to me, seeing my fellow students falling about drunk and telling me what a good night I had missed. A good night it may have been, but the following morning was to be the one and only morning that I would wake up bright and early without any sign of a hangover, unlike the remainder of the section who had even at that early stage broken open the bottles of little yellow caffeine pills to help them stay awake.

During the course we must have spent a fortune on these small yellow wonder pills and probably all left there as caffeine addicts, but one thing was clear - we could not finish the course without them. The first day and in fact the first week were taken up with the issue of uniform, discussions about the contents of the course and familiarizing ourselves with the college and its facilities and other members of staff.

We discovered that we would learn things such as how to be assertive, how to communicate, how to recognize and deal with potential incidents, as well as learning the basic rules and methods we would need to apply when we took up our posts as prison officers. Our instructors explained that we had such a massive amount of information to learn in a very short period that we would not remember it all and would still need to learn much of the required skills once we were actually deployed at our respective prisons.

We were also told that, although we were required to sit two exams during the course, it would be extremely difficult to fail, as after each lecture the instructors would give us preprepared handouts, which would contain the necessary answers relating to that topic in the exams. This practice, we were to find out at the end of the course, went on without the knowledge of the senior college staff and presumably the Home Office and was something the instructors had devised in order to ensure that the vast majority of their students passed. It would also, therefore, reflect on their skills as tutors and would obviously look good on their own staff reports.

During that first week I not only took the opportunity to sample the two watering holes at our disposal, but also found that the college was equipped with a good gymnasium. I decided that I would use this chance to build up my fitness again after not doing any physical training for a year or so since leaving the army. From the second or third day I set a routine for myself that included a three-mile run followed by an hour's session in the gym. Alternatively I would take part in one of the aerobic classes that had been organized by two of the students who were formerly gym instructors. Of course, all this training was being matched by the amount of alcohol I consumed every night. However, the workouts did at least allow my body to sweat out some of the lager every evening before being replaced, and it did help my performance slightly in that it gave me a little more resistance to the overwhelming urge to fall asleep during lectures that we were all experiencing.

It was in the gym that we took part in the daily C&R lessons as well as carrying out the basic fitness tests required to pass the course. The physical training instructors really loved themselves, and were always looking for a way to impress the ladies on the course. One way they tried to achieve this, as an alternative to forcing themselves into the tightest vests and shorts and parading around like it was the mating season at London Zoo, was to tell the most impressing tale of how they battled this prisoner or single-handedly stopped that riot. Once again, the name Charles Bronson seemed to be the favourite prisoner to claim you had conquered. Nearly every PTI on the course, together with some of the other instructors, laid claim to the fact that they had at one time beaten up this man who was reputed to be the worst prisoner in the system. Every tale consisted of a big build-up story in which Charlie had disabled countless other members of staff and riot teams until being overpowered by whichever hero was relating the story to us at the time.

Even though I was used to hearing such ego-boosting tales from many people, I could not help thinking to myself again that I would hope never to come into contact with this man. Although I did not believe the way that each man told us how they had defeated him, I had little choice but to believe the mental picture I drew of this man according to the increasingly alarming descriptions I was hearing about him. My view would of course change later on when in fact I did have the responsibility of looking after this mythical prison legend, an experience that I will describe later.

The first week quickly came to an end and we all climbed into Geoff's trusty Cortina for the journey home and a weekend break to give us an ideal opportunity to sober up, ready for week two.

The start of week two was when we really began to get into the course, and lessons began in earnest at nine o'clock on Monday morning. By nine thirty we were all outside taking the first of our half-hour smoke breaks, which would become as regular as our mealtimes. Although they seemed a little too regular, they were always a welcome opportunity to get some fresh air, stretch your legs and nurse the hangover with some coffee. I did calculate, however, that if you took the smoke breaks out of the course curriculum you could turn out prison officers in about three and a half days as opposed to nine weeks.

I had in fact stopped smoking almost a year prior to going on this course, but started again as I found I had nothing else to do during these frequent breaks. So that was how the course seemed to continue, with smoke breaks being interrupted by the occasional requirement to attend half an hour's worth of lecture. All the stories we heard about the course prior to arriving seemed to be true. It was actually quite a relaxed course and we were well looked after in terms of food, accommodation and the facilities that were at our disposal.

I quickly discovered that the college bar offered no less than The Union

Jack and was a lot more accessible, especially on the homeward journey. To that end, although we did venture to the pub on one or two occasions, most nights were spent in our own bar. F-Section, presumably because we were the only all-male section, quickly adopted the role of the loudest and most dominant of the course. We wasted no time in declaring the college bar our main territory and each night we would assume our positions around the 'Old Joanna' (piano) and from here we would mastermind and execute our various antics.

We soon found that we had generated our own cult following of refugees from other sections to whom, providing we thought they were worthy, we would grant honorary evening membership to the F-Section drinking display team. These members made up for the half a dozen genuine F-Section members who chose not to drink as much as the majority of us. The main core of hardened drinkers and partygoers consisted of Jason, Wilko, Scouse, Fitz and myself.

I have already introduced you to Fitz and you all obviously know me by now, so I will give you a brief description of the other three. Jason was, along with Scouse, not ex-forces like the rest of us, but he did possess the same type of humour and thirst. He was from the Maidstone area of Kent and was, he thought, a bit of a lad. At over six foot he was the tallest in the section, and his main passions were surfing and cars. He was a bit of a boy racer and on the fourth week of the course his passion almost got us kicked out. He returned one Monday morning with a jazzed-up turbo-charged XR2, fully equipped with spoilers, a big exhaust and an enormous speaker which took up the entire rear parcel shelf.

The following Thursday night Jason decided to offer Scouse, Fitz and myself a lift to the local chip shop down the road. The trip went well despite his driving at about one hundred miles an hour down the narrow country lane, and deafening everyone in a five-mile radius with his stereo. When we returned to the college car park, however, Jason obviously did not think he had impressed us enough and proceeded to practise his wheel spins and handbrake turns. Unfortunately, during one high-speed pass of the car park we nearly took out a pedestrian, who narrowly dived for cover to avoid contact with our car. We panicked, and without waiting to identify the man we leapt out of the car and made a run for it. We were halted in our tracks by a bark that we in F-Section particularly had come to know well - Mr Berry the college governor. It appeared that it was he that we had narrowly missed and he hissed out of his bright red face that he wanted to see all three of us outside his office at eight o'clock the following morning. We disappeared to the sanctuary of the 'Old Joanna' and spent the whole night worrying how we would manage to get up and be at his office by eight after drinking all night.

Somehow we did manage it and were soon all stood in front of Gerry Adams' desk awaiting our fate. He screamed and shouted and banged his table, giving us the old speech about being irresponsible and reckless. Then he gave us the ultimatum - he wanted one of us to own up and take responsibility for our actions the night before, otherwise he would sack the lot of us on the spot. Fitz and I were used to these bollockings from our army days and knew he was bluffing, as if he had had the authority to sack us he would have done it straight away. He was just using scare tactics. He gave us five minutes outside to discuss it among ourselves, so Fitz and I used this opportunity to persuade the terrified Scouse and Jason that we had to stick together and all claim responsibility. Reluctantly they agreed; they had no real choice, as the obvious candidate for the chop would have been Jason as the car's owner.

We went back into the breach and stood our ground. Berry was fuming at our show of solidarity and screamed that he would make his decision as to whether to sack us all over the weekend, telling us to report back to him on Monday morning. We knew then that he was bluffing, as he would not bring us all the way back on Monday to sack us - wanker. He was just trying to make us sweat a bit over the weekend. Needless to say, he did not sack any of us and we all completed the course.

The only one of us that returned shaking like a leaf on Monday was Scouse, not because he feared facing Berry, but he had been issued a far more serious and painful threat from his 'tart', as he affectionately called his girlfriend, should he lose his job. Scouse was a natural comedian who was blessed with the trademark Liverpool sense of humour. He was a small, wiry man who when not in uniform was always dressed in his native costume - a shell suit - and he must have weighed all of six stone when wet.

Scouse's story, not surprisingly, was hilariously funny to us. He claimed to have been trapped in a disastrous marriage for years to a rather large lady who he referred to as 'the fat tart'. Apparently he suffered years of abuse at the hands of this woman, who would come in from the pub every night and beat him up for no apparent reason. He told us that she terrified him and for years he felt trapped, until one day he reached his breaking point and decided he could take no more. No, he did not put his foot down and tell her who wore the trousers as she was obviously the one who did, he did the next best thing any man would do when trapped and terrified by an opponent who can't be beaten - he ran away. He bought her a bottle of gin, her favourite tipple, waited until she had consumed the lot and was sleeping peacefully on the sofa, gathered his belongings, crept out of the house and disappeared in his Escort. He feared reprisals so much that he, with the help of some friends, entered a life not dissimilar to that which is offered to supergrasses on the witness protection scheme. He had to change his name, constantly move between different friends' houses and was always looking over his shoulder.

This was the main reason Scouse decided to seek refuge within the Prison Service, as he said with her record even 'the fat tart' would not dare look for him in a prison. He had, at the time I knew him, found another partner and was hoping to get a posting as far away from Liverpool as possible; somewhere like Dartmoor or the Isle of Wight would have suited him perfectly. His new partner still seemed to be the dominant one in the relationship, but she never beat him up and he seemed happy enough.

Scouse was always in the centre of all our practical jokes and was involved in another incident that almost saw us dismissed from the service. He was an expert in winding people up, especially in the bar in the evening, and on one occasion was directing his skills to Fitz, Wilko and myself. We decided there was only one way to deal with him on this occasion and that was to use our newly taught but very basic knowledge of C&R and remove him from the bar. This we did but, as we escorted him down the corridor towards the outside fountain in the garden, we ran straight into two of the senior PTIs in the corridor. We released Scouse, but not before they had seen what was going on. It was strictly taboo to practise C&R outside the confines of the training dojo and they told us to report to the gym first thing in the morning. We all thought that that was it. We had got away with the car incident, but this was far worse and we could not see how we would get out of this mess. Luckily for us, the man in overall charge of the gym was our own instructor and he seemed to like our spirit. Consequently, he just shouted and screamed a lot and gave us some menial tasks to carry out in the gym, and he promised to take it no further, so we were spared to fight another day. My only explanation for these narrow escapes was that the Prison Service must have been extremely desperate for staff at that time, and of course we had Wilko with us who was a favourite of all the PTIs, and the third member of our group.

Wilko was the real blue-eyed boy, a tall, muscular man from somewhere around the Portsmouth area. He was an ex-guardsman, but more to the point and why he got his blue-eyed boy status, especially with the gym staff, was that he was a member of the British Olympic bobsleigh team and had represented his country in at least one Olympic Games. This fact alone, coupled with his looks and physique, made him a hot favourite with the ladies, and he always had at least two female recruits by his side when we were out. This did not deter him from being one of the main faces in the section, and you could always rely on him to organize some great parties. One such event took place in his ground floor room and carried on until the peacock that roamed freely around the grounds gave his usual morning cry to wake us up from the beer-soaked carpet.

I remember one incident from that night, which again seemed hilarious at the time, once our initial feeling of panic was over. We were very wary of allowing gatecrashers in, as we did not want the details of this illegal party getting back to the staff. Well, at some stage during the night, a group of about five or six appeared at the door and tried to gain entry. Fitz and

I, as chief door staff, dealt with them, but as we slammed the door shut we failed to notice that one of their number had collapsed in a drunken state on the floor. The trouble was that his head was blocking the doorway and we only realized this after a few attempts to shut the door had failed. We dragged him into the room and notified Wilko. Between the three of us in our drunken state we concluded that we had killed him, and our natural reaction was to get rid of the body. We nicked some blankets from the store cupboard in the hallway, wrapped him in them and, picking up our dead body, we made our way quietly out of the room to dispose of him.

I don't know how we thought we would get away with it, but in our drunken stupor we really believed we had done him in and thought our only option was to get rid of the evidence. We made our way to the wooded area that surrounded the lake. Our original plan was to use one of the small rowing boats to row out and throw the bundle in the middle of the lake, but this was thwarted by the fact that the boathouse was locked. Funny isn't it, we believed that we had just committed the ultimate crime, but we did not want to break into the boathouse. We decided just to place the body deep into the wood and hope he would not be discovered by anyone on our course. Our mission over, we returned to the party satisfied that we were in the clear. As always it was not until the morning after that the reality hit us and we all woke with that strange feeling that we had done something terrible the night before.

During breakfast we huddled together and decided we could say nothing, not even to our other trusted section members. It was not until the morning smoke-break that I saw Fitz go white, as if he had seen a ghost. Wilko and I turned to see what he was staring at and went equally as white when we saw the man we had 'killed' the night before walking towards us. He came up to us and said "Blimey, that was one hell of a party you threw last night. My head is killing me and I woke up this morning wrapped up in blankets in the middle of the woods. It took me ages to find my way out." We were dumbfounded, relieved but dumbfounded, and as soon as the shock had worn off we laughed about it for hours. It's amazing the effect that large quantities of lager can have on your ability to think rationally.

Most of the section, and especially those I have just described, were good lads with whom I really got on well. I cannot comment on how they turned out once they joined their respective prisons, as I never saw them again once the course was over, but they were good friends when I knew them, who provided me with plenty of good laughs. As the course went on, many of the recruits did start to show signs of changing attitudes towards the way inmates should be treated, but most of this was done in front of the handful of instructors who expressed the same type of attitude. It was clear that, as none of us had any experience of dealing with prisoners, those who showed this change of attitude only did so to try to impress the instructors.

An additional option to the college bar and Union Jack presented itself to us when it was announced that one of the accommodation blocks was to close and the people billeted in there were to be relocated to external bed and breakfast guest houses. As luck would have it, Fitz was one of those who fell into this category and he soon found himself located in a guest house just on the outskirts of Rugby. Until now Rugby had been dreamed of as a good location for a night out, but it was just too far away and too expensive in taxi fares to use. Now of course, we could get a lift with Fitz at the end of the working day, have a good night out, stay in his room and get a lift back in the morning in time for lectures.

Luckily, Fitz's new landlady was quite liberal and had no objections to his having one or two friends stay a couple of times a week. So from then on most nights there were about ten of us crammed into Fitz's room farting and burping after a night out in Rugby's nightspots. We did, of course, continue to use the college bar for its ease of access, but this alternative offered us a welcome break from the same old faces and routine.

We soon all settled into the routine of the course, and the weeks began to really fly past. Before we knew it, we had reached the halfway point and the time had come to put our newly acquired knowledge to the test with the first of our two exams. The word exams suggests to me long two-hour papers that you always struggle to finish, and ones I rarely passed with flying colours. What we sat was actually a thirty-question multiple-choice test. All the questions were relatively simple and there weren't any trick ones slipped in designed to throw us off track. Besides, as I mentioned earlier, the answers had already been given to us by the instructors. Most of us did not even bother revising and those that did got lower marks than the rest, probably because they panicked too much. I was still extremely hung-over from a karaoke night when we sat the test, and I could barely see the paper in front of me, let alone circle the right answer, and I expected to do really poorly.

In fact when the results came back I was amazed to find that I had attained the joint top score in the section and one of the highest scores in the college - maybe it was lager power, I don't know. Although it was only a minor test, the instructors had made a big deal out of it during the week building up to sitting it, and we all felt relieved that it was over. We sat one more test, which was identical to the first except the questions obviously covered the topics we had learnt in the second half of the course.

To my knowledge no one failed the tests. One or two had to retake them, but none was kicked off as a result of failing the first time. It seemed to be a very difficult course to get kicked off, luckily for some of us.

There is not much more I can say about the course, except that I did thoroughly enjoy it. For the first time since the army, I felt as though I were part of a team again and enjoyed the comradeship I found with some of the lads. Some of the content of the course was interesting, and some I felt was totally unnecessary, but on the whole it was true what they said at Wandsworth - it was certainly the best part of the job. As the end of the course began to draw nearer, we began to gain passes in the different aspects, such as C&R, first aid and basic fitness tests, then after we received our final reports came the passing-out parade.

Ours was to be the last passing-out parade of its kind, as all courses after ours were not going to be taught to march as we had been. This was an attempt by the Prison Service to demilitarize its staff. So far as I am concerned they should have tried to do this in its prisons, not just at the training school. It was a shame because, although the parade meant nothing to me, there were plenty of those who felt very proud and it gave them a chance to show their families what they had learnt.

I was only one of two recruits who did not have anyone that came to watch the parade. The other was a girl called Toni from D-Section, who had been back-squadded from a previous course because she had broken her wrist in training. I am not sure why she did not have anyone there, but I just did not want my family there and wanted to get out of there as soon as possible. Toni and I did have a good laugh though, watching all the boys and girls that had been having relationships throughout the course nervously steering their partners away from any possibly awkward confrontations. Everyone was especially wary of us when we approached their family group to play the poor little orphan routine with the threat that we would say nothing as long as the drinks were flowing.

It was, on the whole, a good day and a nice end to an enjoyable nine weeks of constant parties. However, all good things must come to an end, as they say, and the day soon drew to a close and it was time to bid farewell to the majority of the staff and our fellow students for the last time.

My original group of companions from Wandsworth were equally as pleased as me to have been given Belmarsh as their choice of posting, and once we had collected our joining details for our new prison we headed back down the M1 for the last time. We had been granted a few days leave and had to report to Belmarsh by nine o'clock on 17 October. Once back home, we made arrangements to meet at eight thirty by the canteen in Belmarsh's car park to have a cup of tea in much the same way as we had done at Wandsworth, and bade our farewells until then.

8
BELMARSH

Belmarsh Prison is situated in Thamesmead in southeast London and was built on old marshlands that were once owned by the Ministry of Defence and used to test fire various weapons produced in the neighbouring factories of Woolwich Arsenal. There were many stories surrounding its construction, ranging from the fact that it was sinking into the marsh at a rapid rate to the fact that some Irish builders involved in construction had hidden Semtex explosives in the walls of the high security unit designed to house terrorist prisoners. All these were unfounded rumours possibly spread by any number of people opposed to its construction. To the big chiefs in the Home Office, Belmarsh was the new flagship of the modern Prison Service, but in reality chaos reigned within its walls due to poor and incompetent management, a serious lack of experienced staff, and uncontrolled regimes that changed on a daily basis. In short, it was a disaster waiting to happen.

Ninety-nine per cent of basic grade officers had less than six months' experience of the Prison Service and almost all the senior officers and governors who ran the prison had only gained promotion due to the fact that they volunteered to be posted there. I later found out that had they stayed in their original prisons most would not have stood a chance of promotion as their record of service up to that point had not been good enough. In short, they did not have a clue about how to manage staff or inmates and could not organize a piss-up in a brewery let alone deal with a serious incident. They were the service's dead wood; people with no hope of furthering their career elsewhere or old dinosaurs sitting out their final days to retirement, who had no interest in the future of the Prison Service and were put out to graze in the most expensive prison built to date.

Belmarsh provided the Prison Service with a perfect opportunity to promote a new, modern Prison Service and lose some of the stigmas that have become attached to it over the years since its formation. In reality they just did not handle it correctly and it was destined to earn itself a reputation that was at one time far worse than the most notorious prisons in its history.

I was obviously unaware of all this as I pulled up in the car park for my first day of a one-week induction programme. To give you an idea of how desperate the prison's situation was, our induction was cut down from two weeks to one as there had been so many staff off sick following assaults that they needed us on the wings as soon as possible.

My first impression of this huge prison was how different it appeared from the outside in relation to Wandsworth. It looked more like a huge Barrett housing estate hemmed in by a huge grey wall, which had a strange rounded steel construction to finish it off at the top. From over the top of the wall I could make out the cell windows of the various accommodation blocks. All around the wall and car park it appeared as though every conceivable entrance and blind spot were covered by moving closed-circuit television cameras. The exterior did not make me shiver with fear as Wandsworth's had done, but its sheer size and the thought of some of the prisoners incarcerated behind its walls made the prospect of entering through its gates every bit as terrifying.

With that all too familiar feeling of nervous anticipation, I went into the staff canteen to meet up with the others and await the arrival of our welcoming committee. We had only to wait about fifteen minutes, and were studying the scaled-down model of the prison located in the main conference room of the officers' mess when PO Webster and PO Johnson arrived. We took our places in the semicircle of chairs arranged in the room and - yes, you guessed it - began with the ritual of the creeping death. Of course we all knew each other well enough by now, but this was for the benefit of our new training staff and it also gave them the opportunity to introduce themselves to us.

PO Webster was an older man with a mop of grey hair and a nicotine-stained moustache. PO Johnson, although roughly the same age as his colleague, looked younger in years and appeared to enjoy keeping himself fit. Both were fairly quiet men, but PO Webster seemed unable to resist drifting into the storytelling that we had become used to. We learned that both men had come from Brixton Prison to take up their posts here, and they began the morning with a verbal introduction to Belmarsh.

We discovered that the prison held both remand and convicted prisoners of all the different categories from the lowest risk, category D, to the highest, Category A. There were five main accommodation blocks as well as a separate hospital within its walls. The four main blocks were called house blocks and numbered accordingly from one to four. House block one held short-term convicted inmates as well as having a separated wing that housed sex offenders, or rule forty-three prisoners to use the politically correct term. House block two held mainly convicted working prisoners who had jobs in one of the prison workshops, kitchen, farms and gardens or as red band cleaners. House block three, which had the nickname Beirut due to its hectic regime, housed all the remand prisoners awaiting trial as well as being responsible for running the induction programme for newly convicted prisoners. Finally, house block four at that time housed the longer-term convicted prisoners but was later refurbished to house Category A inmates.

At that time all Category A inmates were housed in the purpose-built Category A unit, which was a small unit set within its own perimeter wall at the rear of the main prison. Within this unit at the time were what were considered to be some of the most dangerous prisoners in the system. Some years later this unit was to be refurbished at tremendous cost for the purpose of housing the extremely high-risk Category A prisoners. It was, however, never to assume this function as shortly before its completion the government announced the news that all Irish terrorists serving sentences in British prisons were to be transferred back to Irish prisons. When I returned to Belmarsh after my time at Wormwood Scrubs only two European prisoners were being held in the unit, which was designed to hold forty-eight in total.

For the duration of our induction programme we were to be based in a small classroom on the top floor of the main administration building, which was located inside the main prison walls but within the sterile area, which is the piece of land found between the main wall and the inner fence and that surrounded the prisoners' accommodation blocks.

Although we had passed the training college course, we were still unable to draw our own set of keys until we had completed our induction. This was to prove extremely annoying, as when we were moving about without a member of staff we would have to wait at every gate for someone to pass and let us through. Not only that, it could have been dangerous, as potentially we could have been trapped somewhere in the event of a fire or other serious incident. This lack of keys together with our brand new uniforms proved to be a dead giveaway to the prisoners that we were fresh out of training despite our best efforts to appear as hardened veterans. This was all too apparent during our first visit to one of the residential house blocks on that first afternoon.

At one thirty that afternoon we met PO Webster at the main gate of the prison to venture inside its walls for the first time. The gate lodge here was very different from that at Wandsworth. There were three sets of electronic doors to go through before you even got to the sterile area, and the main area of the gate lodge where the staff were situated was full of complicated-looking electronic control panels and CCTV screens.

It was no simple task to get through the gate into the main prison. First you had to pass through the double electronically operated doors. Then you had to pass through a metal detecting porthole before being searched both physically and with a hand-held metal detector. And finally you had to place any bags, coats, loose change, key chains and sometimes even your boots or shoes through an X-ray machine. Only when you had been through this procedure each and every time you entered the prison could you finally draw your keys at the key chute.

As we made our way across the courtyard towards house block one, I was able for the first time to appreciate the sheer size of the prison. To give you some idea of the size, the total distance around the main outer wall was reported to be almost two miles and, if my memory is correct, the prison could hold approximately one thousand six hundred prisoners.

The interior decor of the house block was less grim than the wings at Wandsworth. There was, however, still a distinct smell unique to prisons, although the addition of integral toilets in all the cells meant our nostrils were not assaulted by the choking smell of human waste rotting in slop buckets. One difference I noticed immediately was the familiar noise level being generated from all areas of the house block. It was not only keys and doors banging like the noises I remembered from Wandsworth, but also the air was filled with the din of hundreds of people shouting and running about everywhere.

The main difference here was that all the prisoners were wearing their own clothes and not the blue prison uniforms we were used to seeing. As we made our way into the control 'bubble' at the centre of the house block, the scene we could see through its windows was chaotic. The bubble was the modern equivalent of the 'Wendy house' we saw at Wandsworth, from where all the prisoners' movements on and off the house block were controlled.

There were staff and inmates all over the place coming and going through various gates or just hanging around on different landings talking, playing pool or watching television. The sheer number of inmates and the way the whole scene appeared totally disorganized made it even more intimidating than the worst wing at Wandsworth despite the altogether brighter decor.

We were given a confusing explanation of the bubble officer's job, which basically comprised overall responsibility for the whole house block's movements. As well as arranging all the work parties, visits, doctors' appointments. etc., which on its own appeared to be the most responsible job in the prison, they were also responsible for keeping a running total of the prisoner roll and controlling any incidents via phone and radio. This position seemed all too much like hard work to me and one I thought I would never be able to master. We also got a brief account of the house block's regime, which accounted for the chaotic scenes before us.

It appeared that Belmarsh was the first if not the only London prison at that time that offered its prisoners association periods on a regular basis. On each house block they broke down the day of each of the three separate spurs or wings into what was called up time and down time. Each morning between about nine thirty and twelve one or two of the wings would be on up time when they received association and/or exercise, during which they had unlimited access to the phones, television, pool table and showers. Usually it was during these periods that the inmates were also given controlled access to the canteen, which was located on each house block. The remaining spurs used this time to attend the workshops, educational facilities or gymnasium. At Belmarsh at that time it was compulsory for every inmate to attend some type of workshop or education class as soon as a space became available, unless he was excused for medical reasons. This process was repeated during the afternoon between two thirty and four, but this time the wing that had association in the morning attended work and vice versa.

After this explanation it was time for the bit I had been dreading. We were split up into groups of three and told to report to the officers in charge of the spurs on association. As soon as we edged our way onto the spur we became surrounded by inmates who instantly recognized that we were 'fresh meat'. They couldn't resist the opportunity to make us even more uncomfortable with a barrage of questions such as, "How long have you been prison officers?" and "Could you sort this or that out for us?"

We, in turn, made matters even worse for ourselves by nervously stuttering replies to the effect that we did not work on that house block and advised them to see the spur staff. The officers working on that spur offered us no support and remained seated at their desk laughing along with the inmates at our awkward attempts to answer the questions. I don't mind admitting I was terrified and felt a terrible feeling of vulnerability.

As the hour or so we spent on the spur passed, I watched how the other officers walked in and around the large group of prisoners and seemed so relaxed and confident in doing so. I began to question whether I would ever have the ability to carry out my duties in this way. I thought I would spend my career as I did that hour - glued to the same spot, too nervous to move and greeting every prisoner that came within two feet of me with a stupid, nervous grin. Relief came when a message for the NEPOs to report back to the bubble came via the yellow telephone located on the gates at the front of the spur. This sense of relief was short-lived, as when we reported we were told to accompany an officer who would observe us whilst we did a couple of 'spins' (cell searches) on the bang-up spur. The officer was not there to assist us in any way, but rather to observe and report on our cell-searching skills. He picked the cell, which looked to be occupied by the largest pair of inmates in the prison, and after he had briskly opened the door and barked, "Cell search", he passed the pair over to Mickey Mc and me. We entered the cell and, much to the amusement of the prisoners and the observing officer, we began to carry out the task exactly by the book as taught at the college. We went through the whole list of correct questions, such as asking the inmates if they had ever had a cell search and if they knew what one was. The thing that the officer found the funniest was how we replaced everything we searched neatly back where we found it and searched absolutely everywhere including the toilet bowl, with the use of rubber gloves, of course.

The whole cell search took us almost forty minutes to complete and later on in the debrief we were told that you rarely got forty minutes to do ten cells let alone one. To cut down this time in the future, the advice given to us was to get the prisoners out, make a good mess, and sit down for five minutes reading their dirty magazines or looking at the pictures of their wives or girlfriends on their picture board. I always found cell searching a task I did not enjoy, as it always caused an element of friction even though all the parties involved knew it was a necessary requirement.

To that end, I did not take the advice offered in this first search and always left the cell as tidy as possible, even if I was under pressure from the other member of staff to wreck the place. As for the photos and magazines, I always imagined how I would feel and react if I caught someone staring at photos of my girlfriend and I always asked before looking at the magazines. In fact later, in an attempt to ease my discomfort of searching, I would open the door and declare that I was on a dirty magazine hunt. Most prisoners would tell you where their stash was just to prevent you tearing up the cell to look for it, as well as the fact that so long as we were reading the magazines we would not find anything they didn't want us to.

Some staff would take any opportunity to place a prisoner on report after a cell search, such as for having two Bic razors in their possession or having a ripped sheet or pillowcase. I could never be bothered with all the paperwork involved for such petty offences. Still, if nothing else it helped boost our confidence a little in dealing with prisoners, and the inmates commented on how nice it was to be searched by two polite and tidy officers.

During the week we visited all the other house blocks in the same way and found the routine in each to be very similar. One place where the routine was different was the high-security Category A unit, which we would visit later that same week. To enter the unit you had to undergo the same searching process as at the main prison gate - metal detector porthole, physical search and the X-ray machine. The unit was set over two floors with two spurs housing twelve prisoners on each floor. Staffing levels were incredibly high with no less than two officers on each spur and one in the individual spur offices required before you could unlock a cell. In addition to this, there had to be a minimum of four officers and one senior officer to run the visits complex and two senior officers in the main unit office. There was also a daily cleaning officer responsible for collecting the food and organizing the feeding, and finally an officer was permanently based by the unit's main entrance to search and book in anyone entering or leaving the place.

On the day of our visit, one of the inmates from the unit made an escape attempt whilst on escort to Maidstone Crown Court. Tony Bolden had allegedly smuggled a can of CS gas and a home-made knife from the unit into the police cellular van. On his arrival at the court, he attacked the escorting staff with the gas and knife and tried to make good his escape. Unfortunately for him, his status as a Category A meant there was a large police presence at the court and he was quickly overpowered and recaptured, but not before injuring two of the escort staff.

As we entered the unit, the stories of the injuries sustained were beginning to spread, with various levels being reported. The favourite was that he had sliced open one officer's face with the knife before breaking his arm, and sprayed the gas in a female officer's face. The broken arm report proved to be false, but I found the speed at which news travelled back to the inmates quite incredible. We had no sooner left the office after hearing the news ourselves than we passed an inmate grinning at us whilst making a gesture to us as if breaking his own arm.

This inmate was a man called John McFadden, a small but incredibly powerful man who enjoyed nothing better than a good row with a couple of screws. In fact it was this very inmate who, later that morning, was to pick me as the target for his threatening abuse over the fact that he did not get his milk for his cornflakes. He did not listen to my stammering pleas of ignorance on the matter; in fact he seemed rather pleased that he had chosen me to confront, as he had a more chance of persuading a new boy to run and get his milk. And, in my inexperienced state, I would have done so had I known where to find the milk he claimed was missing. Once again, I was offered no support by the three regular officers that were on duty, despite the fact that at one point I came extremely close to living out my days with a pool cue sticking out of my head. It was this sort of 'look out for number one' attitude, which I encountered among many staff, that I despised and it made me always more than willing to offer support and help to the new staff I encountered in later years.

The remainder of our induction took us to all the other house blocks, the hospital, which housed some real nutters as well as the genuinely sick but sane inmates, and the workshops. One area that differed greatly from the one we saw at Wandsworth was the control room. Auxiliaries staffed the control room at Belmarsh. These people were not trained to deal directly with inmates as is a fully trained prison officer, but they did have a senior officer in overall charge. It looked like the shop window of Dixons, as the whole of the claustrophobic room was a mass of television screens and videos. It was very dimly lit and, as well as monitoring every camera in the prison and controlling all the electronic gates, a member of staff was also on permanent radio duty communicating to every officer that had a radio.

It was from this room that radio and camera would closely monitor every incident. In short, it was the nerve centre of the prison. It was rather like the bridge of a ship, although looking around at some of the characters that were working there it looked more like the bridge of the Starship Enterprise. It was also from this room that the two electronic doors that led from the main Category A unit to its exercise yard, segregation unit and visits hall were controlled.

Later I was to encounter many times the frustration of waiting by these doors whilst the auxiliary on the controls refused to override the system and open the two doors together. This procedure was meant to be applied in the event of an incident in order to allow the staff to respond as quickly as possible and not get delayed for valuable seconds waiting for one door to close before the other opened. I remember on one occasion standing on the wrong side of the inner door screaming at the control room through the intercom to open the doors whilst watching in horror as the officer that was bringing in the exercise party was being seriously assaulted on the other side of the door. The excuse was that because he had already opened the outer door and was in the corridor, but had not been able to close the outer door before being assaulted, the auxiliary could not get authorization to override the system. It only took about three or four minutes for the doors to finally be opened, but that was long enough for the officer to sustain serious injuries, which put him off work for months and left him mentally scarred forever.

On our final two days, we were required to take tests on basic security including which key opened which door, first aid in the workplace and also a food-handling hygiene course in case we became cleaning officers in the future. It was also the time we would learn of our new places of work for the next couple of years. Although we could give our preferences as to where we would like to begin our career, the ultimate decision was left to manpower services, who placed us where the staffing levels were at their lowest.

9
CATEGORY A UNIT

I and the other lads from my course all asked to be put in the Category A unit, a request that baffled most of the staff we told. The reason for this request was because we all agreed that, although the unit held the highest category and some of the most dangerous prisoners in the system, it was a lot smaller and seemed less daunting than the chaotic scenes we saw on the main house blocks. It was true to say that, although the unit had fewer daily incidents than the house blocks, when it did kick off you could expect it to be on a much larger scale. This was due to the type of prisoner held within its walls. There was a large Irish contingency convicted of various terrorist attacks carried out on mainland Britain, and the very nature of their training within their organizations meant they all stuck together during any acts of disruption. Most of the other prisoners at that time were what I would class as the 'old school' or 'gentlemen villains', who rarely complained so long as they got what they were entitled to and no one gave them any unnecessary grief.

I held a great deal of respect for many of the men in this category and like to think that I earned some of their respect in return for treating them with decency. In addition to these two groups, there was also a small group of nutters and one or two what just hated screws for different and possibly very valid reasons. This minority took every opportunity to join in any of the other inmates' attempts to disrupt the regime when they felt they had cause to do so.

One such incident was to greet me on my very first day as a fully trained officer on the unit and kicked off not even one hour into my shift. We had unlocked spur one on the ground floor for breakfast and one of the inmates who was due to appear in court that morning approached us and declared that he was not going. He was informed that we could not make the decision to honour his request and he would have to go to court and take it up with his solicitor once there. He stated quite clearly that the escort staff would have to drag him onto the van by force if he did not get to see his solicitor before he went. I nervously told him that his solicitor would not make it as he was probably already on his way to the court. I then made a big decision, bearing in mind it was my first day, and told him I would try to arrange a brief phone call to his solicitor before he left.

He seemed happy with this compromise, but it was short-lived as my request was disapproved by the unit senior officer who favoured the alternative of dragging him onto the van. No sooner had I delivered the news to him than he and the rest of the inmates began to smash up the spur with some ferocity. The drill at the time for such an event was to evacuate the spur and lock the inmates inside it and, considering there were only two of us on there at the time, it seemed like the sensible thing to do. However, as soon as we did this the inmates obviously gained complete control of the spur and began erecting a barricade across the main door whilst continuing to destroy the furniture. By the time the duty governor had arrived to assess the situation the spur was almost demolished and the inmates had well and truly formed very good defensive positions from where they could fight off any attempt to regain the spur.

After an hour of talks had failed to bring a peaceful end to the dispute, the riot squads were sent in and eventually regained order. It had not been an easy task and about four or five officers and inmates had sustained injuries. The damage was estimated at about two thousand pounds and all the inmates on the spur were charged with a number of offences against prison rules. I could not help thinking how it could all have been avoided if I had been allowed to let the inmate make his telephone call. As it was, the inmate in question did make his court appearance and was dragged kicking and screaming onto the van.

Most of the incidents in prison are caused in a similar way, by staff refusing to bend the rules slightly even if it means it could avert a serious problem. This method of handling incidents was very common at Belmarsh and indeed throughout the prison system. It is, I agree, difficult always to find a peaceful solution to all disagreements between staff and inmates in prison, as often the rules laid down by the Home Office do not allow for the types of compromises that would satisfy the prisoners' requests. I always believed, however, that when you were the man on the front line, facing possible injury both to yourself and others, you should have the strength of character and the authority to make a decision based on your first-hand evaluation of the circumstances. Most prison staff, especially the senior grades, that I came across during my career were incapable of making a command decision other than the one ordered at the time by a higher authority, or the one written into the contingency plans as the textbook way to deal with a particular incident.

As far as I am concerned, each and every incident you come across in prison, as indeed outside, is unique and as such you may only use the rule books as a very loose guide on how to deal with them. I would go so far as to state that ninety-nine per cent of the incidents I have been involved in that turned nasty were as a result of the staff handling them in the wrong way. The majority of inmates, especially the majority of those on the Category A unit during my time, never asked for anything unreasonable or anything that we could not have delivered without breaching security or that they were not entitled to as part of their basic rights.

It became very apparent to me, even at that early stage in my career, that many staff perceived their jobs as one big game. This element I am referring to went out of their way to incite trouble in order to gain the status of being worshipped by those with similar mentalities as good, hard screws that gave the cons fuck all and didn't take any shit. In reality, they are cowards who would run a mile if the shit really hit the fan and who made the job of the rest of us half-decent officers more difficult than did the most disruptive prisoner in the system.

It was not long before I was to come across two young officers who had exactly the attitude I have just described and who both worked on the unit when I arrived. Both were two young Yorkshire men whom I shall call Steve and John. I am not in the game of grassing people up, but they and the prisoners and staff who have come across them will know exactly who they are.

These two boys were in my opinion a right pair of pratts who led each other to believe they were the hardest things that walked the earth. Many other members of staff idolized them for the way they treated every inmate and member of staff that seemed too friendly with the prisoners as though they were the scum of the earth. I never actually saw these two hard men in a row, but they were involved in instigating almost every incident that occurred when they were on duty, before retreating to the safety of the tearoom to write up their reports while leaving other staff to sort out the tear up that usually followed.

I soon discovered to my horror that they had a bet going between them to see who could secure the most guilty verdicts on prisoners in adjudication for a substantial amount of money payable at the end of their tour in the unit. This bet was no secret among the staff or prisoners and one governor in particular, who regularly held the adjudication hearings, would enquire as to whom was winning before hearing the case, and I am sure he would pass judgment in a way that kept the score as close as possible.

During my career I hated placing prisoners on report because the whole process was time consuming and I preferred to deal with it my way and prevent the inmate's record being blotted by some petty offence. Obviously I came across some real arseholes who deserved to be nicked or left me with no alternative, as they would not let me help them avoid it. There were also times when we were ordered by senior members of staff to nick prisoners, despite the rule book stating that the decision to take such action is entirely up to the officer in question.

I remember one such occasion when the Irish contingent on spur three decided to refuse to be locked up at five o'clock one evening in protest at one of their visitors not being allowed to give him a kiss and a hug on a visit. Yet another incident was sparked off by a simple non-threatening request being refused. All the inmates on the spur, even the English ones, had to stick together and respect the others' wishes to stage this process. The spokesman for the Irish stated that they would not cause any problems but would not return to their cells until they had talked to the duty governor about the reason the request had been denied. At this time I had been working on spur three for about six months and had begun to get on well with all the inmates on there. In particular, I had a good relationship with a man called Ronnie Johnson, a big old fellow from Bermondsey. The order came back that we were to go into the spur and verbally give the inmates a direct order to return to their cells. When I returned to the spur, Ronnie, who had a heart condition, was in his cell complaining of chest pains, so this being the priority I called for the medical team who promptly arrived at the scene. They took Ronnie to his cell and laid him on his bed in order to examine him and I carried on with my previous task.

As expected, every inmate refused the orders and stated again that they wanted to speak to the duty governor. When I reported this back to the senior officer, he asked me what Johnson had said. I explained his current position, but was told to get back in and give him the order. Even if Ronnie had obeyed the order, I could not have locked him up as he was still undergoing medical treatment in his cell.

Again, as expected, Ronnie told me that he had to stick with the others and I told him that I felt it was ridiculous for me to give him an order in his position anyway, so I left without giving it. The following day I and the other officer involved attended the unit adjudication to give evidence against the twelve members of spur three's population. The incident passed by peacefully in the end, with the duty governor admitting that the decision had been wrong and assuring the inmate in question that he could greet his loved ones with a kiss and a hug on the next visit.

All involved pleaded guilty to refusing direct orders and were given three days' cellular confinement and seven days' loss of canteen access. Ronnie was the last inmate to attend and asked the governor to ask me one question. He asked if I had actually given him the direct order or not. This was my first time in adjudication and I was taken by surprise when I had to answer something and not just read the standard details of the incident I had read five times already. As soon as I was asked, I noticed the huge figure of the unit's principal officer glaring at me and nodding his head to tell me just to say yes to the question. I could not lie about the facts, however, and had to say that I had not given him the order due to his position at the time. I thought the PO was going to explode over the desk and kick the shit out of me, and the governor did not look too amused either. He told Ronnie that on the evidence I gave he was not guilty, but said he was worried what the others might think if he returned as the only man on the spur not to be locked up for the next three days.

Ronnie agreed and stated that he would have refused the order anyway had I given it and he accepted a guilty verdict and the same punishment as the rest of them. Once he had been taken out, I tried to leave but the PO screamed at me to get back in. He and the governor spent the next half an hour yelling at me about how it is always our word against theirs and I should never tell the truth when put in that position by a prisoner.

When I returned to the spur, Ronnie apologized for putting me on the spot but commended me on my honesty, especially as he had seen the PO glaring and nodding his head and knew I had got a right bollocking after he'd left. Big Ronnie and I got on quite well after that incident and I held a lot of respect for him. He was what I considered to be one of the old school, the likes of whom I had met growing up in south London. I also got on well with his wife and other members of his family when they visited him, especially his two young boys, Liam and Alfie. Both boys were proper little tearaways but the youngest, Alfie, had the most mischievous character.

On one occasion I had picked up the Johnson family at the main visit area to drive them round to the unit in the small battery-operated milk float type vehicle we used at the time. I stopped at the first gate to open it and no sooner had I done so than the van with its passengers went driving past me with little Alfie at the wheel. I could not give chase until I had closed the gates, which gave the little bastard quite a good head start, and I didn't catch up with them until they were almost outside the unit. Meanwhile, the control room had seen me on the cameras running after the vehicle and my radio was jammed with various different call signs desperate to find out what was going on. Luckily, due to his age and the fact that I took responsibility for leaving the driver's door unlocked, the Prison Service did not take any action against Alfie.We did, however, receive a proper new minibus to transport visitors in future. Not that I ever got to drive it, as that little episode cost me a lifetime ban on being the visits bus driver - shame.

Although Ronnie could not show how well we got on for the sake of the other prisoners and more so the other staff members I worked with, he did stick up for me on more than one occasion. Once I remember we had these two racing car drivers on remand for drug offences, who had a bit of difficulty adapting to their new lifestyle. In an attempt to get in with the faces on the spur, they tried to put me down by saying that they could at least go into any pub in London without fear of retribution, unlike myself. Big Ronnie immediately replied that I would be welcomed in any pub he used for a drink as his personal guest, an invitation that he definitely would not extend to the two boy racers.

One of the pair had perfectly permed black hair and always reeked of aftershave, even when going to the gym. He commented once in my presence to another prisoner that he could not wait to get to a dispersal prison and deal with proper screws. The other inmate turned to me and said, "As soon as he hits a dispersal smelling like that and with his hair, they will have him on his back quicker than a basted turkey at Christmas."

The unit was full of different characters from various avenues of the criminal world from convicted and remand IRA terrorists to some very nasty high-risk sex offenders. All the nutters and sex cases were held on spur two and included some inmates charged with some of the most high-profile and disgusting crimes you could imagine. The 'main man' at the time was a particularly horrible creature called Childs. He was an older man who had been accused and convicted of some terrible crimes, many against minors. In one he was accused of murdering a young boy and then hacking up his body and putting the bits through a meat-mincing machine before burning the remains in an attempt to get rid of the evidence. The trouble with Childs was, although he had been convicted of these stomach-churning crimes, he thought he was the dog's bollocks and carried on as the spur's very own barrack-room lawyer.

I hated him and every time I had to be in his presence my skin crawled and I had this overwhelming urge to smack him in the face. One afternoon I was on the spur to pick up an inmate for visits and Childs was once again on his soap box preaching about his rights. I had had enough and told him to shut the fuck up and with that he picked up a jug of boiling water and threatened to do me with it. I snapped and picked up a pool cue and the plastic dustbin lid and charged at him like a knight on a joust. He threw the water at me but I deflected it with the dustbin lid and caught him a cracker with the thick end of the pool cue right across the nut and put him out sparko. Childs, being the type of tosser he was, tried to raise a formal complaint, but it was decided that no further action would be taken as I had only acted in self-defence and I had only struck him once and so had not used unnecessary force.

I never had any further problems from him, and he was always as nice as pie to me whenever I was on the spur. I took a lot of stick for deciding not to charge him with attempted assault but, as I said before, that was not my way and I felt happy enough that I had been able to put him in his place in the way that I did.

Another high-profile prisoner with whom I had a good working relationship was 'Dingus' Magee, a convicted IRA terrorist who was apparently of a very high rank within his organization. You may think it odd that an ex-squaddie could strike up a rapport with a convicted IRA man, especially when it was rumoured that he had been part of the M60 machine gun team that had ambushed a Green Jacket patrol in Crocus Street, West Belfast, killing three and injuring many more.

I discovered that the way to be a successful prison officer was to judge the inmates as people, not for what they had done to be in prison. The only ones you could not treat in this way were the sex cases, as I am sure most of you will agree that it would be almost impossible to ignore crimes of that nature. The only two screws that 'Dingus' would really talk to for any length of time were myself and a good friend of mine, Brian B. Brian had the same sort of laid-back attitude as me and had served for twenty-two years in the Paras. He hated the senior management as much as I did and thought they were all incompetents. His favourite phrase to sum up the daily carry-ons we endured was, "This place is a right cake and arse party." He was the only person I met that did not give a fuck about who he upset, and between the two of us we gave the management more headaches than any prisoner ever could.

We began to have a problem with the Irish prisoners on the unit at weekends due to the fact that they only received visits on weekdays and there was nothing to occupy them at the weekend. The gym staff did not lay on any training for them like they did during the week and, as a result, they were getting increasingly restless and more fights and petty arguments were breaking out. So Brian and I got together with Dingus to see if we could sort something out to relieve the boredom. Our solution was that we would organize training sessions for them on the exercise yard and take them out twice a day on both Saturday and Sunday. It took us a while to get our ideas cleared by security, but Brian and I, being the persuasive type, endured and eventually got the go-ahead.

We used to come in wearing tracksuit bottoms and Brian had his maroon Para sweatshirt on and I had my Green Jacket Northern Ireland one on. I am sure you can imagine what this sight looked like - two screws, both in their army sweatshirts, chasing a group of about twelve high-risk IRA inmates around an assault course we had constructed on the exercise yard. All the inmates loved it and it put an end to all the problems we had faced on previous weekends and the whole idea was a great success. However, when Brian tried to expand the assault course and asked for permission to add some climbing ropes, which he wanted to suspend from the caged roof of the yard, his request was denied.

10
CHARLIE BRONSON

If you put an animal from the wild in a cage and each day you torment it, beat it, starve it, deny it contact with other animals, or tie it up and restrict its movement, it will eventually attack its tormentor out of sheer frustration. Man, it is scientifically believed, evolved from animals and therefore we surely must all possess that basic animal instinct for survival. Animals only attack when hungry, threatened, injured or out of self-defence or protecting members of their group. Some people, I agree, attack others for no apparent reason at all. All these type of men or women generally attack people that are weaker than themselves or have the benefit of others to back them up. These are the bullies of our society. Of course most animals attack creatures smaller, slower or weaker than themselves, but they only do this for survival, to eat and live, not just for fun or self-gain egotistically.

I was told that Charlie Bronson was an animal in every story I heard about him. It did not take me long to realize that, yes, perhaps he was an animal or at least had had to become one during his years of incarceration. He had indeed attacked prison staff and had destroyed prison property - facts that he has or will never deny - but these acts have not been carried out for no good reason. Charlie carried out these types of prison offences after enduring years of torment, deprivation and solitude, as well as suffering mental and physical pain and torture inflicted on him by the very breed of man I have described in the last paragraph - 'THE BULLY'.

If you put a bully in a position of authority such as the one a prison officer holds, it gives him the perfect opportunity to prey on as many victims as he can and then cover up his cowardly acts by claiming he was acting within the realms of his duties. I have worked with these scum and witnessed first hand the way they work. They are insecure little pricks as far as I am concerned, and it would be an insult to every creature to call them animals. The only thing they have in common with some animals is that they hunt in packs, they prey only on the weak and vulnerable, and they use strength in numbers to carry out their attacks and solidarity to cover them up.

It is this breed of prison officer that dealt with a young Charlie in his early 'career' in prison and thereafter over the many, many years he has been incarcerated. Their bully-boy tactics have been covered up by their superiors and passed on to their prodigies whose actions they in turn have covered up as they progressed up the ranks within the service. It is a vicious circle that has been going on for years and will likely continue due to public ignorance.

The way Charlie got sucked into the secret world of bullies and solitary suffering was textbook in prison terms. He made one fatal mistake very early on in his prison career, a mistake that played him right into the hands of the bullies. For over three decades they have not let him forget this mistake, and have lied and exaggerated to cover up their own violent and unprofessional conduct to create the ultimate prison 'monster'.

Charlie was involved in a 'sit down' in a workshop at Parkhurst Prison, a common and usually peaceful protest whereby prisoners refuse to work until they get the chance to speak to a governor regarding some dispute or other. These disputes are generally over food visits or exercise, the three most important things in an inmate's daily routine and therefore the most common aspects of prison life deliberately disrupted by staff intent on causing upset among the inmate population. Many times I have witnessed certain elements of staff deliberately denying inmates their preferred diet, holding them up for visits or harassing visiting relatives, and refusing to unlock certain inmates for exercise or association.

On this particular day, Charlie was informed by the other inmates that they were all going to refuse to work, an action he would have had no choice but to participate in, as there were some pretty big boys in Parkhurst at the time. When a group of inmates refuse to work, the officers have to issue an order individually to each inmate in turn so that they can then be placed on report for refusing an order. When this time came, Charlie was first in line to be given the order to return to work, which following the brief he refused. Unbelievably all the remainder of the inmates backed down and agreed to go back to their workstations. Whether this was a deliberate plan to drop Charlie in it, or whether all the others just lost the will for confrontation on that day, the result for Charlie was the same - he was nicked.

The 'mufti squad' (the forerunners of the modern control and restraint team) arrived to take Charlie down the block to await the governor's orders the following day. I know from experience that in these situations the members of the mufti squad used the opportunity to go in as hard as possible and rough the prisoner up as much as they could while being able to cover it up in their identical reports.

Charlie was upset and confused as to why he had been let down by his fellow inmates, and he was also terrified as he had heard the screams of men being dragged to the seg and beaten by the mufti squad's long sticks. He tried to reason with the staff that now stood poised to leap on him with their riot helmets and sticks just visible above the mattress he was huddled behind, but his pleas were in vain; these wolves had the smell of blood in their nostrils. They had no intention of settling for a non-physical outcome and were eager for a roll around the floor to break up the boredom of their shift and give them a good story to brag about in the officers' club at lunchtime over a few celebratory pints.

Charlie did what I think most of us would do in that situation - he picked up a broom and began swinging it in front of him in an attempt to keep the mufti at bay. You must imagine the scene - Charlie is terrified he is going to get the shit kicked out of him, a concern probably being confirmed by verbal threats coming from the psyched-up members of the mufti squad. The inmates, who would be shouting from the sidelines as more officers flooded the area to herd them back to their cells, are also encouraging him. There would be a delay of some minutes before the mufti would strike, as they would need to wait until the area was cleared of all other inmates to ensure they were not outnumbered and there would be no potential witnesses of the removal.

Unfortunately, during this stand-off period, in all the confusion and noise, an officer was caught by the broom Charlie was swinging around. The mufti squad immediately overpowered a stunned Charlie, and whoever else was close enough also jumped in, and a bruised and dazed Charlie was dragged off to the block. Once in the block he received the welcoming strip search and a 'know your place' roughing-up by the seg staff before being trussed up in a body belt and placed in a strip cell.. A prisoner in a strip cell with a body belt on is supposed to be visited by a doctor and, as far as I can remember, the belt is only meant to be worn for a maximum of a few hours. Charlie on this occasion saw no doctor and the belt remained on for days rather than hours. He had committed the cardinal sin in prison of striking a prison officer and so began his out-of-control spiral into a journey to hell, with a little help from the prison staff who would never let him forget that he had struck one of them.

I have seen so many times the way that certain officers victimize inmates. It is common knowledge that if an inmate is involved in an incident with staff or tries to stand up for his basic rights he becomes a target for the vigilante-type bully staff. This abuse of authority went on daily and was an art handed down by older members of staff and accepted by senior management. More often than not, selected members of staff would receive an unofficial briefing by management informing them that inmate 'A' was causing them problems and would need to be 'removed' to the seg unit. This select group would then hatch an elaborate plan to carry out this order, which would always be done when the rest of the wing was locked up.

The usual method of carrying out these premeditated removals would involve at least four hand-picked officers. The mere fact that they were chosen would be enough to boost their already enlarged egos and make each of them more determined to impress the others with their over-the-top macho methods. The officers would enter the cell aggressively, and before the inmate knew what was happening he would have three or four officers on him, usually dangerously, unnecessarily and extremely painfully over-exaggerating the control and restraint techniques. During this scuffle they would take any opportunity to stick the boot or fists in before dragging the inmate down the block. Once here he would receive a strip search together with some equally over-the-top violence from the block staff, who were regarded as the hardest and most elite of the prison staff.

The control and restraint techniques taught to officers are very effective and very little pressure needs to be applied to immobilize even the biggest man. They are, however, like all martial arts, extremely dangerous when abused, which is why their use is supposed to be closely monitored at all times. If an inmate has received injuries after being restrained, such as bruising, lacerations or even quite often broken wrists, a Prison Service nurse or doctor has to attend to treat the wounds and write a report on their findings. Almost all the so-called examinations I witnessed were carried out with the medical staff just looking through the spy hole of a locked cell door, then completing the necessary paperwork in the seg office with the 'help' of the officers involved with the removal. At the same time these officers sit down and discuss what story to write down on their reports, usually stating that the inmate attacked one of them first. This is then copied down on all the other reports to seal the inmate's fate. Thus when the inmate is brought before the governor the next morning, he faces a charge backed by four or five 'sworn' statements from officers. The governor would always discuss the case with the staff prior to carrying out the adjudication and would have decided the inmate's fate before he had even seen him.

So many inmates fell foul of these carefully planned take-outs and, once found guilty in the kangaroo court style adjudication of assaulting a member of staff, they would never be able to shake off that title. It was exactly in this way that Charlie began his nightmare journey into the belly of an archaic, corrupt prison system that, with its bullies, beatings, cover-ups, dungeons and brutal, inhumane regimes, had not changed much since Victorian times.

At one time during my career I applied for a transfer to Long Lartin Prison in Worcester. Long Lartin is a dispersal prison housing long-term prisoners and is supposed to offer a more stable type of regime. On my arrival for an interview I met the governor, who was the head of custody and who immediately told me he liked the look of me because I came from Scrubs and I looked like I would not take any shit from "these scumbags". He was, of course, referring to the inmates, although I did wonder briefly if he was on about the staff. He explained, without carrying out an interview, that the job was mine and went on to express his wish to recruit half a dozen or so officers like myself who could on his orders, quote, "Stick a riot helmet on and crack a few heads open." He said he would handle any subsequent allegations about inmates being hit with truncheons and claimed to have full Home Office approval to form this attack squad in the hope of deterring a rise in prison violence. He said we would be exempt from other duties and would have our own rest room and would be on standby to react to any part of the prison, sort the problem and return to our room with no questions, almost like a Prison Service version of the SAS.

Needless to say, I declined his offer and told him I had applied for a transfer to get away from the bullies and unnecessary violence I had witnessed at Scrubs and Belmarsh. They had formed a squad like this at Belmarsh and it was full of all the arseholes who spent the day strutting around the wings trying to look hard and intimidating in ill-fitting boiler suits. They did not last more than a few months before being disbanded, apparently due to staff shortages.

It is exactly this type of bully-boy mentality and victimization that Charlie has endured for almost thirty years. It became as much a routine part of his daily life as a trip to Tesco is for us on the outside. Just try to imagine yourself in his shoes for just twenty-four hours, waking up alone and afraid, not knowing if you will get through the day without an officer wanting to goad you into confrontation, and unsure if the powers that be will decide to 'ghost' you to another prison, which will lead to more uncertainty and a fresh lot of bully-boy screws wanting to make a name for themselves.

Going back to my initial comments about Charlie being an animal, well perhaps I would agree he is a bit like an animal, a very scared animal. This is not because he attacks people for no reason, because animals don't do that. There is only one species that attacks for no reason or to boost their ego and that is the bully. Animals only defend themselves in a kill-or-be-killed scenario. I can tell you now that Charlie is certainly no bully. He detests bullies and I never saw any evidence in his character that would suggest that he would attack another human being for no reason. On the other hand, I have met countless 'psychos' in uniform who are capable of half killing a man just for looking at them the wrong way, and then use their position of authority to cover up their actions by blaming their victim. The only thing Charlie is guilty of is having too much self-pride to not allow himself to sit in his cell for thirty years and accept the mental and physical torture dished out to him by these bullies. He has chosen to try to fight back even though he knows he can never win a fight inside because, to quote a governor I once worked with on the unit at Belmarsh, "Don't worry lads, our gang will always be bigger than theirs in here." At least Charlie can say to himself when he's lying naked and bruised in a strip cell that he still has his pride and what little dignity he could salvage from his position fairly intact. It is this very part of Charlie's character that has kept him sane over the years of pain and suffering, because, despite all the bad press you may hear and a careful hiding of some of the true facts over the years, the medical boards have actually certified him sane. This certificate of sanity is an acclamation that very few of us can say we have. Perhaps we are all mad and Chaz is the only sane one among us, and that's why we have kept him locked up in solitary confinement for over thirty years.

Time and again the courts have refused to take into account statements from qualified doctors who have examined Charlie in the same way that they have denied me the opportunity to speak in open court about my experiences and the premeditated brutality I have witnessed. Why would an establishment that has nothing to hide be so afraid of one former employee going public in a court of law? I can only assume they are afraid of any subsequent investigations that may be ordered and the can of worms it would open up, not only on Charlie's case but also hundreds like his of unprofessional misconduct carried out by staff in prisons and special hospitals going back for years.

For many prison officers, to "roll around the floor" with an inmate is all they come to work for. It not only breaks up their usually boring routine, but also gives them status with other staff and maybe even a week or two off on full pay. Apart from that, it also gets the officers away from the wing for a couple of hours while they sit and write their reports, and then they can return to the wing like conquering heroes returning from battle. The whole scenario is viewed as a game by most staff and is a great way of widening the 'them and us' divide between staff and prisoner.

The Prison Service would describe Charlie as a monster, but I would wholeheartedly disagree. The man I met and worked with is far from a monster. Charlie is extremely talented, caring, witty and very clever and, surprisingly, even after all these years of torture he bears no grudge and takes everyone he meets at face value. The Prison Service has spread the myth about Charlie Bronson in order to keep a lid on the appalling treatment they administered to him and others like him, not only in prisons but also in the special hospitals such as Rampton and Broadmoor. Patients were injected daily with the liquid cosh, which renders the body paralyzed, or were subjected to electric shock treatment in an attempt to stabilize the brain. Perhaps they had hoped he would just die and no questions would be asked, but it obviously caused them a great deal of embarrassment, if not a great deal of concern, when he was certified sane and had to be released back into normal prison society.

It is my belief that the powers that be have done their utmost, with the cooperation of their bully squads in prison who have become experts in fabricating the truth and covering their tracks, to prevent Charlie having the opportunity to prove that he is capable of being released into society to lead a normal, law-abiding life with his family. And for the first time in many, many years Charlie has everything to live for. He has found his long lost son, and he has a loving wife and stepdaughter and many good friends, myself included, all of whom have offered him and his family full support. One friend, Andy Jones, owns the Crime Through Time Museum and has offered Charlie full-time employment on his release. Charlie has set up his own children's charity and has told me he would love the chance to talk to youngsters about the pitfalls of getting involved in crime and wasting precious years of your life in prison.

The following pages are an account of my first meeting with Charlie when I worked with him on the super-max unit at Belmarsh. This was the first time I had ever met the man behind the myth and it was the beginning of a very unusual friendship struck up in the most unlikely of circumstances. I was fortunate enough to work with Charlie once more further on in my career, which I will talk about later in the book. Since leaving the Prison Service I have carefully monitored Charlie's plight, and have been involved in television and video documentaries as well as newspaper articles. I have also been fortunate enough to have been invited to a couple of parties on Charlie's behalf, where I was able to meet some great people and strike up more unlikely friendships.

I had been on the unit for almost nine months and, shortly after introducing the training programme with Brian, I and about four other officers were pulled into the governor's office and told some worrying news. In the office stood the governor, the unit's two principal officers and a senior officer, all looking very sombre. The governor broke the silence to tell us that we had been chosen to look after a special prisoner who was due to arrive in the next few days. He told us that we would be keeping him in total isolation in the unit's segregation block and his name was Charlie Bronson. We had all heard of the name from various people throughout our training and I think everyone in the room felt as terrified as I did at the prospect of this man's arrival.

We had heard some real horror stories about this man's violence towards staff and his superhuman strength, but up until then he was to us like a mythical creature that had been created to scare young prison officers. Now we had just found out that he was actually a living man and we would have to look after him while he was at Belmarsh.

We were told by the governor that he was so unpredictable that if he even looked at us the wrong way we were to jump all over him and do whatever was necessary to immobilize him. He told us not to worry about using excessive force and that we would receive full backing from the management should we have to take this action.

On the day of Charlie's arrival, I, Tony Lebatt and Mick Regan waited nervously in the seg unit for the escort to arrive. We had prepared the end cell for him and spoke anxiously about what to expect during his stay. At this time we all anticipated a long, hard period of time ahead and all expected to be off sick by the end of the week having been assaulted by this powerful and unpredictable man that we awaited.

The telephone rang with the news that he was on his way through and we caught a glimpse of about ten or so staff surrounding a man with a shaved head and large handlebar moustache, strapped in a body belt, coming through the corridor from the main unit. When he reached the seg we saw just how powerful this man was. His arms and chest were huge and my first impression was that he resembled an old circus strongman. He said very little as we escorted him to his cell except to say "All right guv" to us as he gave each of us the once over. This was his first time at Belmarsh, so he was obviously as anxious as we were about what to expect during his visit.

The senior management was terrified at his arrival and the governor at the time made a fatal mistake in an attempt to ensure that Charlie behaved himself whilst he was there. He made a promise to Charlie that if he behaved himself for two weeks he would ensure that he was moved onto one of the spurs in the main unit. Charlie told him that he would look forward to that and gave his word that he would not be any trouble.

The first few days were a little tense as both we and Charlie adapted to working together, but I quickly began to see a different man to the one that had been described to me by many people in the past. True to his word, Charlie behaved impeccably, and as the days passed we began to get on really well. He began to tell me a bit about his past and some of the places he had been within the system, including suffering some appalling treatment in Broadmoor and Rampton special hospitals during the seventies.

Although he had obviously suffered some terrible treatment, he did not appear to have any hate or bitterness towards me. He had some really funny stories and also really enjoyed listening to my stories of life outside the walls of the prison. I quickly built up a healthy respect for the man and lost all the feelings of fear and nerves that I had experienced before I had met him. Even as early as those first two weeks, I knew this was a man with whom I could have a great friendship. I saw a little bit of my own character in him in the way that he would not let the system push him around and stood his ground for what he believed in. I certainly did not see a madman, rather I saw a highly intelligent man with a great sense of humour and self-pride. Despite suffering years of brutal torture, both mentally and physically, he had the amazing strength of character to judge each officer and situation individually and not let his past experiences cloud his judgement. However, this progress we had made between ourselves was to suffer a setback when the initial two-week period came to an end.

Two weeks from the day of his arrival, Charlie greeted us in the morning with his bags packed and ready to move to the main unit as he had been promised. When we made enquiries as to when we could move him we were told that there was no way he was going onto the unit and we would have to tell him that he was to remain in the seg. Despite our concerns that Charlie should hear the news first hand from the person that had made the decision, no one responsible came forward and it was left to us to tell him. Charlie was devastated at the news and, although he appreciated that we were only the messengers and had no intention of harming us, he did ask us to lock him back in his cell and get the governor who had made the promise to come and see him.

Strangely enough, the governor in question had gone on leave the day before and could not be contacted as he was on the ferry to the Isle of Wight. Meanwhile, Charlie was getting pretty pissed off and we knew we had to get someone to try to explain why the promise had been broken despite the fact that Charlie had kept to his side of the bargain so well. In the end Mr Outram, who was then a principal officer on the unit and had known Charlie some years ago at Leeds Prison, arrived to talk to him. Along with him came about four teams of three officers in full riot gear, who were briefed to stay out of sight but to steam in if Charlie looked as if he were going to have a row.

So, whilst Mr Outram was chatting to Charlie in his cell, the riot teams stood outside physically shaking at the prospect of taking Charlie on. The senior officer in charge of them whispered encouragement by telling them that they had to hit him hard and fast and give him as many blows as necessary to immobilize him. He also told them that once it was all over they could boast to other staff that they had given the famous Charlie Bronson a good kicking. Thankfully they were not deployed, as Outram managed to explain to Charlie what had happened and assured him that he would be well treated by us while he was at Belmarsh. He also promised that he would receive no more false promises and that he would ensure that the governor in question would stay away from him.

We, as the staff dealing with Charlie, felt just as let down as he did and decided that from that moment on we would set our own regime for him. Outram agreed to this so long as we kept within the security requirements of the unit. After allowing Charlie some time to accept this setback, we sat down with him and told him of our proposals. We explained that we would come to work in tracksuits and, providing he remained the only prisoner in the seg, we would allow him plenty of time out of his cell during which time we would help him train on the yard. He loved the idea and we set about scrounging any type of sports equipment we could find and soon had a badminton set and a scrabble game and had arranged access to the unit's multigym once a day.

In addition to this, we rescued Charlie's beloved medicine ball, Bertha, from his stored property box so that he could carry out his trademark medicine ball sit-ups. So began some of Charlie's best days in his twenty-two years of incarceration to date. During the next few weeks I was to strike up the beginnings of a strong friendship that remains to this day with a man who turned out to be nothing like the reports I had heard prior to meeting him. We had some really hot days that summer and we all thoroughly enjoyed training with Charlie on the yard and beating him at scrabble, and Charlie enjoyed the trust and companionship that he had experienced so little of during his years in prison.

Charlie had arrived at Belmarsh after being arrested during a brief spell of freedom for an alleged conspiracy-to-rob charge. He was due to appear at Luton Crown Court shortly after his arrival and was glad of the regime we set for him as it gave him a chance to focus on his forthcoming trial. For possibly the first time in his life in prison, we had given him the opportunity to prove to all his critics that he was more than capable of interacting with us and caused us no problems at all. The Home Office, however, had yet another surprise in store for him, and just two or three weeks before his trial date decided to move him to Bristol Prison. We, of course, protested at this on Charlie's behalf and were given no reason as to why this decision had been made at this stage. Charlie had done nothing wrong and had behaved himself impeccably while at Belmarsh, but the Home Office still insisted on moving him to the other end of the country just days before he had to appear in a serious criminal case.

We felt that not only had the Home Office once again failed to give Charlie the best help they could, but also they had failed to recognize all the hard work that we the staff and Charlie had done over the past few weeks. The only conclusion I could come to was that they were afraid that he was getting too comfortable and doing so well that they would not have been able to keep him in solitary conditions legitimately for much longer if he stayed.

Despite our pleas, the decision stood and the day arrived when we were to transfer him to Bristol. At that time Charlie always travelled naked and restrained in a body belt. I had managed to secure a place on the escort and ensured that I had acquired a bag of hard-boiled eggs from the kitchen for the journey. We travelled in a small Category A minibus with tinted windows and, although unhappy with the move and anxious about what to expect, Charlie was in fairly good spirits.

Shortly after our departure we stopped at a set of traffic lights next to a coach of old ladies going on a day trip to the coast. Charlie has a great respect for the elderly and stood up in the van to wish them a good trip through the window. I noticed many of them staring at our vehicle and commented to Charlie that they might be able to see through the windows and see Charlie in all his glory. Charlie assured me not to worry as he had been in more of these minibuses than anyone had and there was definitely no way they could see through the glass. I did not share his confidence as more and more old ladies pressed their faces against the windows of their coach. It was not until we reached Bristol that I had my fears confirmed and discovered that you could see quite clearly through the windows of this particular bus.

It was on this same journey that I received my nickname from Charlie, which has stuck to this day and is used each time we communicate. About halfway down the M4, Charlie asked me to crack a few eggs and hand feed him. I had just moments earlier broken the aerial on his prized Roberts radio attempting to get a clear reception. I turned white thinking that Charlie would return the favour by pulling my head off, but he took it well and we laughed it off. With this still fresh in my mind, I gingerly shelled a hard-boiled egg and fed it to him. No sooner had I popped one in his mouth than he wanted another, then another. I ended up stuffing more eggs into his mouth than he could chew and he had to spit them out in order to prevent himself from choking. He commented that I had almost succeeded in killing him with half a dozen eggs when the Home Office had failed for years in all their attempts. So, from that day on, I was known as the hard-boiled screw. Today this has been changed to the ex-hard-boiled screw, but it has become the name I am called by many of the new friends I have made through Charlie.

When we arrived at Bristol, the usual reception committee was out to greet Charlie. As is standard in every prison when receiving a 'difficult' inmate, a group of some twenty or so of the biggest screws are mustered to meet the van. As soon as we left the vehicle they surrounded us and all gave Charlie the standard stares in an attempt to intimidate him from the start. When we arrived in the seg unit, Charlie asked to be put into the strong box as he just wanted to get on with his time here without any aggravation. He had no sooner gone into the cell than the reception committee's leader screamed the standard welcome in which he pointed out, in no uncertain terms, that if he even looked at one of his staff the wrong way he would get the kicking of his life. He also made it perfectly clear that he would get fuck all during his stay at Bristol, unlike what he had become used to at Belmarsh.

I heard this speech and felt great sadness for a man who I had grown to respect a great deal over the previous few weeks. I was in no position to do anything, but I was confident in my friend's ability to do hard time when he had to. With our paperwork signed it was time for us to leave, but not before I pushed past the mass of screws surrounding Charlie to shake his hand and tell him to keep his head down.

The following is a letter I sent for the attention of the parole board on Charlie's behalf, after the judge at his appeal at the Old Bailey in 2004 directed that the parole board must set a release date for him. I am unsure whether the letter ever reached the board, but I was asked by Charlie himself if I could send a letter documenting my views and experiences. I have met some really nasty pieces of work in my time both in and out of prison, most of whom will be released within a fraction of the time Charlie has served behind bars. Comparing Charlie with some of these people, I strongly believe he deserves the chance to be released and I am convinced he will use his experiences to help young people today realize what a waste of their lives it is to spend years in prison missing out on so much that life has to offer as he has.

"To Whom It May Concern:

I first heard of Charlie Bronson during my first two weeks' training for the Prison Service at HMP Wandsworth. He was described as almost a 'mythical monster' by a number of older prison officers, Most of whom claimed to have "rolled around the floor" and "got the better of him" in a boastful manner as if to try to impress the new recruits, at the same time exaggerating stories to make us fearful of this man, who they branded the most dangerous man in the prison system. These stories were continued when we arrived at the Prison Service college, where a certain element of instructors again were obviously out to impress us with their accounts of how they "beat up Charlie" and "taught him not to mess with them". I quickly realized that these men had probably never even seen Charlie, much like the men in the army who had been shot by snipers in Northern Ireland but had never in fact been to the country. All these stories did ,however, convince many new recruits and many therefore had already formed a biased opinion of Charlie without even meeting him. They were under the impression that this man had to be attacked on sight before he got the opportunity to attack them.

I first met Charlie in person at the secure unit at HMP Belmarsh in 1994. I must admit I was nervous about the initial meeting as I had only heard the Prison Service side of his story. The first time I met Charlie I noticed that he was probably as nervous as I was, as this was his first time in Belmarsh and he was unsure of the reception he would receive. Putting on a brave face, I had a nervous first meeting but pushed aside the stories and decided to form my own opinion of the man behind the myth. I quickly built a working relationship with Charlie and within a day or two we had formed a good bond of trust between us. For the month or so that followed I heard his side of the story, which I believed to be genuine as he never denied doing some bad things whilst in prison, but I appreciated he was only reacting to some of the brutal treatment he had received over the years. He felt remorse for his actions and even at that early stage wanted the chance to prove he could change. I was surprised to discover what a great personality he had, bearing in mind the years of solitary confinement he had endured. He had feelings, needs, and a sense of humour and was highly intelligent and talented. I enjoyed games of scrabble, helping him with exercise routines and even sat alone in his cell enjoying cups of tea, which he made me! I was of course aware that he had taken hostages in the past, but I never felt threatened in any way at any time when I was working with Charlie. There were still officers who would try to wind him up in an attempt to get a name for themselves so they could brag that they had wound Charlie Bronson up. As I have mentioned, Charlie will openly admit that he has done some bad things while in prison, but he was sucked into a system that almost needed a myth like Charlie to use as an instructional tool for its new recruits. Yes he has taken hostages, damaged prison property and tried to fight the system in the past, but he has only reacted to years of mental and physical torture by an element of bully-boy prison staff.

Since leaving the Prison Service I have kept in touch with Charlie and have met some of his friends, including his wife Saira who has done so much to keep Charlie focused in recent years. Over the past few years he has achieved so much when even now the Prison Service has tried to deny him many of his basic allowances. He appreciates that he will need a pre-release programme, but is as confident as I am that given the opportunity to do this he will react positively as I found he did when I worked with him. He is in my opinion not a danger to anyone. He has got so much more in his life now: his wife and her daughter, whom he loves very much, his friends like Andy Jones, who has offered him full-time employment in his museum, his writing and artwork for which he has won many well-deserved awards. He loves children and has done much for charity including setting up his own children's charity. There are far more dangerous prisoners in the system that have been released or are on softer regimes than Charlie. He has psychiatric reports, which all counteract the Prison Service reports, to state that he is completely sane and focused. All he needs is a chance to prove that he is a different man and is capable of leaving prison and leading a normal life. He could do so much to educate the younger generation of the dangers of wasting your life in prison. My personal experiences of Charlie have all been good with no exceptions; I have never felt threatened by him and would be more than happy to sign a declaration taking responsibility for him on his release. Both he and his family will always be welcome at my home. I would have absolutely no reason to feel he would be a danger to my family or me any more than I feel he would be a danger to others. He deserves a chance to prove himself and if given that chance I know he

Me and some of the lads waiting for helicopter to insert us on a seven day close observation patrol on border crossing point 101 near Rosslea county, Fermanagh, 1989

Me and Mark patroling Carrickmore, a Republican border town in Fermanagh, prior to Gerry Adams making a speech for the Easter parades, 1989

Me and Simon making up for lost drinking time in Kos on leave after Fermanagh tour July 1989

Steve, Jim, Trisha, Simon and Me at the London Final of Rose of Tralee contest, Penta Hotel, Heathrow 1989

Me and Mark receiving an award for best
G.P.M.G.S.F. Team Dover, 1989

Me taking a breather during live
firing exercises in Canada, 1990

Me and Mac on Leach Lake on R&R in
Rockies, Canada, 1990

Me on top of the world on R&R in Rockies,
Canada, 1990

Me on patrol on Irish border,
County Tyrone, 1990,

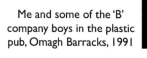

Me and some of the 'B'
company boys in the plastic
pub, Omagh Barracks, 1991

"Tooled up"
Me, 'Little Mac' and
Freddie Fryer in our
accommodation, ready to
go on another border
patrol, Tyrone, 1991

Me waiting to go on shift after a heavy night, Belmarsh, 1994

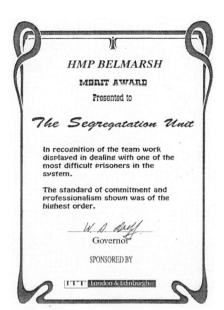

Award presented to us for our work with Charlie, note how they describe Charlie!

Me and Charlie, Belmarsh Seg, 1996

Signed Photo from Charlie, 2006

Me and Joe Pyle, 2006

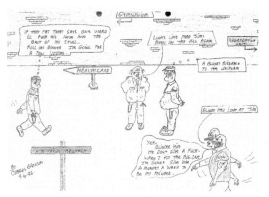

The first piece of art Charlie did for me,
Belmarsh Seg, 1996

A section of artwork Charlie has done
for me and my family

A section of artwork Charlie has done
for me and my family

The first oil painting done for me
by Charlie, 1997

A rare photo of Charlie and
his beloved mother, Eira

Me with Eira and Roy Shaw,
'Free Charles Bronson Campaign'
in Derby, 2006

Charlie's angel, his faithful medicine ball 'Bertha' being well looked after at Dave Courtney's Place

Me at the 'Crime Through Time' Museum, 2000

Me and Andy Jones, museum owner
and firm friend and supporter of Charlie

Needles and Louise from the punk group
'Swellbellies' at the museum

Charlie's ex, Joyce Conner and some of the chaps
wifes at the party thrown for her by Charlie in Woolwich, 2001

The badge we wore at Charlie's
appeal in the Old Bailey, 2004

Me with Dave Courtney at his home, 2006

Me with Dave Courtney and Roy Shaw
at various events in 2006

Me with Dave Courtney at his
'An Evening with...' in 2006

"Boys and Their Toys..."
Me with Dave Courtney

Me at a book signing with Dave Courtney and
Chris Cowlin (Apex Publishing Ltd) Gravesend, 2006

will do it to the very best of his ability.

He is a good man who has survived some of the most horrendous treatment in an archaic Victorian prison system, but after all he has been through he holds no grudge or any bitterness. He has grown old in prison and the system now owes him the chance to prove that he can go home and live the reminder of his life with his friends and family. A Prison Service code states that it has a duty to care for people in its custody and help them to lead law-abiding lives upon their release. They have failed to give Charlie this chance up till now and it is time they give him his chance and disregard what I believe is a personal grudge the system has with this man.

Give him a chance and he will not let you, me, himself or, more importantly, his family, down."

11

DAVE COURTNEY OBE

What can I say about this man that you have not already heard or read about. Well, all I can say is that it is all true, however unbelievable you may think the stories are.

I first met Dave in the high-secure Cat A unit at Belmarsh in 1996 when he was brought in on remand for a charge of importation. He had a fearsome reputation as one of the top London gangsters at the time, and the general feeling was that he was going to be a right handful.

It had only been a few days since we had taken delivery of Charlie and everyone's nerves were shot at the prospect of having him on the unit, so you can imagine how most of the screws took the news that 'Big Dave' was coming for tea. I will tell you how they took it - they all went fucking sick, that's how they took it. You see, your average screws strut about the landings and wings of our prisons as if they are the hardest men to ever walk the earth, but, as I have maintained all along, most are bullies who act by preying on the weak and always ensure they outnumber their intended victims before they strike.

Well there is certainly one thing Dave Courtney cannot be accused of - and believe me he has been accused of a great many things by some very dodgy coppers over the years - and that is that he is weak. In fact the staffing levels dropped to such a desperate level when Dave arrived - due to a strange outbreak of 'Davecourtneyitis' that spread through the officers - that I began to think we would have to make Dave the honorary governor of the unit. Imagine that - 'dodgy' Dave in charge of forty-eight of the most dangerous men in the prison system! How funny would that be? Still, one thing's for sure, he couldn't do any worse than the fat idiot who was currently filling that position.

The difference in the screws on the unit at that time was that they not only had to worry about dealing with the consequences of their actions at work - that was easy to do, as they could always rely on a fellow officer to back them up with false witness statements to incriminate inmates, they also had the worry of possible reprisals on them outside work. Due to the reputation of men like Dave and a good few other big names on the unit at the time, the fear of reprisals outside the walls was continually drummed into us by intelligence briefings given by the security department.

We were told, for example, that we should not use our full names in front of the inmates and should certainly not discuss things such as where we lived or socialized. All these briefings succeeded in doing, however, was spread fear and paranoia through the ranks of the bad apples amongst us and give them just cause (or so they thought) to attack inmates at every opportunity. My belief was, and still is, that so long as you didn't behave in a way that led to fear of reprisals you didn't have anything to worry about. Most of the guys I came across doing bird, including the top boys like Dave, had enough on their plates without worrying about getting people to follow screws home, and they would deal with the bully-boy element in their own way.

One of the ways Dave dealt with the sneaky-beaky way in which the screws went to great lengths to disguise their identities was as he dealt with most things - by applying a little bit of forward planning and combining it with a little bit of his famous cheeky wit. He was so amazed at the paranoia, which was rife and plainly obvious to anyone observing from the outside, that he devised a cunning plan that still makes me giggle today when I think about it.

Dave was, and still is, very well connected with the London club scene and he noticed that a lot of the staff on the unit at the time were fairly young and many were single. So, over the space of a few weeks, he began dropping into conversation with the more paranoid members of staff snippets about his connections with this club and that club. It didn't take long for the screws to start taking the bait and they began to quiz Dave on where were the best places to go and what nights were the good ones, etc. Dave turned round and said he would have a word and get a crowd of them free VIP entry into one of these clubs. Of course many members of staff jumped at this opportunity to gain free access into a top club, with the chance of rubbing shoulders with the rich and famous.

When they arrived at the club, however, Dave's kicked into action and, having briefed the door staff about the party's arrival, they were all given star treatment and ushered to the front of the queue. Once inside, they were offered exclusive gold membership for free, courtesy of Mr Dave Courtney, which being slightly stupid they all eagerly accepted.

Of course you know what's coming - in order to register for gold membership you are required to fill out a form, giving your full name address and contact details. How easy was that after they had spent months painstakingly trying to conceal their names from the inmates on the unit? In one night, Dave had succeeded in compiling a dossier of the full names and addresses of about half the unit's workforce!

Can you imagine the panic that this little caper caused amongst the ranks of the already paranoid Prison Service? The Home Office actually issued an official memorandum forbidding any member of staff from attending any establishment with links to Dave Courtney or his associates, which was pretty much everywhere in south London at the time. Dave did not escape reprisal from the Prison Service officials, who were obviously greatly embarrassed by the whole issue. As a consequence, he was placed in solitary on a trumped-up charge of attempting to condition staff, which we all know is bollocks - he was just being nice. Of course a little bit of solitary is not going to bother someone like Dave, despite the fact that in a further attempt to wind him up they only allowed him to exercise handcuffed to 'Dingus' Magee, who at the time was in the middle of the longest dirty protest ever held in a mainland British prison and was permanently covered in shit. Imagine having to walk round the cage next to that stench for an hour a day, but, as always, Dave stuck two fingers up at the authorities and took it all in his stride.

As I said, when Dave first arrived at the unit nerves were on edge, so when the staff who were strip-searching him discovered that he was in possession of two Rolex watches, one of them couldn't wait to use that information to do a bit of stirring up. He was not part of the regular team assigned permanently to look after Charlie, but he used to come in to assist us with serving Charlie's meals. To try to impress Charlie and make conversation, he couldn't wait to tell him about the right flash bastard who had just come in wearing two gold Rolex watches. Well Charlie and Dave had never met before, though both were aware of the other's reputation, and in the enclosed world of a high-secure unit this comment from an insecure officer was just enough to cause a bit of verbal conflict between them for a few days.

Evidently Charlie didn't like flash jack-the-lad characters and, due to the officer's description, this was the picture he had painted of Dave, so he began issuing threats to him out of the window. Dave, not being a man to back down from anyone regardless of their reputation, of course replied with his own shouts of retaliation. This went on for a few days and the tension at one time got pretty tense, so we had to be particularly careful that these two didn't meet whilst moving to and from the gym or visits. There was even talk of setting up an unlicensed bout on the exercise yard at one time and some officers began opening books. Talk about the clash of the fucking titans - what a row that would have been to watch.

Thankfully this stand-off didn't last for long. Both men soon realized that the screws were deliberately antagonizing the situation, as not many had any love for either Charlie or Dave. In fact the two men became firm friends and have remained so to this day, so once again the system failed to break two of the highest-risk inmates they had had in the unit at any one time.

The truth about why Dave had arrived on the unit wearing two gold Rolexes was far less sinister than the authorities would have liked. He had been asked by a friend, who needed to raise a bit of cash, if he could sell the watch legitimately and he still had it in his possession at the time of his arrest. Of course the authorities didn't have any of that story, so they confiscated the watches with the intention of proving they were in fact the proceeds of some dodgy drug deal or robbery, as if they didn't have enough on Dave as it was. They were obviously worried about the fragile charges they already had him on, so felt they should formulate a plan B. Nevertheless, despite an extremely conscious effort to prove the watch was not legitimate, all their investigations proved futile and once again the authorities had to eat humble pie and were forced to return the watch eventually.

Dave quickly settled into his own unique way of handling the monotonous routine on the unit with his own brand of humour. He quickly realized that everything that had to be done for the inmates on the unit involved a great deal of effort from various members of staff. One exercise, which you may think is a simple one but for a Cat A prisoner is in fact one of the most drawn-out processes, is a simple trip to the prison hospital.

Whilst still in solitary, Dave made a basic request one morning to see a prison doctor. The officer was persistent in his demands to know the reason for this request, and Dave insisted that it was personal and he would rather just tell the doctor. However, when the officer eventually said he could not authorize the appointment unless he knew what was the problem, Dave told him that he just needed a doctor to look up his arse.

Well, you can imagine how the rumour that Dave Courtney had piles spread through the ranks of the officers - everyone thought it was hilarious. A few days later the day of the appointment arrived and preparations began to move Dave from the unit across the three-hundred-yard sterile area from the unit to the main prison building and into the hospital wing.

I had been attached to the six-strong team of officers detailed to accompany Dave to the hospital. Now, to move a Cat A inmate from the unit is no mean feat. They were deemed such a risk that before any move could take place the rest of the unit and the main prison had to be locked down and secured. We then had to ensure we had two dog handlers to accompany us across the sterile area from the unit to the hospital, as well as notify the control room by radio exactly when we were leaving the unit and when we had arrived and were secure in the hospital wing. All the way across to the hospital, during the visit and until we were securely back on the unit, Dave was to be handcuffed to an officer and the control room would track our every movement through the dozens of closed-circuit television cameras that covered every square inch of the unit and prison grounds.

Well, after all these preparations we finally began to move out of the unit and across the open space between the unit and the main prison. As I said, it was only about three hundred yards or so, but to Dave, who had not focused on anything further than about four feet away or seen any greenery for the past six weeks, it was like crossing Siberia. He played along with the novelty of it all the way across, performing his 'kid in a sweetshop' routine and staring at the trees and the sky.

We made our way into the main prison and up the stairs to the hospital and then secured ourselves in the examination room, which was located at the front of the prison and overlooked the road towards Thamesmead. When the doc arrived he asked Dave to bend over and drop his trousers so he could carry out his examination. Dave obliged, propping himself up on the window sill and looking out of the window whilst pulling his arse cheeks apart to assist the doc. Whilst in this position he kept commenting on the cars and people he could see through the window - a sight he had not seen for some time. In no time at all a bewildered doctor commented from the rear that he could see nothing wrong with Dave's behind and asked again what the problem was.

"Problem?" Dave replied. "There is no problem, doc. I just said I wanted someone to look up my arse and, now that you have, I will be off, thank you very much."

Well I nearly pissed myself there and then at the comment and also the sight of the senior officer, who had taken the original request from Dave to see a doctor and whose face had gone purple and looked as though it was going to explode.

"You fucking told me you had piles, Courtney, you twat! Do you think I am some sort of mug or something?"

"Gov, I never told you I had piles - you came to that conclusion all by yourself. I just told you I wanted a doctor to look up my arse and now he has done we can go, thank you very much."

The senior officer was fuming and, had he not been such a spineless twat, he would likely have jumped all over Dave there and then. I was too busy laughing to have been of any help if it had all kicked off, so I was glad when we got clearance to make the move back to the unit. All the way back the senior officer was having a dig at Dave, telling him how he thought he was the daddy of the unit, that no one had ever left the unit with less than eighteen years served in the four years it had been open, and that he would go all out to have him at every opportunity.

Of course these were just idle threats in Dave's case, but that's not to say that these threats were not carried out on other, shall we say, less well-connected prisoners, even in the unit where it appeared that every inch of floor space and every blind spot was covered by closed-circuit television cameras.

I witnessed countless attacks by staff on inmates for no apparent reason other than that they could and had been getting away with it for years. Don't forget that we knew the position of every camera, we had seen the monitors in the control room and we had been told where the blind spots were and who to contact if we wanted a certain camera to 'malfunction' for a few minutes. Believe me, this went on day in, day out, and all the stories you have read from people's accounts of the time they spent as an inmate in one of our prisons and having suffered brutality or psychological torture at the hands of power-crazy screws are true. I can confirm that, as I saw it with my own eyes, and it was witnessing on a daily basis this behaviour by my fellow prison officers that disgusted me so much that I felt I had no choice but to turn my back on the Service. I was ashamed to be associated with such cowards. I detest people with no backbone who hide behind authority in order to inflict such pain and suffering on others.

One such incident, which occurred whilst Dave and Charlie were with us on the unit, was the particularly vicious attack on an older prisoner we had on the unit at the time. This guy had never been in prison before and was a fruit and vegetable stall owner in his fifties, who somehow had ended up on remand in the max secure unit because of some people he knew outside. Guilty or not, the guy was like a fish out of water. He didn't have a clue and was obviously terrified and extremely intimidated by the surroundings in which he now found himself. All that apart, he was a genuinely nice man; well spoken, polite and seemed to get on well with the other inmates on the unit, who realized he was out of his depth and took him under their wings.

However, the fact that he was obviously totally inexperienced in the art of 'doing bird', coupled with the fact that he was an educated man who thought that the screws were there to look after the inmates and provide them with advice and support whenever they needed it (which of course was exactly our job description but was not recognized by most members of staff), made him a 'pain in the arse' and a definite victim for the bully squads.

For weeks this man was ridiculed and tormented by a number of officers in an attempt to goad him into even the slightest sign of aggression towards them, but he never rose to it. You could see the frustration rising in the faces of these officers and around the tea-room table during lunch they made no effort to disguise their hatred for this man. One thing I was certain of was that it was not so much IF this man would be attacked by staff, but WHEN.

From the main unit leading out onto the exercise yard there was a corridor, which was about twenty foot long and at each end was closed off by means of an iron wicket gate and a further electronically operated, reinforced door, which was controlled via a buzzer and intercom by the main control room. This corridor was known by both staff and inmates as 'muggers ally'. One Saturday afternoon two northern officers, who liked to think they were the ultimate law on the unit and who had been the main characters in the conspiracy to target the fruit and veg man, were bringing in the members of spur three, including Dave and Joe Pyle, from the yard.

In a carefully pre-planned move, they had arranged for another two officers to meet them and assist in bringing the inmates back onto the unit. They remained on the yard as the inmates filed off and passed through the first door to wait in the corridor. Both doors could not be opened at the same time unless there was a serious incident either on the exercise yard, the seg unit or on visits, or indeed inside the corridor. The two officers on the yard had deliberately arranged for their target to be the last prisoner to come off the yard and, as the three of them approached the first gate, one of the officers in the corridor closed it in their faces, leaving them alone in the sterile area between the corridor and the exercise yard.

Due to the nature of the timing mechanisms on the doors, before they could reopen the first door the second door had to be opened to allow those waiting in the corridor to get back onto the unit. This in itself is bollocks, as all they had to do was override the system, but this just confirms that the staff in the main prison control room were in on what was about to happen too. Once the inmates and staff had passed through the second door and it had been closed behind them, they opened the first door to allow the two northerners and the old boy into 'muggers ally'.

Once inside, and with the doors locked again, the two officers without warning set upon the prisoner and subjected him to a vicious and unprovoked attack, all because they had taken a dislike to him and they could get away with it. After a few minutes, as planned, one of the officers pressed the green alarm bell situated on the wall in the corridor and continued to beat the prisoner until some other staff responded to the bell and gained access.

Of course all the staff knew what had actually happened, but they just reacted as if the inmate had assaulted the officers first, and so he would be subjected to a bit more pain by the adrenalin-pumped officers arriving at the scene. Once he was relocated in the unit's segregation area and the staff had allowed themselves a period of celebration, he would be required to be seen by a medical officer to check for injuries.

This particular incident, as with so many others carried out on a daily basis in our prisons, left the inmate in question with some pretty serious injuries. He was found to have two broken ribs and serious bruising to his face and body. The problem was, however, that the medical staff were all in on the cover-up too. You hear the authorities all the time going on about the criminal code, whereby one criminal will never grass up another one. Well, let me tell you, the authorities also abide by this same code and use it far more than those in the criminal world and to cover up far more heinous crimes.

For what those officers did to that man you would be looking at a custodial sentence on the outside, but because it was carried out in prison on people that the public don't know or care about by staff who are expert at making up false statements and getting them endorsed by however many other members of staff that are needed, the incident goes unnoticed and the inmate in fact receives further punishment for breaking the worst rule of our prisons by assaulting an officer.

This particular inmate did attempt to contest the allegations made against him and his solicitor made an attempt to view the video taken that day through the twenty-four hour closed-circuit television camera located in the corridor. He was told by the senior staff at the prison, and also had it confirmed by the Home Office, that unfortunately that particular camera was offline on the day of the assault as it was experiencing technical difficulties - yeah, right, course it was.

This may be a good time to mention a particular inconsistency that I began to notice relating to certain prisoners and members of staff. It is common knowledge that many members of the Prison Service and the Police, as well as many others that hold very senior positions in our society, are also members of the Masons. Funnily enough I have never been invited to join and as a result have no knowledge of the inner workings of the Masonic movement other than the well-known fact that they are all duty-bound to look out for one another.

Although a secretive sect, it soon became obvious which members of staff were either fully fledged or trainee members, and the more I observed the daily regime in the places I worked the more apparent, if not blatantly obvious, it became that some members of staff were giving certain prisoners preferential treatment. The type of additional privileges a Masonic prisoner would receive ranged from extra time allowed on visits or exercise to the smuggling in for them of various items of contraband by

Masonic prison officers. I often wondered, if this sort of 'favouritism' could be demanded for relatively minor rewards in prison, what types of mutual favours were being done at the higher levels of government or within the judicial system. I used to hear rumours, for example, as I am sure many of you have, that certain high-ranking police officers or members of parliament would 'get off' charges such as drink-driving or various other such allegations and that they had done so because they were members of their local Lodge, and I believe even more strongly now that such things do go on after witnessing the events I have described above with my own eyes.

Every movement and activity was videoed in that unit, and I know for a fact that not only were those tapes passed on to the police and other criminal investigation departments but also they were used by psychologists who analyzed them in an attempt to gain further understanding of the criminal mind. It fascinates them how a criminal ticks and they would analyze everything from what they ate to how many times they had a wank a day. Good job there were no cameras in the cells, as Dave was constantly getting caught in this act by the same officer, an old bird who we called Zelda from a children's show called Terror Hawks that was popular at that time. If you remember the show you will understand why we gave this officer the Zelda nickname. I am sure that she quite enjoyed catching Dave in the act of daily relief.

For all these reasons the mood amongst the prisoners on that unit was not a good one. There was a real feeling of 'them and us', as most members of staff felt unable to build any type of relationship with the inmates due to the paranoia that had been built up by the reprisals briefings I spoke about earlier. Also, as the senior officer explained to Dave during that hilarious hospital trip, during the four years the unit had been opened I think there had only been two inmates who had served sentences of less than ten years. Such was the hype at the time about the category of prisoner held on that unit that the judge only needed to hear that an inmate standing before him was residing there and he would usually award the maximum sentence. So it was little wonder that morale was at an all-time low. It really was a case of ABANDON ALL HOPE ALL WHO ENTER.

Dave quickly realized this and, as he was more than confident that he would be found not guilty of the charges against him (he was, I believe, the first inmate to be released from the unit with a 'not guilty' verdict at that time), he made it his mission to try to boost morale amongst the other residents. Obviously his pranks, such as the hospital outing, had people talking for months afterwards when word spread, but he was constantly playing the joker in an attempt to raise a few laughs.

One particular caper I witnessed while I was working on spur four one Saturday morning was his 'Groutie' impression. We had unlocked the spur as normal for the inmates to collect their breakfasts and make their morning applications, which most were doing when this classical regal piece of music burst through the air. As we looked around, bewildered, for the source of this music, we saw Dave strutting out of his cell with his nose up in the air. He was dressed in a prison-issue dressing gown and had fashioned a cravat around his neck using one of the legs he had torn off his prison pyjamas, and he was sucking on what looked like a giant spliff, which he had inserted into the outer shell of half a Bic biro to look like a cigarette holder.

He glided over to our desk in his prison-issue slippers with a copy of a rolled-up newspaper under his arm and said, "Morning, gentlemen. Has my post arrived? I think I will take my breakfast in my room this morning. Please let me know when my Racing Post arrives, there's good chaps. Do carry on."

It was just this sort of spontaneous prank that kept us all laughing, cons and screws alike; well, some of us screws anyway. There were one or two that really took a dislike to Dave's brand of humour and extended their animosity towards him far beyond the usual hatred that most screws are encouraged to develop early on in their careers towards all inmates. This vindictiveness was apparent each and every day when these members of staff came into contact with Dave, but there is one incident I recall that in my opinion highlights the mentality of most of my colleagues at the time.

We had a prisoner called Ronnie Fields on the unit at the time, who to the inmates was an icon and to the officers a pain in the arse. He didn't give a fuck and absolutely hated screws and wasn't shy of letting them know this. He was, however, a gentleman and, so long as you didn't try any of the usual mind tricks or attempt to fuck up his routine, he just got on with his bird with dignity. He was a great friend of Dave's, but once again was hated by the bad element of staff. He could, however, handle himself very well and had demonstrated this by knocking out a good few screws and cons in his time. So, although he was the centre of most ego-boosting conversations in the officers' tea room, no one would ever have had the bottle to take him out in the way they did other less hardy prisoners.

One afternoon the Irish lads decided to stage one of their regular weekend protests, which usually culminated in the spur getting flooded with a dozen or so officers from the 'elite' security department, who would use heavy-handed tactics to get all the inmates secured back in their cells. Whilst this was going on it became apparent that Ronnie had collapsed on the floor and was clearly having trouble breathing. Dave went to his aid immediately and sat on the floor with him in his arms, trying to help him control his breathing. Shortly afterwards the remainder of the spur had been secured and the alarm had been raised, but it appeared that Ronnie was suffering a heart attack and was in a pretty bad way. Due to the security procedures involved in getting an ambulance into the unit, it usually took a minimum of half an hour for the paramedics to arrive.

What happened next will surely highlight to you the severe lack of common sense and humanity that your average screw had, let alone the basic inability to assess a situation and react appropriately. Basically, most were unable to make any decisions that involved deviating from the textbook method of dealing with an incident, especially when they were confronted with two incidents to deal with at the same time.

Instead of allowing Dave to remain outside his cell with Ronnie to comfort him while they awaited the arrival of the paramedics, they insisted that he return to his cell and leave Ronnie lying on the floor in the middle of the spur. It is a fact that many officers hated Ronnie with a passion and

Dave realized that they would love the chance to watch him suffer and possibly die on the floor of the unit that day, so there was no way he was willingly going to return to his cell and allow this to happen.

I witnessed on many occasions throughout my career staff deliberately forgetting to give inmates medication or ignoring a cry for help or cell buzzers from inmates who were either quite ill or even threatening to harm themselves. It was a well-known fact that if you had a death on your wing you were treated as something of a hero in the officers' mess, as an inmate's life was the lowest of the low to a great many screws - they were expendable.

The officers dealing with this particular incident showed the same disregard for Ronnie's health, and their main priority was to get Dave back inside his cell. When he repeatedly refused the order to return to his cell, he was jumped and the staff began to drag him across the floor. There was no way he was going to let go of his mate, and at one time there were six big screws dragging both him and Ronnie, as he was still gripping him firmly in his arms. The only way they managed to get Dave to release his hold was when two of them stuck their fingers into his mouth and began to pull him by his jaw back to his cell whilst also applying strokes across his back and shoulder area with their truncheons. Eventually Dave had no choice but to release his grip and he was banged up, but I still believe that he saved Ronnie's life that day by staying with him for as long as was possible, thus giving the paramedics time to arrive on the scene.

This incident caused tension to rise within the unit, as Ronnie was such a well-respected man, but yet again it was Dave who came to the rescue with his latest morale booster. He received an audio tape through the post, put it in his tape recorder in his cell and cranked up the volume, and for the next few days all you could hear from pretty much anywhere in the unit was the sound of the 'Laughing Policeman' booming out from his cell. It certainly had the desired effect! I am sure some of you will remember those little laughing bags we used to get, and how much fun they were - well, Dave's prank caused the same sort of infectious laughter.

The senior management on the unit did not appreciate the benefits of

Dave's piped laughter, as they were under the impression that everyone - staff and inmates - had to be as miserable as they were. However, every time an officer was detailed to go and turn off the tape, it just came back on louder than ever, so eventually they gave up and the 'Laughing Policeman' became a permanent feature on the unit for a good few weeks. It was rather like that elevator music you get in posh hotels.

All the inmates' correspondence on the unit at that time was closely scrutinized by both the security department and the police if they found or heard anything suspicious. This included all mail and conversations either on the wing, on the telephone or on visits. To that end, one of the busiest men on the unit was the Cat A censor, who was responsible for reading all the incoming mail and deciding whether any of it should be passed on to the relevant authorities.

Dave realized this and, being a man who always liked to put a bit of extra work your way, he devised a plan to keep the censor's office busy. He was at that time involved with some men's magazines such as Front, so when he was asked to judge a readers' wives competition he saw two opportunities. Not only could he partake in his favourite pastime (wanking), he also saw it as a great chance to provide the censor with plenty of work. He got his wife to forward all the correspondence relating to the competition to his new address, and before long he was receiving two or three bags of mail a week.

Whilst Dave had almost dislocated both wrists giving each photo and letter his personal attention in his official role as judge, the censor had slipped two discs in his back and had lost about six stone in weight carting the bags over from his office in the main prison two or three times a day. He had, I heard, also almost paid off his mortgage with all the overtime Dave was putting his way. In an attempt to help him become mortgage-free even quicker, Dave stepped up his campaign a notch and began ordering all sorts of stuff via the mail-order pages of the newspapers and Sunday magazines.

Fairly soon the Home Office heard about Dave's sudden popularity, probably when they realized the censor could no longer get into his office due to the huge backlog of mail that was stacking up behind his door. They were then forced to publish their second official memorandum in as many months relating to Dave. It warned all staff and inmates that no prisoner must be allowed to enter any competitions or order any mail-order item to be delivered to the prison during their stay at any of Her Majesty's establishments. It became apparent that they had also received a rather large bill from various publications, as most of the stuff Dave had ordered was on a 'send no money now' deal and, as the Cat A unit was the delivery address, the Home Office was automatically responsible for payment.

Shortly after the mail scandal, Dave's bail hearing finally came to court and, in line with the reputation he had built up whilst on the unit, it was to prove to be the final two fingers up at the establishment. The judge set bail at a ridiculous one million pounds cash, obviously thinking that this would be a totally unreasonable amount for anyone to produce and would therefore ensure that Dave remained incarcerated until the trial date. He had, however, underestimated the high regard in which Dave was held by many of his well-connected contacts, and he was to stun them all in court a week later when he returned for a second hearing. I would have loved to have seen that judge's face when one of Dave's pals arrived in court clutching a holdall containing one million pounds in cash for his bail bond. This was raised by, among others, Peter Stringfellow and Nigel Benn, both very good friends of Dave who were willing to help him out in his time of need.

This was the final smack in the face for the Prison Service and a very fitting end to his extremely humorous and eventful stay in the unit. Dave went on to get a 'not guilty' verdict on the charges for which he was originally brought in and he made history not only by being the first man in the unit to produce one million pounds in cash for his bail but also by being released with a 'not guilty' on all counts. He also made the headlines by appearing in court dressed as a court jester complete with bells on his hat and everything.

This was good news for Dave, not only because it meant he was a free man again but also he had been able to get out of the Category A unit, I believe, just in time. Dave's antics during his stay with us, while providing all the other prisoners with a great deal of entertainment and being a great moral booster, had also earned him the utmost respect from the other chaps. It soon became common knowledge in the tea room that his growing popularity with the other prisoners was really antagonizing a lot of the staff at all levels, and I was aware that sinister plans were afoot to set Dave up with some similar treatment to what was served up to the fruit and veg man, only it was said that it was going to have to be a much more ferocious attack as most knew that Dave was going to be much more of a handful than the previous victim.

A few years after Dave's release without charge from the unit, a little story hit the headlines that I am sure most of you will remember seeing in the media. Dave was travelling along a stretch of the M25 motorway in his Range Rover when he was involved in a near fatal crash. Dave's recollections of the incident are obviously vague, but the one thing he does remember just prior to the crash is that the road was surprisingly quiet when he noticed a car approaching him from the rear at speed. The next thing he remembers is the Range Rover cartwheeling not sideways but bonnet to boot over and over again. Each time the car turned, another piece of the bodywork was torn off the vehicle, and within seconds the still conscious Dave began to register the extreme pain from his shattered pelvis and legs. He told me that at one point the sunroof was ripped off and he could see the tarmac just inches from his head each time the vehicle landed on the roof. I asked him what was going through his head, apart from bits of the M25, and he said he was just hoping that he would get a crack on the head to knock him out as the pain from his injuries was becoming unbearable. He thought the car would never stop and at one point had resigned himself to the fact that his time was up and he would not walk away from this one.

Eventually the car came to a stop some 200 yards away and a semi-conscious Dave recalls being astonished that he had been aware of the CD player playing all the way through the incident, despite about 80 per cent of the car being torn apart by the impact, and as he lay there drifting into unconsciousness he was amazed to hear Elvis still singing away through the car's undamaged stereo. 'All Shook Up' would have been an appropriate Elvis number to have been playing at this point.

I am mentioning this incident because, although not related directly to a prison incident, there are a number points that don't add up to me regarding the circumstances of the crash, which when compared to what I witnessed in prison makes mentioning it worthwhile I think.

Firstly, there was no other car involved in the accident or indeed on the road at the time, and I am sure those of you who have been unfortunate enough to witness or be directly involved in a high-speed crash on a motorway will agree that such a crash will almost inevitably involve at least a couple of other vehicles due to the natural reaction times of the human brain in such situations. Apparently this stroke of luck was due to the fact that travelling just behind Dave that night was a plain-clothes police car. It was those officers' lightning reactions that enabled them to stop their vehicle and set up a roadblock in time to prevent any other vehicle becoming involved as the Range Rover hurtled down the carriageway.

Speaking from experience of being involved in countless incidents where you are required to react fast, not least in Northern Ireland while patrolling in vehicles around built-up areas, I have always found that if you do not know the exact time and place something is going to happen your human instinct initially is one of shock, which can slow your reaction time down by valuable seconds no matter how highly trained you are. So my conclusions are that it would be highly unlikely that a car travelling at speed and so close behind such a high-speed crash would be able to react so quickly as to prevent any further knock-on incidents, unless of course they knew exactly what was going to happen, if you know what I mean.

The second thing I find strange relating to the incident is that initially the air ambulance was scrambled to attend the scene, which I am sure is the usual method of extracting a seriously injured road traffic accident casualty with multiple fractures and internal injuries such as Dave received. The air ambulance was, however, recalled minutes after getting airborne by an unknown party, and even before any medical assessment of the extent or seriousness of Dave's injuries had been carried out, and instead a road ambulance was dispatched to the scene. Who knows - perhaps someone somewhere was hoping Dave wouldn't last long enough for the slower road ambulance to arrive?!

Eventually Dave was transferred to hospital where he remained in a coma for several weeks and the first request by the police was to take blood for an alcohol test, which proved negative. When Dave eventually came round, the first sight was his mate Brendan, who had with many other good mates kept a vigil at his bedside throughout. Just before Dave regained consciousness, Brendan had been talking out loud to his comatose friend, stating, "You should see the state of the car - it's a complete write-off! You've made a hell of a mess of it!" Unknown to Brendan, Dave had been able at that stage to hear the whole statement and they both still wind each other up today about Brendan's apparently greater concern over the state of the Range Rover rather than Dave's condition.

Following the incident all subsequent inquiries made by Dave's legal team hit a dead end. For example, when they requested the CCTV footage for that night they were informed that at that particular time all the CCTV monitors for that specific stretch of the M25 had for the first time in their history all been shut down for maintenance work. Doesn't that sound familiar, going back to the cameras in the Cat A unit? Also, when an interview was requested with the two plain-clothes policemen who were conveniently driving behind Dave that night, the excuse for not being able to oblige was that they had been transferred to another force and it was force policy that they were no longer allowed to comment on incidents that had occurred prior to transfer.

I can only draw my own conclusions based on my experiences and knowledge of how easy it is to erase CCTV footage or attain false statements or give official-sounding excuses as to why officers can't comment, but I know what I think about the whole incident. You, of course, will have to make up your own minds. I just can't help thinking of another similarly controversial incident that occurred in Paris some years ago. All a bit funny, don't you think?

I am privileged to have remained in contact with Dave over the years, and he always welcomes me into his house and to the numerous shows he does around the country. He has been a great help and support in writing this book and for that I am grateful. Some people love him, some people hate him, but that's the way of the world. I think he is a great guy who will help anyone out if he possibly can. The inscription on the gravestone that stands outside his front door sums him up perfectly. It reads:

DAVE COURTNEY OBE
A RIGHT FLASH BASTARD
BUT A NICE FLASH BASTARD.

12

EXTERNALS

Back at Belmarsh I returned to normal duties on the Category A unit, although I didn't have long left before I would be deployed to another area within the prison. My final days on spur three were to see me witness one more incident, which was to remain in my mind forever.

One of the inmates on the spur at the time was an old boy called John who, although convicted of playing a role in the Warrington bombing, had always protested his innocence. I began the normal routine one morning by unlocking the cell doors on the spur. I had unlocked John's door and moved on to the next, when something told me that all was not right. I returned to his cell, pushed the door open fully and nearly threw up at the sight that greeted me. The whole of the cell was covered in blood, even the ceiling, and John's lifeless body lay in his bed with a jagged gash on his neck from ear to ear. The stench was almost unbearable, so, after turning to my colleague and advising him to lock up the rest of the spur and call for assistance, I entered the cell to open the window. As I carefully trod around the pools of blood, I put on some surgical gloves and picked up the tin lid that he had used to cut his own throat.

As I turned to go back out of the cell, I was greeted with about three other Irish prisoners staring in disbelief into the cell. You can imagine what this looked like - there I was, standing in the cell with a man whose throat was cut, holding the bloodied tin lid in my hands. My delicate situation was not helped by the ever witty big Ronnie, who had also arrived and began making comments like, "Oh, Mr Dawkins, what have you done? I always knew you were working for MI5." In a final bid to shatter my delicate nerves, the lifeless body of John groaned from behind me, "It's all right, I'm not dead. I can't even get that right."

I knew at this point that I had to move fast if we were going to stand a chance of saving him. The wound in his neck began spurting blood again and I was not sure what damage he had done to his jugular vein. I called for urgent medical assistance on my radio, as I appeared to have been left on the spur on my own. I then explained to the other inmates that they would have to get back behind their doors while we treated John. Luckily I had a fairly good relationship with them and they realized the urgency of the situation so returned to their cells with no problem.

By the time I had secured the spur, the paramedics were on the scene and, after carrying out some first aid in the cell, they took John off to hospital. He did make a full recovery despite the fact that he had actually caught his jugular with the tin lid, although he would have a nasty scar to remind him of the incident for the rest of his life. I cannot comment on whether the man was guilty or innocent, but the reason he told me that he had tried to take his life was that he could not live with the fact that people would associate him with the appalling bombing in Warrington.

That incident, as I have said, was almost at the end of my tour in the Category A unit, and in September 1994 I was to be redeployed to the externals group responsible for escorting prisoners to and from the courts and other prisons. I had not really wanted to leave the unit, as I had become confident in carrying out the duties involved there and enjoyed building a good working relationship with most of the inmates on it. However, the Prison Service policy was that, due to possible conditioning, members of staff would not be allowed to do more than two years there before being moved to another area. I was lucky to get the post with externals, as it was a much sought after position and I still did not fancy the prospect of working on the house blocks.

The man who ran the office for the externals group was Dave Bartlett, and over the next few months we were to become good friends. He was a very laid-back sort of man and believed in the give-and-take method of working. By that I mean that if you had finished your escort early and he had nothing else for you to do he would tell you to bugger off quick before someone else found you something to do. That was how we worked then. Some days you would not get back to the nick until ten o'clock at night, but the next day you might have finished by twelve.

The best job on the list was the Inner London Crown Court run, where we would take a vanload of inmates up for their daily appearances. Although this particular duty meant you would not return to the prison before five, once you had handed your inmates over to the court staff the rest of the day was yours. I got on really well with the two auxiliary drivers of the vans, Del and Andy, and in no time at all we had set ourselves a nice little routine for inner London runs.

We would get to the court as quickly as possible, which meant that I had to collect and push my inmates through the reception process and onto the van as fast as possible. Then it was over to Del or Andy to use their knowledge of the London roads to get us to the court by the fastest route possible through the rush-hour traffic. Once at the court, the unload was carried out as quickly as the load, and as soon as all the inmates were secured and my paperwork was complete we were off.

The only thing that would impede our escape was if a member of staff at the court had gone sick and the PO needed to use an escort officer to man one of his docks. In the event of this happening, our contingency plan would be that Del or Andy would ring the court office from the cellphone in their van and pretend to be the prison with an additional job for the van and the escort officer. It was important that you were the first van there for this plan to work, as if a second van had pulled up then the PO could have decided that they could do the additional run.

The additional run was always the same every morning, straight out of inner London and straight into Tower Bridge Police Station for one of their famous 999 full English breakfasts. Once we had spent an hour or two in the police canteen, we would return to the court after a phone call to ensure that they had sorted out any staffing problems. We would then park the van and disappear over to the Rose and Crown for a liquid lunch.

We would usually leave the pub at about two thirty and make a beeline for the delicatessen to get a hot chicken escalope to help soak up the three or four pints we had just consumed. We would then stagger in through the legal visits entrance back down to the cells where we would grab an hour or two's sleep to sober up before our return trip to Belmarsh.

How I managed never to have lost any prisoners by the end of the day is beyond me. I can only be thankful that none of them ever fucked around too much when we were loading them on the van. By that time of day the majority had had a gutful of sitting in court all day and just wanted to get back to their cell and relax, so they took little notice of the half pissed escort staff. In fact I think most of them enjoyed travelling with me as I always sat in the front of the van, which was taboo when you had prisoners on board, but I piped the van's radio through the intercom so they could listen to the music in the back.

When I was not on the road, most of my time at Belmarsh was spent in reception where inmates came as their first and last port of call as they went in and out of the prison. The place was almost always chaotic and seemed to have a constant stream of prisoners and staff flying around. Reception also had to accommodate escort staff from other prisons, and it was here one day that I first came across some staff from Wormwood Scrubs. I heard them mention my old pal Charlie Bronson in their conversation with the reception SO so decided to join in.

They were not, however, speaking highly of him as I had hoped, and two of them in particular were commenting on how we at Belmarsh pandered to his every need. When I heard the same two bragging that they were directly involved with the vicious beating he received while on a previous visit to the Scrubs, I was disgusted and felt I had to get involved with the conversation to stick up for my pal.

At first I let them describe in detail how they gathered the biggest bully boys on duty down the seg to await Charlie's arrival with the calculated plan of giving him a good kicking to teach him what he would get if he fucked about at that prison. This practice is not unique to the Scrubs and goes on in almost every prison in the country at some stage or another. The Scrubs, however, as I was to find out later, was one of the worst offenders in terms of such brutal welcoming committees.

The pair went on to describe how they had taken all their chains and watches off and had lain in wait in one of the strip cells until the escort bringing Charlie had left. Then they went into the cell where Charlie was and before he had a chance to do anything they all attacked him. Charlie is still pursuing the assault all these years later, but it is proving very difficult for his legal team to break through the wall of silence that the Prison Service puts up in all these cases to protect the bullying element within their ranks. The assault on Charlie at Scrubs, like so many before and after, was totally unprovoked and vicious.

The two officers that claimed to be involved described how they tore out lumps of hair from his trademark moustache and smashed his fingers and hands with their feet and truncheons. All the time they were describing the incident they were smiling and seemed to be very proud of their involvement. They then went on to describe the officers whom they had heard about who had looked after Charlie whilst he was at Belmarsh and how they thought they were all cowards due to the fact that they had not beaten Charlie up.

This was the point during the conversation that I blew up and began screaming at them that I was one of those officers. I was livid and it took a couple of members of staff to prevent me from smacking them right in their smug little faces and exacting some revenge for Charlie's treatment. I told them that both I and the other officers who worked with Charlie were all far better men than they could hope to be. I left them with one final thought that Charlie is like an elephant - he never forgets, and one way or another all ten or more of those involved in that attack would get their comeuppance.

It is people like that who are the cowards. They would not have dreamt of having a go at Charlie or any other prisoner unless they had a gang of other like-minded bullies behind them to back them up. It is just this type of officer that gives the decent ones a bad name and makes the difficult job of being a prison officer even more difficult. Unfortunately, they are looked upon as idols by many other members of staff, who in turn often get involved with the bullying in an attempt to gain the respect they crave from these sorts of officers. I never looked upon them as anything less than cowards, and it was the fact that I was working alongside them and hated the feeling that people would think I was like them that made me ultimately take the decision to leave the Prison Service.

By this stage of my career, I had made good friends with a couple of decent officers. My main partner in crime was Geordie P and we spent many good nights in various pubs and clubs around London. On one particular night out we went to the Queen Vic in Belvedere to watch a live group perform. The pub was packed by the time we arrived after our twelve-hour A shift, and before long we had attracted a small group of young girls who flirted round us all night. They could only have been barely eighteen and we were not interested, but we chatted to them when they came to our table just out of courtesy. The interest they were showing to us had, however, drawn us to the attention of a group of rowdy young lads who appeared to be with the same crowd as these young girls. One of them, a tall boy with a baseball cap, staggered into our table and started gobbing off that they were his birds and if we did not stop talking to them he would do us. I told him to piss off and drink his lemonade and called him a silly little boy. He was most upset by this and tried to grab me but was restrained by the girls who took him back to the rest of his gang.

Shortly afterwards, two of the girls came back over and were looking really worried. One of them explained that the boy I had upset was the 'hardest boy' in Orpington and he said he was going to stab me after the pub shut. She offered to distract the gang long enough for me to get out of the pub. I thanked her for her concern, but explained that I had never run away from trouble before and was not really worried about some 'Kevin', the teenager wanting to have a go at me. The rest of the evening went by without further incident apart from the 'intimidating' stares we received from Kevin and his gang.

As we left the pub Kevin shouted "All screws are wankers" to us but made no attempt to follow as we left. It was not until we had crossed the road and were making the important decision whether to have a Chinese or kebabs that the gang of about five kids came charging out of the pub and up the road. They spotted us on the other side and Kevin made a beeline straight for me. As he approached, I again told him not to be a silly boy and to go home before his mum got worried about him. With that, he pulled his arm out of his jacket and was clutching a very large black diver's-type knife in his right hand. This was now serious and I had to disarm this kid before he got hurt. I was laughing in my head as I remembered a recent episode of *Coronation Street* when Jim McDonald assaulted a burglar with a crowbar only to find out he was a minor, and Jim nearly ended up inside. With this in mind, I knew I could not afford to hurt him too much, so remembering my unarmed combat from years before I grabbed his knife hand. As I did this I instinctively pushed the fingers of my free hand into his throat, causing him to drop the knife and fall to the ground gasping for breath.

I picked the knife up, straddled his body, put the blade across his throat and told him never to pull a knife out unless he has got the bottle to use it. Overcoming my urge to stick him with his own weapon, I got up, pulled him off the ground and, with a swift kick up his arse, sent him crying down the road. Geordie, in the meantime, had another member of the gang in a neck hold when I noticed a third boy pull out a small lock knife and run over to where Geordie was. I intercepted him with a flying kick in his back that sent him hurtling over a garden wall.

The incident was over quickly, and once the boys had run off we disposed of their knives down a drain in the road. Someone had called the Old Bill and we decided that we should wait and give our side of the story before they got a different version from the gang of boys. In short, we spent the next four hours being interviewed at Belvedere Police Station about the incident.

To our surprise the case came up at Croydon Crown Court almost a year later and we were called to give evidence. It turned out that my Jim McDonald theory had been correct as the boys were only sixteen, a fact that their defence team referred to a great deal while cross-examining our evidence. I could not believe the sight as I entered the witness box and saw these two angelic-looking schoolboys all dressed up in their best suits and giving the jury their best puppy-dog eyes. Geordie and I somehow had to explain to the court that these little angels had attacked a pair of big rufty-tufty prison officers.

We did manage to convince them but made it clear that, whilst we thought they should learn for their own sake that they should not go round with knives picking fights at their age, they should not receive a prison sentence. The judge listened to our mitigation on their behalf and awarded them some sixty hours' community service, which, at the age they were, would have been a hard enough lesson I hope.

My relationship with Jackie at that time was getting worse despite the fact that the birth of our daughter, Lauren, on 20 February 1994 had given us a bit of renewed hope. I began spending more time out drinking and eventually Jackie had taken all she could and we decided the only way forward for her was for us to split up. By November 1995 I had left our house in Sidcup and had moved into the grim prison flats in Brockley, nicknamed Heartbreak Hotel.

I had not really thought about my feelings until I was sitting on my bed in my new room staring at the three bin liners that contained my worldly possessions. I had rung Jackie to arrange to collect my stereo and could hear Lauren crying in the background. The sound of my eighteen-month-old baby girl crying tore me apart, as I realized that I would never again be able to put her to bed each night and get her up each morning. I thought at that point that I would miss out on so much of her growing years and might even lose touch with her altogether. Luckily that has not been the case and I have always maintained regular contact with her, and when we do see each other we have a great time. She has grown up so much over the years and is now doing well at school and has turned out to be a real little character in her own right. Those of you that have kids will agree that they are the best thing that could happen to you and I never tire of watching them, although they do grow up too fast so every moment is precious.

Shortly after my separation I began to go a little off the rails and began to hit the drink a bit too much. I started to become a regular feature at all the functions and you could always rely on me to liven up the party a bit. I added a little too much life to one such party and the consequences could have cost me my job.

At the time a civilian catering firm ran the officers' mess and I was invited to the mess manageress's leaving party, which was held at a pub in Thamesmead. On the day of the party I was not working, so began drinking at lunchtime as I slowly made my way to the venue. By the time I had arrived, I was well on my way to getting the prize for being the most pissed person there. I met up with a group of fellow officers, but shortly after arriving we noticed an unwanted guest in our midst. Wandering around and telling us that we had drunk enough was a certain governor who shall remain nameless, but those of you who have dealt with him will know who he is when I say he had a dicky bow on as usual. Some of our group took great offense to this man's interference with our love of lager, and it was decided that something had to be done. I was nominated as the one to go and tell him to leave, as his presence was no longer required.

I staggered over to him and basically told him that he was upsetting the other guests so we wanted him to piss off. He agreed and stated that he was about to leave anyway as he was ashamed to be seen in our company. Pleased that my task had been carried out with apparent ease, I returned to the group only to hear some alarming news. Scouse informed me that as I had walked away the governor had gestured something behind my back and had not left but in fact had just moved to another position in the pub.

Furious that he had ignored my warning, I went back over to him and asked him why he had not gone. He made some sarcastic remark which, in my inebriated state, I felt left me with only one option. I gave him a cracker of a right-hander, which did not have its usual effect due to the fact that I could see three of him and tried to hit the one in the middle. It was, however, effective enough to make him leave and cause everyone else to stare on in disbelief.

The rest of the evening went well until I had obviously had enough and went outside to throw up in some bushes. Whilst doing so I lost my false tooth and, despite scouring the area on my hands and knees, it appeared that the tooth fairy was too quick for me as I never found it. My memories after that point are a blank and the next thing I remember was waking up in a strange room the following morning.

I awoke wrapped in an army-issue sleeping bag on a top bunk bed, and as I tried to remember where I was I looked around the room for clues. Scattered all over the floor of this strange room was an array of martial arts stretching equipment. In my bewildered state I thought I had been captured by a gang of triads and immediately checked to see if I still had my boxer shorts on. Thankfully I did and they were still on the right way round, so I was fairly confident that my kidnappers had not gang-raped me. It turned out to be 'steady' Eddie's house, who was a fellow Green Jacket as well as an officer at Belmarsh. He had found me asleep outside the pub and had taken me back to his place for the night.

I made my way into work only to discover that I had no uniform other than a spare pair of trousers in my locker. As a result I had to struggle through the day with a bright blue key chain, a belt with 'loan belt' engraved in large letters on the back and wearing a female officer's blouse, which I had borrowed from another friend, Tracy. You can imagine the stick I got from other members of staff, let alone the inmates.

I was still oblivious to what had really gone on the night before, although I had that feeling you get after a night out that something serious had happened. It was the way in which everyone I came across gave me that look while shaking their heads and tutting at me that made me worry more. It was not until I passed the telephone exchange that Kim came out and asked if I was on my way to apologize to the governor for my behaviour the night before. After she had explained what I had done, I spent the next few days waiting for the summons to his office to get the sack. I have got to give the man his due though. He did not take the matter any further, although he did make a meal out of it every time he had to pull me up about anything in the future. That incident occurred right at the end of my time with externals. With the new privatization of all the courts looming, there was only a requirement for about four permanent officers to remain on the externals group. Maybe the governor incident had something to do with the fact that I was not chosen to stay, who knows, but I was once again to be redeployed and this time it was to one of the house blocks.

13
HOUSE BLOCK THREE

By late 1995 I was unable to avoid doing a tour of duty on the house blocks and soon found myself thrown onto the worst one. As I mentioned before, house block three was given the name Beirut due to the chaos that reigned within its landings. The house block's primary role was to act as an induction wing and as a result we took all inmates straight from the courts and police stations. We also seemed to be a dumping ground for any inmate that had problems on the other house blocks. With such a mixture one thing was certain - that amongst its population house block three had some of the worst inmates you could find in a prison. Many were hardened drug users and as a result spent the first few days 'clucking', or withdrawing, from the various drugs that they were hooked on. If anything should be used to educate young people on the pitfalls of drug abuse, then it should be the sight of these pathetic souls sweating and shivering for days unable even to get off their beds.

The house blocks were a rich haven for drug pushers, who were normally the stronger and most well-known inmates. They took every opportunity to prey on newly arrived addicts, knowing that in their desperate state they could sell them any cocktail of drugs, which they mixed with anything from sugar to powdered bleach to increase their supply. Heavy debts would be run up in this way, debts that many inmates were unable to pay when called upon to do so.

The ones that could not pay would normally have to repay the debt by being recruited into the pushers' little empire and carrying out smuggling operations by getting their visitors to bring drugs into the prison. By getting others to do this meant that the pushers themselves rarely risked getting caught and getting time added onto their sentence. Drugs in prison are a major problem and one that most inmates that are against their use will agree is ruining day-to-day life in our prisons.

I think it would be fair to say that no one minded the inmates having the odd joint of cannabis after lock-up, but there are very few that actually encourage the use of harder drugs such as heroin. Apart from the obvious dangers of AIDS through shared needles, a man on heroin is very unpredictable and, if you are locked in a cell with such a person when he goes into one, you have not got much of a chance of defending yourself. There is also the well-known fact that heroin addicts who are desperate for a fix will do or sell anything. This could mean he would steal your personal effects or even be persuaded to seriously injure or kill someone in return for some drugs.

The presence of such addicts not only made life unpleasant for the majority of other inmates and staff; but also they became easy prey for the bullies, amongst both the inmates and staff. It was generally believed that you could easily get away with giving a prisoner high on heroin or crack a good kicking and he would not remember a thing about it when the drugs wore off. Whilst I personally do not agree with drugs, I disagree even more strongly with bullies and do not see that just because a man is on drugs it gives someone else the right to give him a kicking.

I remember one such heroin addict who was suffering so badly from withdrawal symptoms that he was almost unconscious on his bed most of the time. One officer who I worked with at the time thought this man was a great plaything and took me into the cell to show me his new toy. At first I thought he was just amused by the lethargic nature of the inmate when he asked him to get out of bed. When the inmate could not get off his bed the officer told me to watch and then proceeded to do something that I could not believe I was seeing. He got up onto the bed and began to kick the inmate straight in the head several times with the full weight of his heavy boots. The inmate could do nothing in his current state apart from cry out in pain and take the kicks. This officer thought it was a great game and assured me that the inmate would never get an assault allegation to stick because he was a heroin addict.

I was horrified and grabbed the officer, threw him against the back wall of the cell and slapped him right across the head. I warned him that the next time I even heard of him carrying out this sort of behaviour I would kick him in the head a few times. I then told him to piss off and helped the inmate to the treatment room to get his head looked at. I did not mention the officer's actions purely because I do not like to grass people up, so I told the nurse that he had fallen off his bed. I later told the inmate that if any officer ever treated him that way again he should come and find me and I would deal with them my own way.

There were one or two good officers working on the house block. My old pal Brian had started at the same time as me and, as usual, always made me laugh with his anti-management attitude. Unfortunately, like all areas in every prison, there was a large element of the bully boys who loved nothing more than to hear the sound of their own voices as they screamed orders around the landings. I soon discovered why so many members of staff preferred to work on the house blocks rather than the unit.

It was a well-known fact that because the unit housed such high-profile prisoners the staff who worked there never got involved with using the restraint techniques on any of them except in very rare incidents. The general guideline was that any disagreement between the inmates and the management was dealt with, wherever possible, without the use of force. You may think, as I do, that this method should be practised in all situations regardless of who the prisoner is. The reality, however, is that the staff on the house blocks used force at the first opportunity and even went around the landings in groups looking for any excuse to use their restraining methods on a prisoner who might be provoked into an argument with them.

Some staff loved every chance they had to use force and used the opportunity to inflict as much pain on the inmates as possible. The louder an inmate screamed, the more respect the officers involved seemed to get from the large crowd of staff who always quickly gathered on the scene to witness such incidents. It was no secret that many officers carried on in this way not only because they loved the feeling of power but also simply because they knew they could get away with it.

Most of the inmates who received such treatment were hand picked because it was felt that they would not have the chance of proving that they were struck first. The staff would get together and, often with the help of senior management, would draw up a watertight story of the events in which they would always blame the inmate for starting the incident.

This sort of behaviour made the job of a decent officer even more difficult. Not only did these bullies disrupt the regime of the house block and alienate the prisoners from us, when a whistle or alarm bell sounded you were never sure if it was a genuine incident or one set up by a member of staff. Although you knew this went on, there was little or nothing that could be done to stop it. In most cases the prisoner was too fearful of reprisals to contest the officers' version of events, and if another member of staff tried to protest he would receive a lecture on how it may not do his or her career much good to drop fellow officers in it.

Once again, I tried to rise above this way of carrying out your duties and began to try to establish a good working relationship with the good officers and the more permanent inmates such as the cleaners. I began to earn respect from many of the lads on my spur and, as Christmas approached, I was confident that I had established a good regime for both them and myself. However, my methods did not meet the approval of some of the other staff, who would stab me in the back with comments that I was a 'care bear' and too soft. They could not have been further from the truth and all the lads knew that, although I was easy going, they could not take the piss out of me.

I appreciated all the hard work the cleaners and tea boys did and always rewarded them with an extra shower, the chance to get on the phone or even half an ounce of tobacco now and again. They trusted me enough to let me in on the fact that they had begun to brew a batch of hooch for the Christmas period and offered to let me taste it when it was ready. I was not sure whether this was a great honour or if I was just to be their guinea pig, as some of that stuff can stop a man's heart with one mouthful. I declined the offer but then made the decision that as I was working on Christmas Day I would bring in my small hip flask with some brandy to give them a drop in their coffee. I took a serious risk in doing so as not only could I lose my job and be charged with smuggling contraband into the prison, but also there was always the possibility that the inmates would use this gesture to bribe me in the future. I was, however, fully confident that the select few I had chosen to do this for could be trusted one hundred per cent and, true to their word, I never had any comebacks from any of them. I had to laugh later in the day though when they were all staggering around half pissed and the other members of staff were going mad trying to find out where the hooch was stashed, a secret that I also kept to myself.

To be fair, Christmas Day was run on a very relaxed regime and we even organized games and competitions between staff and inmates. Each inmate received a bonus of some extra chocolate bars and tobacco and the kitchen laid on a good turkey dinner. The number one governor even made a brief and rare appearance on the house block to wish the staff and inmates a Merry Christmas.

After a month or two, I had forgotten all my fears of working on a house block and had become happy carrying out my duties there. We had our fair share of fun and games as well as our fair share of nutters who passed through our doors. One group of inmates we received shortly after Christmas was a gang of about eight Chinese triads on remand for kidnap and arson. These boys were scary and wasted no time in establishing their authority amongst the other inmates. They spoke very little English, or so they made out, and the first incident we had involving these budding Bruce Lees occurred moments after their arrival on the house block. They had been brought up from reception and placed in the holding room with about half a dozen other inmates to await allocation to a vacant cell.

Minutes after they had arrived we heard an almighty commotion coming from the holding room. When we arrived we saw the Chinese beating the shit out of one of the other inmates in the room. We opened the door and intervened and all the Chinese bowed politely to us and retreated to the back wall of the room. It turned out that one of their number had wanted to go to the toilet and so had just pissed in the corner of the room. This had disgusted the other inmates and the one who had just got the kicking had been nominated to vent the feelings of the rest of the group.

We removed the injured man and made the Chinese inmate mop up his pool of urine. Satisfied that the incident had been dealt with, we locked them back up again. Not five minutes later we heard someone frantically banging on the window of the holding room. When we investigated, the inmate who was banging shouted through the glass that the Chinese were tooled up and ready to kick off. This was obviously a far more serious threat to us and the other inmates in the room than the previous incident. The fact that a knife had been mentioned meant that we would have to tackle the incident wearing riot gear and using shields. The use of such equipment was standard procedure when dealing with armed inmates should a peaceful settlement be unsuccessful.

As we donned our overalls, helmets and protective leg gear, Governor Outram began to use his powers of persuasion, which he had successfully executed when Charlie had been given the news of his setback on the unit. This was a difficult task even for him, as the language barrier severely slowed down the negotiations and we could not afford to wait for a suitable interpreter to be called in.

Eventually Outram took the unusual decision to be the first to enter the room without any protective clothing but closely followed by those of us that now formed the four three-man riot teams. You may think this was a foolish decision, but had we rushed in with guns blazing the Chinese inmates who were armed may have had a chance to injure some of the other inmates or some of us before we could disarm and restrain them all. With Outram leading the way in a non-aggressive approach he hoped to minimize casualties on all sides.

The plan worked and, whether it was down to his approach or the sight of the riot teams, luckily we did not have to remove any inmates aggressively as they surrendered their home-made knives and walked out peacefully. This particular gang caused a few problems during their stay with us, as I have already mentioned. The main thing they would practise was intimidation of other inmates by preying on them in the recess or in the phone queue. They met their match though when a large gang of Jamaican yardies arrived on the house block and made it quite clear that they would not stand for any nonsense from the Chinese.

That is the way prison life goes. It is a constant battle to survive and it really is survival of the fittest or hardest. As an officer you have to learn to judge each and every incident individually and try to act accordingly depending on that particular situation. This may mean that you turn a blind eye to certain things or you may have to steam in to help an inmate who is in trouble.

Whatever the Prison Service claims, I stand by the belief that the inmates run the landings and wings of our prisons. The most successful way to run a prison is to find a happy medium where the inmates and staff can work together. There are very few prisoners in the system that go out of their way every day to cause disruption, and the majority of the ones I have witnessed doing so have all had very good reasons. How many of you would smash up your living room and destroy your television just for the fun of it?

When a prisoner gets frustrated over not getting a valid explanation to a certain problem, the main way that he can get heard is by smashing up his cell. I have witnessed many, many officers refuse to speak to an inmate and forcibly lock him up to get rid of the problem. They then ignore the cell call bell that inmates use to get a member of staff, and sit and wait until the prisoner gets so frustrated and angry that he starts to smash things up. This then gives those officers who love to wind up inmates the 'valid' excuse to get on their riot gear and go into the cell to remove the inmate by force.

To many members of staff it is part of their daily routine to play such mind games and ultimately get 'hands on' a prisoner before taking him down to the segregation unit and nicking him for assault on staff and damaging prison property. Both these charges are considered very serious and can result in the inmate receiving many days added to his sentence as well as weeks spent in isolation. This sort of behaviour only helps to breed hatred towards the staff by the inmates and can send a man who just wants to do his bird and get out into a deep black hole that can be very difficult to get out of.

By about January 1996 I had begun to find it increasingly difficult to work with many of my fellow officers and felt under pressure more and more each day to help them cover up some of their acts of brutality or false accusations against some inmates. I was being talked about in the staff room more and more and was beginning to find it almost impossible to carry out my duties in my own unique way. I felt that I might not have any option but to resign, although financially I knew I could not afford to do so.

When a position in the segregation unit came up my name was put forward by the senior management on the house block as they wanted me out because they had grown worried that I might report certain officers' behaviour to a higher level. The fact of the matter was, I knew that if I had done so no one would have taken any notice and I would have been transferred or sacked and totally alienated from other members of staff.

I took up the position in the seg as I thought it might give me a break from the pressure I was under, not that I was given a choice really. At about that time I had moved out of Heartbreak Hotel and had moved in with my old army pal Harry in his flat in Uxbridge. The main reason for this was the fact that I felt I could not have Lauren to stay in a flat with twenty or so pissed-up screws bringing all sorts of birds home at all hours. The other reason was that I was beginning to get tired of other officers' company at work, let alone twenty-four hours a day. Also, the travelling was becoming difficult and the shift pattern in the seg unit was slightly more flexible than the one on the house block and allowed me an extra forty-five minutes in the morning to travel across London.

Taking all those points into consideration, I felt I had nothing to lose by transferring to the seg, and so at the end of January I reported to the acting senior officer for my first day's duty.

14
BELMARSH SEGREGATION UNIT

Belmarsh prison boasts one of the largest segregation units of all British prisons. The unit was laid out over two floors and was equipped with approximately twenty single cells, two strong boxes, its own exercise yard and its own kitchen area. Its appearance was certainly less grim than the seg unit I remembered from Wandsworth.

I walked to the office, which was situated on the first floor of the unit, and entered it to find about six officers slouched around on various chairs. As I entered, the young officer who was sat behind the main desk looked at me and stuttered, "Y-y-your la-la-late". Fighting back the urge to laugh at this strange-looking kid with his college boy baby-faced features and silly Tintin haircut, I just told him to fuck off and made my way to the kettle to make a cup of tea.

As it turned out, this Tintin lookalike was actually the acting senior officer of the segregation unit, which will give you some idea of the state of things at Belmarsh at that time. To make matters worse, he was quite a big bloke and really fancied himself as a bit of a hard man. During my time there I learnt to tolerate him because I had to work with him, but his arrogant nature and opinion that he knew everything about everything was typical of the type of person I despise.

After I had finished my cup of tea, Tintin paired me up with his mate Simon, an ex-navy officer, who was also a pain in the arse who thought he was the dog's bollocks, for a tour and brief induction into the seg unit's regime. In his opening speech to me he more or less said that we were a law unto ourselves in the unit and it was a cushy little number as we got to give some of the arseholes a dig when they stepped out of line. He told me that when a prisoner was first brought down to the seg we would always take over from the escorting staff and place the prisoner into one of the two strip cells on the ground floor. We would then carry out a full strip search on the inmate and, once done, we would vacate the cell, leaving the prisoner a special suit to put on and a heavy-duty grey blanket on the floor. The prisoner would remain in these conditions until he had been seen by a prison medical officer, usually a nurse not a doctor.

Many of these nurses, both male and female, at that time were fully fledged prison officers and not agency nurses like some are now. The problem with this was that if the inmate complained of injury the nurse who examined him would not report the full extent of these injuries on their form or they would state that they were self-inflicted during a struggle with the staff. Don't get me wrong, I have witnessed many prisoners harming themselves by splitting their own heads open on cell doors in order to claim they have been assaulted. Such incidents are, however, rare whereas cases of nurses covering up genuine injuries are more common than you may wish to think.

The seg unit, as I was made aware of on that first day, was the end of the line for an inmate involved in problems on the wings. It was also the place where most of the reports were written with the help of other more experienced members of staff to cover up any over-the-top behaviour carried out by staff whilst restraining an inmate. This procedure would involve all the staff involved in the initial incident, the governor who was present during the removal and even some of the seg staff, who liked to give their previous experience on dealing with such delicate reports.

Once an inmate was in the seg he would remain in a cell on the ground floor until the following morning, when he would go in front of the governor to be adjudicated on for his crime against the prison rules. In the vast majority of cases he would be found guilty and some would receive an award, i.e. they would stay in the seg, while others would be sent back to the house blocks. If an inmate were sentenced to remain in the block, he would be relocated to a cell on the first floor for the duration of his stay.

It became apparent to me at a very early stage that even though the seg staff usually had very few inmates under their charge at any one time, they were even less eager to give them their daily rights than those staff I had left on the house blocks. To ensure that their daily workload was kept to a minimum, they had devised an unwritten rule between themselves and one that I had to swear never to reveal to any senior management. This rule was called the 'first day rule' and as its name suggests was carried out on all inmates during their first day of incarceration in the block.

The daily routine always began with the taking of applications during the serving of breakfast. Each inmate had this one and only chance to make an application for all his basic rights for that day. He would have to request a shower, a telephone call, a medical appointment with a nurse, and even his one statutory entitlement of one hour's exercise. If the inmate was asleep when we went to his door, no attempt would be made to wake him and he would be marked in the book as having refused breakfast and applications.

Similarly, if the inmate wanted to report sick he would be told that he would be placed on a three-day rest-in-cell routine, during which time he would not be able to make applications. This particular 'rule' was done without the knowledge of any medical staff. The theory behind this, according to the brainchild who introduced it, was that if the inmate were genuinely sick he would still be sick in three days' time, at which point he would be allowed to book an appointment with the nurse.

During an inmate's first day on the block he was advised that due to the 'first day rule' he was not entitled to any applications or privileges and would spend the first twenty-four hours locked up in his cell. Most prisoners feared reprisals too much to question this rule, as they knew that down the block there was only ever one prisoner unlocked at any one time and he was always faced with no less than four officers.

With all these schemes in place for denying the inmates their routine and rights, it meant that we had nothing to do all day except feed them and sit in the office watching television. If an inmate insisted on taking his exercise, the staff would usually cancel it at the last minute for a number of excuses ranging from "We had an incident" to "It looks like rain". Although I did not agree with this method of working, the fact that all the other members of staff did very little but sit in the top office telling war stories, I could escape and enjoy my own company in the bottom office, which was vacant.

One of the first prisoners I came across in the seg was a young but big and loud man by the name of Strachan. He had run into problems on the wing basically because his face did not fit, but he was not going to allow anyone to push him about. Many officers regarded his large physique and loud personality as a threat to their authority and so orchestrated an incident, which would ensure he was restrained and removed to the block. His first period with us was for fourteen days and he settled in well and seemed to be enjoying the time on his own away from the hectic routine and certain officers on the house block.

When the time came for him to be relocated back to his house block he refused the order to move and so was placed on report again. He explained to the governor that he feared for his safety from certain inmates and staff on the normal location, and he even made claims that certain officers were in league with certain inmates to do over prisoners that those officers did not like. The governor told him he did not believe his theory but still awarded him an additional fourteen days' respite from the house block.

This went on for another six weeks and by this time Tintin and his mates were getting the right hump because they believed the seg should be used only for punishing inmates and not for offering them shelter from staff or inmates on the wing. During this time no attempt was made to investigate Strachan's claims of officers targeting inmates. I arrived one afternoon for a late shift and was told by Tintin that they had worked out a plan to get rid of Strachan and get him back to the house block. I was told to follow them to Strachan's cell and to stand back and get involved when needed. They opened his door and Strachan emerged his usual cocky self, but when he saw that there were six of us on the landing his expression looked worried; he knew his time had come. He had barely left his cell when Tintin and three of the others jumped him and dragged him to the floor shouting remarks like "We'll teach you what a seg is all about" and "You won't take the piss out of us any more, you wanker".

I stood bewildered as they threw punches into his head and body and I listened to his pleas for them to stop and for an explanation for what was happening, but felt I could do nothing. After about five minutes or so they dragged Strachan to the box where they stripped him, put him in a body belt and left him for two hours without notifying a governor. After this time they went and removed the belt and told Strachan not to mention that he had had one on and they hoped he had learnt a valuable lesson not to try to take the piss out of the seg staff.

The plan did not stop there, and I was told I had to nick Strachan for attempting to assault me when I unlocked the door. I of course protested, but had been told that the report had already been written into the book and could not be changed. I knew this was a test of my loyalty and unfortunately my inexperience forced me into going along with the false report. It did not end there as Strachan was then told that if he pleaded guilty to attempting to assault me they would speak to the adjudicating governor and see that, so long as he moved back to the house block, he would get away with a caution. With this option as an alternative to at least twenty-eight days added to his sentence, not to mention an assault on an officer against him for the rest of his time in prison, he chose to plead guilty. On the morning of the adjudication the governor was told the whole story and the reason for the false charge and agreed to go along with it and gave Strachan a caution for attempting to assault an officer.

Shortly after that incident we received a young prisoner nicknamed 'Rat Boy' from Pentonville Prison. He had apparently been scaling the drainpipes in the exercise yard at the 'ville, and was sent to us as, being a modern prison, all our drainage pipes were cemented to the wall in such a way that you could not get your fingers around them. He was nothing but a skinny twenty-year-old who looked terrified when he arrived and stepped off the bus, but to one officer, who shall remain nameless, he was to become his personal plaything.

This officer quickly discovered that whenever he opened Rat Boy's cell door the boy cowered under his blankets in fear. Bored with just watching this, he then began going in the cell and kicking the mass of blankets under which the boy was hiding and laughing at his cries of "No, please,

please stop, you're hurting me". He took great pleasure in showing this circus stunt to most of the staff who passed through the unit.

The final straw for me was when I was taking this inmate out on exercise with the officer in question. As we reached the back metal stairs leading to the unit, the inmate collapsed, fell to the bottom and appeared to be having a fit. The officer immediately kicked him right on the top of the head with full force and told him to get up and stop fucking around. When he did not respond he dragged him by his hair and jacket back up the stairs, threw him back onto the floor of his cell and said, "That's another one who has refused exercise."

I looked through the spyhole on the door and noticed that the inmate was not moving and still appeared to be unconscious. I went and told the other officer that I was concerned that the boy was badly injured, but he had already sat down and just said he was faking it for attention. Not satisfied with this, I entered the cell, picked the boy up and placed him on his bed. He was still breathing but was not conscious, so I returned to the office and called for medical assistance.

The medic arrived and confirmed that the inmate had been having an epileptic fit and was suffering from concussion, and he was immediately transferred to the prison hospital. The medical examination did not mention that a blow to the head had occurred other than that received from falling down the stairs. Again I felt I could do nothing, but on my return I had a little word with the officer involved. Had that inmate died, I would have been equally responsible for his death, and even if I had told the whole truth there would have been no way of proving that I was not involved in kicking him while he was on the floor.

It was not all as shocking as the two incidents I have described and I do recall one inmate who brought a smile to my face while he was with us. He was an old boy who had been living on the streets, but at one time he had served for a good few years as a Royal Marine commando. Due to his age and eccentric behaviour he too had problems settling into the house block routine and as a result spent a few weeks with us. His favourite pastime was singing old war songs to the back wall of his cell and shouting market trader phrases like " Get your lovely tomatoes here, tuppence a pound ".

He was harmless enough but one thing was clear - he, like Strachan, was not going to be sent back to the house block without using every effort to stay on the block first. On one particularly hot day we noticed a smell coming from the old sea dog's cell. When we looked in we saw that he had lined up his breakfast and lunchtime meals in neat lines behind his door. He had a line of tomatoes, one of mashed potato, another of beans and even one of porridge. When asked his reasons for this he replied that he was on hunger strike and was growing his own food in his allotment, which is what he had named his line of food.

His protest, however, took an even more unpleasant turn when he announced that he was progressing on to a dirty protest. Most of us had witnessed this type of protest before, as IRA prisoners favoured it after it had been used to such effect by the hunger strikers at the Maze. We did not think that this little old boy would be capable of sustaining his protest for more than a day or two, and our guess appeared to be right when on the first day he called us in to see his cell and show off the start of his protest.

We entered the cell and looked around it, bewildered, for signs of excrement smeared over the walls, but none was apparent. Then he proudly pointed to the floor in the rear corner of the cell where lying there was a tiny lump of shit that was no bigger than a single rabbit dropping. We were all in stitches when we left and told the old boy to keep up the good work. However, we would grow to regret these taunting words, as for the next two weeks he really went to town and the whole unit stank like a sewer for a fortnight.

The routine when someone is on a dirty protest is that you move them to one of two adjoining strip cells immediately. Then, on a daily basis, as they cover one cell full of shit you move them into the clean cell next door. If you are lucky they come quietly; if not, then special white protective clothing, gloves and masks have to be put on to remove the inmate by force. Once in the next cell a volunteer cleaner or officer goes into the dirty cell fully dressed in the protective clothing I have just described, with the addition of a pair of safety goggles and a power-jet hose. He then spends as little time as possible hosing the walls down until they are clean or he can no longer take the smell or cannot see anything because his goggles have become covered in shit.

This process goes on daily until the prisoner decides to end his dirty protest or is moved to another prison. It is a filthy process to be involved in and many of you would agree that the inmate should be kept in the dirty cell and not moved daily. That the cell has to be cleaned daily is as much for the sake of the health and hygiene of other prisoners and staff as it is for the inmate undertaking the protest. It is not a pleasant way to get your point across, but sadly it remains the best option as a last resort for some prisoners who have been ignored previously when attempting to go through the correct channels.

Soon after I joined the unit, I heard the news that my old pal Charlie was due to come back to Belmarsh and this time he was to be housed in the main seg. I was pleased with this news as I had not seen Charlie since I left him at Bristol over a year earlier, and I looked forward to working with him again. I remember thinking how funny it would be to see how some of the other big, brave members of staff would react to working with him. I knew that Charlie would be happy to be returning to Belmarsh, as he had received fair treatment from us during his last stay. I only hoped that the staff I now worked with would be as professional as Mick and Tony and the others had been when we looked after him in the Category A unit.

Shortly before Charlie's arrival, we had a visit from Governor Outram who, although he was our immediate governor at the time, would soon be taking over house block four, which was undergoing a refurb to enable it to house standard risk Category A inmates, and, in brief, Mr Outram's goal was to work with Charlie with a view to transferring him eventually onto the house block where he could mix with other prisoners. This sounded like a good idea to me and I was certain that Charlie would rise to the challenge and enjoy the fact that someone in authority was putting so much faith in him and giving himself the chance to prove himself. Everyone that knew Charlie agreed it would not be an easy task, not because we lacked faith in Charlie's ability but because we knew that ultimately the decision would rest with the muppets at head office.

On the day Charlie landed back at Belmarsh I was actually off duty, and when I returned to work a day or so later I noticed a distinct change in his appearance. He still had his head shaved, but his trademark handlebar moustache had evolved into a full beard, which was almost down to his chest. This was obviously the first point I raised with him and the explanation he gave was typical of Charlie's character. Apparently, since we had last seen each other Charlie had run into some problems at Long Lartin jail in Yorkshire and had ended up in the box. As usual, he was denied access to most everyday items such as a pen or pencil, but the governor had also refused him the use of a razor for shaving. Despite repeated applications for this basic necessity, the governor stood firm and continued to deny Charlie his request.

Annoyed at this pettiness and in a last-bid attempt to have a shave, Charlie stated that if he were continually denied the use of a razor he would not shave until 1 January 2000. On this date he promised to shave off the beard, put it in a box and post it to the governor concerned. We both laughed when Charlie remarked that it was only very early in 1996 at this stage and "the fucking thing is pissing off already, Jim, but I am a man of my word and I will have to suffer it for another four years."

True enough, despite numerous attempts by Governor Outram to persuade Charlie to lose the beard, he stuck to his word and did not shave it off until the set date. I am not sure if it ever reached its intended destination, as the last I heard it was in the possession of Charlie's old solicitor, Martin Oldham, who let Charlie down greatly during the Woodhill hostage trial. I am sure that the matter was resolved, as it was left in the very capable hands of his new solicitor Mr T, and not a lot gets past that man.

The formal catching up over, it was time to sort out the routine for the duration of Charlie's stay. As is usual with any of Charlie's time in an individual prison, the powers that be felt it unnecessary to let us know for how long he would be with us. This, of course, made it extremely difficult for us to plan any real long-term programme. It seemed to me that the main reason that no time limit was set was they were afraid that we would make some real progress with Charlie and they would then have to review the policy of keeping him in permanent isolation.

Charlie's first priority was to establish whether he would get adequate access to the exercise yard. I told him he would get the minimum one hour per day which, if we were not busy, could be extended should he wish to carry on training. He was, as usual, pleased that he would get the designated hour. In fact he never once asked for the period to be extended, but always welcomed the extra time when I offered it. Once the question of exercise had been clarified, Charlie told me that he would begin at once a revised version of the Bronson Olympics as part of our training programme.

Over the next few days we quickly settled into a good routine and soon the pair of us and John Howis, an extremely fit young officer whom Charlie grew to respect, could be heard laughing all over the prison. I was fortunate to have John working with us because, although relatively new in service, he possessed a similar attitude to mine and as such we were able to work well together. Not to mention the fact that, after throwing 'Bertha' to Charlie a thousand times during his sit-up workouts, John was always at hand to take over and throw her another two thousand times when my lungs were hanging out of my mouth. In fact Charlie and I both agreed that John was possibly the only man we knew that could almost match his own incredible stamina.

Mick Regan, although based in the security department at this time, also used to make regular appearances for the daily workouts and soon the competition between the four of us began pushing us all to our own limits of physical endurance. Sadly, Big Tony Lebatt was missing from the old crew as he had seriously damaged his knee tackling a prisoner high on crack and, as a result, was on sick leave for some months as they tried to save his kneecap.

Apart from the training side of the regime, Mr Outram had also set in motion other activities for Charlie. He had managed to secure Charlie access to art materials so he could carry on with his drawing and writing. He even managed to get him a mock computer keyboard on which Charlie soon taught himself to type. I had also conferred with John and Mick and we had decided to make Charlie the number one cleaner in the seg. We did this completely off our own bats, knowing full well that we would not get clearance through the correct channels, but we had the utmost faith that Charlie would not let us down in any way. He never did and, in fact, was the best cleaner we had ever had. No one threw rubbish out of their windows and everyone's plates were always washed immaculately by the time we took Charlie round to collect them after mealtimes. This job suited Charlie as it kept him active, which he loved, and he also got first refusal on any food that was left over to satisfy his huge appetite.

It did not take long, however, for the news of Charlie's new position to reach the security principal officer, who in turn phoned us up with the order that we were to sack Charlie immediately. Our response was that if he wanted to sack Charlie he would have to grow the balls to come down and do it himself. Obviously he did not want to do that, but he made a real fuss by reporting the matter to the governor and head office, who in turn all became involved. In the end, good old Mr Outram came to the rescue and said he stood by our decision to employ Charlie and would personally take responsibility from then on.

The only thing Charlie said he would not do as a cleaner was clean the office or make tea for the staff, which was fair enough as this was not part of the cleaner's regular duties anyway. He did, however, make one exception - one day when we were alone in the unit he offered to make me a cup of tea. To this day, I think I can lay claim to the fact that I am the only screw that has had a cup of tea made for him by Charlie Bronson.

The only occasion I felt a little nervous when working with Charlie was when he asked me to cut his hair one day. I managed to find a set of clippers in the store and sat Charlie on a chair in the middle of the landing to begin shaving his head. The clippers coughed into life and I ran them straight down the middle of his head from front to back. Then, to my horror, the clippers died on me, leaving Charlie with a bald stripe right down the middle of his head. I almost fainted as I frantically tried to get them working again, but to no avail, and Charlie kept asking, "How's it looking, Jim? Go on, son, take it all off."

Fortunately there were no mirrors visible and, as luck would have it, at that moment I heard the audible tone on the office radio, which signalled an alarm bell somewhere in the prison. As quick as a flash I told John to wait there and informed Charlie that I would have to respond to the bell but would finish his hair when I got back. Off I ran with the clippers in my hand, but in the opposite direction to where the alarm bell was ringing. I went round all the house blocks, the Category A unit, the stores, and even the dog section looking for a serviceable set of clippers, but with no luck. I was on my way back to the seg, contemplating how to break the news to Charlie before he broke my neck, and I took a short cut through the hospital wing. As I entered the main entrance, I heard a distant whirring sound of hair clippers in action and followed the noise. I ended up on the top floor and found one of the cleaners halfway through cutting a patient's hair with a gleaming pair of clippers. I could do nothing but commandeer the clippers and leave the cleaner and patient to slag me off for nicking them before they were finished while I ran back to the seg - well, I was a desperate man!

Luckily, on my return, Charlie was still sitting in the chair talking to John. With the new clippers I was able to finish the job with no further problems and Charlie was over the moon with the end result. Until he reads this, I can only assume that Charlie will still recall that day when I tackled an alarm bell with a set of clippers in my hand. I certainly never told him the real truth of how he nearly had to spend a couple of days with an extra-large centre parting - that would not have done his image, or my health, any good at all.

Our work with Charlie continued and he responded so well that Mr Outram was able to secure his move to house block four once it was operational. We were all a bit sorry to see him go as it meant we would have to return to a normal routine, but we knew Charlie had earned the right to move forward and we were pleased for him. Charlie had achieved a great deal and had provided me with some of the best days I had seen in the Prison Service, not to mention the fact that he had managed to smash his world record of medicine ball sit-ups. We wished him well and I promised to visit him on the house block whenever I got the chance.

At this time I had been living in Uxbridge for some months with my old army mate, Harry, and the travelling through London was beginning to take its toll, both financially and with my timekeeping. Consequently, I had applied for a transfer to Wormwood Scrubs, which was the nearest jail to where I was living. This decision was taken purely for practical reasons. I could not afford the travelling costs as well as paying maintenance for Lauren, and I have always tried to put my kids first before anything else. I knew that if I moved to the Scrubs I would save a great deal of money and would also be able to have Lauren at weekends, which I was unable to do at the prison flats in Brockley.

However, I was not looking forward to working there, as I had heard some real horror stories about the prison and some of its staff, not least from Charlie. He commented on how sorry he was to hear I was going to "that piss-hole" when I told him of my transfer. He did, however, fully understand my reasons, as he knew how much I loved Lauren and wanted to see more of her, so he wished me all the best and just advised me to watch my back and keep my head down. With those words in my head, I left Belmarsh on 15 August 1996 to take up my new position at the Scrubs on Monday 18 August.

15

WORMWOOD SCRUBS

I arrived at the infamous twin-towered main gate of Wormwood Scrubs at eight o'clock on Monday 18 August 1996 only to be told that no one had been made aware of my arrival. I was directed to the training room only to find that the training officer, Senior Officer Denman, also had no knowledge of my transfer, even though it had apparently been arranged for two months. Denman made some calls to various staff in the personnel department, all of whom denied any knowledge of my transfer. It appeared that Governor Jackson, whose name was on the transfer confirmation I had received, had retired without telling anyone about my arrival.

I was told that all I could do was go home and ring the prison the following day to see if anything had been sorted out. Although I was not too disappointed that my first trip inside this grim-looking jail had been delayed, I was extremely worried by the fact that no one knew I existed. The answer I got when I phoned the following morning pissed me of even more. I was told by a lady in personnel that my transfer had never been agreed and the Scrubs was not taking on any more staff as they were undergoing an audit on staffing levels. I was advised that I would just have to go back to Belmarsh and reapply the following year.

Not being happy with this answer, I decided that I would not take the lady's advice and would take the matter up with higher authorities myself. I returned home and immediately began the first of hundreds of phone calls, which would continue over the next two months, to head office. Basically, my case was passed from one area manager's office to the other, each denying responsibility, while for two months I stood my ground and refused to go back to work until I had an answer.

Eventually, as a last-bid attempt, I contacted staff care and welfare and a lovely lady called Angela sorted the problem out within days and contacted me with a start date at the Scrubs. I have no idea who she spoke to, but I was amazed at the speed with which she managed to get a response considering that for two months I did not exist as far as head office was concerned. It just goes to show how well the Service cared for its employees under the new Investors in People scheme that had recently been introduced!

On 14 October 1996 I once again approached the imposing twin-towered gates of the Scrubs to begin my induction week. The first thing I had to contend with was the arrogant attitude of the gate staff. As I was a strange face and the gate staff considered themselves 'old sweats', they wasted no time in talking to me as though I was a three-year-old. I was saved further humiliation by the arrival of the training Senior Officer, Mr Denman, who turned out to be a fair man.

I spent the following week under the supervision of Mr Denman, although he appreciated my experience and basically gave me free rein to wander round the prison and visit the different departments. The main thing I noticed about the Scrubs, which was uniformed in every department, was a distinct 'them and us' divide between the inmates and most of the staff. I appreciate that this is necessary in such controlled environments, but many of the staff seemed to have a real hatred for anyone wearing the blue striped shirts, blue jeans and grey sweatshirts issued to all convicted prisoners at the jail.

This is not to say that prisoners on remand, who could wear their own clothing, were spared this 'them and us' treatment. Some of the worst allegations of assaults by officers on inmates came from remand prisoners serving on C-Wing, although I did not personally witness any as I rarely went onto that wing. At the time of writing this, there is still an ongoing investigation into such allegations at the Scrubs and criminal charges have been brought against some of the officers concerned. I only hope they do not meet any of the inmates they are accused of assaulting if they get a custodial sentence, as I am sure the alleged victims will not hesitate to dole out their revenge whilst the officers have no uniform to hide behind.

As I explored the different areas of this vast Victorian prison, I received the same hostile greeting from staff in every department - with the exception of C-Wing, which was still very much as it was when the prison first opened its imposing gates and conjured up the typical image you would expect from an old London 'gaol'. The rest of the prison had undergone a half-hearted makeover. The addition of integral toilets and a lick of green and magnolia paint on the walls may have been easier on both the nose and the eye, but it did nothing to mask the hostility of most of the staff that worked there. It really was a different world once you entered the belly of this imposing structure, and the sheer arrogance and aggressive, obnoxious attitude of the staff I met left me feeling nervous and intimidated. After all, I was supposed to be on their side, so you can imagine how the prisoners must have felt.

This, of course, was very much the image the Scrubs wanted its staff to portray, and they took great pride in the fact that they were resisting any outside pressure to move towards a more modern regime, as had already been adopted in most other prisons. For example, they were still refusing to offer inmates any periods of association or access to showering facilities more than once a week.

Unlike Belmarsh, the majority of staff here were older and longer in service, a fact I had hoped would have meant a more relaxed and professional working environment. Unfortunately I could not have been more wrong. The vast majority of staff I came across were lazy and arrogant and had this inbred hatred of all prisoners. Consequently, they would take advantage of any opportunity they had to show this contempt, through either mental or physical abuse.

Any new members of staff, as I was, were treated with total distrust and disdain until such time as they proved themselves to be loyal enough to be welcomed into the inner sanctum of these cliquey bully squads, which roamed the landings at will. The only way to prove this in their eyes was to be involved in one of the daily 'takeouts' of a prisoner, usually arranged after a lunchtime session in the officers' bar. Here the alcohol would fuel the contempt eating away at these officers and they would return to the wings thirsty for some ego-boosting action.

The vast majority of these takeouts were unnecessary and totally random, with officers often picking victims from the landing roll board in a twisted version of 'pin the tail on the donkey'. Alternatively, they would act on 'intelligence' passed on by another member of staff who had taken a dislike to a particular inmate. This would be reason enough to set up a takeout on an unsuspecting inmate.

These incidents were all orchestrated to relieve boredom, to boost egos, or much of the time to initiate new members of staff into the 'way we do things at the Scrubs' and test their loyalty. If you didn't participate you became an outcast, and if you attempted to report their behaviour to a higher level you were told not to be silly and to think very carefully about your career before making such allegations about senior officers. Usually four or five officers would go to the allocated cell and begin an aggressive cell search. Of course the rest of the inmates on the wing were on twenty-three-hour bang-up, so although they might hear a commotion there would be no eye witnesses to back up any complaint the inmate might submit later.

Most of the inmates targeted in this way were recent arrivals to the Scrubs and so at some stage during the search they would more often than not question the officers about their over-the-top methods. This was the trigger they needed to 'wrap up' the inmate and, after a violent removal to the segregation unit, he would always be placed on report for assaulting an officer. This was considered as educating the inmate in the way we ran things at the Scrubs, and I can tell you that very few prisoners escaped this unofficial and hostile induction.

The worst part was that the senior management on the wings were not only aware that this practice was going on, but also they seemed to encourage it. They even had their own early-warning system in place to prevent any outsiders, i.e. members of the board of visitors or visiting teachers or clergy, walking in whilst these takeouts were being executed. If such outsiders arrived at the prison, the gate staff would ring the wing or department they were destined for to forewarn the staff of their imminent arrival. Then all their subsequent movements within the prison would be monitored and pre-reported in the same way.

Although all the officers involved in the incidents, and sometimes others who were not even at the scene, would submit almost identical statements swearing that the inmate attacked an officer in a totally unprovoked manner and had to be restrained using approved methods of control and restraint for reasons of 'good order and discipline', it was almost always left to the newest member of staff to place the inmate officially on report. He would always be the one that claimed he was assaulted, and on adjudication the governors and senior management would always back the officer's version of events. They would therefore almost always find the inmate guilty and were also under extreme pressure from the staff to award the highest possible sentence for that particular offence. Basically, the better the officer's story, the higher they expected the awarded sentence to be; and the higher the sentence, the greater the status that the officer gained when he returned to the wing. It was reminiscent of the 'trial by combat' scenarios endured by the medieval knights in order to win their king's trust.

I was always reluctant to get involved in these premeditated takeouts and, as a result, I was always treated with contempt and mistrust by most of the other staff at the Scrubs. Consequently, I was never accepted as an accredited member of staff - not that I would lose any sleep over not being a recognized thug and bully boy. Having said that, I am certainly no angel and would be lying if I said I never got dragged into certain incidents where I felt I had no choice but to submit false statements. It is certainly something I am not proud of, and this is partly the reason I am writing this book - to expose this corrupt behaviour, but I certainly avoided these situations wherever possible and was never involved in setting up these takeouts or subjecting an inmate to an unprovoked attack.

On the other hand, I am not campaigning for the abolishment of our penal system. I agree that such institutions are an unfortunate but necessary part of our society. My concern is that the people trusted to run these volatile establishments are failing us as a society by being unprofessional and by being allowed to get away with carrying out illegal acts within their walls that amount to nothing less than ABH or GBH. Committing these offences outside would almost certainly incur a custodial sentence, and such offences are in fact the reason why many of the prisoners suffering this treatment are in prison in the first place. How can we teach violent criminals to lead law-abiding lives on their release if they are being subjected to violent confrontations each day by prison staff?

Anyway, back to my introduction to the Scrubs. By the end of the week I had visited each department within the prison and, to be quite honest, I was worried about which area I would prefer to work in. None of them was particularly appealing; not least of all because I was unsure if I could ever work with many of the staff. I was informed that I was to be placed on B-Wing, which was the induction wing and was much the same as house block three at Belmarsh. I was quietly relieved, as the staff there seemed to be closer to my own age than those in the other wings. I also thought that at least I had some experience in dealing with newly convicted prisoners and some of their needs and requirements.

I was greeted on B-Wing with a certain distrust from the majority of staff, as they had all heard that Belmarsh was a 'soft nick' where staff treated prisoners with kid gloves. They seemed concerned that I was some sort of governor's grass, and it actually took some time for many of them to begin talking to me. One of the only officers that accepted me almost straight away was 'Hutch', who was in charge of the threes landing - my new designated place of work.

To look at Hutch, you would probably categorize him as a 'right horrible cunt', which is how the inmates would describe a bad screw. His appearance did not reflect his nature, however. He was a fair man with a personality quite similar to mine. Don't get me wrong, he did not take any shit and he could get into a row if a prisoner took the piss out of him, but he was an even-handed man who commanded respect from the majority of inmates. Like me, they knew where they stood with him, and if we said we could not do something they knew we had genuine reasons and it was not just that we could not be bothered.

I quickly got to know the inmates on the landing, in particular 'Sully' and

'H', the cleaners. Sully was in his thirties and was a keep-fit fanatic. He worked hard both on the wing and in the gym, where he was doing a course to qualify as a games coach. He passed all the relevant courses and, so far as I am aware, he secured himself a job in a sports centre on his release. Unlike many of the other prisoners who often found it hard to adjust to life outside and consequently ended up back inside, we never saw Sully again, and that was something that Hutch and I were really pleased about.

H was an old hand and had done a lot of bird in his time. He knew the system better than most of the staff, but never used this knowledge to gain anything he was not entitled to. Most of the other prisoners respected him and he was good at resolving disputes with other inmates. If H told anyone that Hutch and I were okay, they never questioned his judgement and knew they could trust us. There were one or two officers who worked the opposite shift to Hutch and me that took a dislike to H and went out of their way to try to push him into breaking prison rules so that they could sack him and get him put in the seg. He was, however, too long in the tooth to fall for their mind games and knew he was winding them up even more by not taking the bait. He would, of course, tell Hutch and me all about any agro he had had when we came back on duty.

It was not long before I was involved in my first incident on the wing, which occurred in the threes landing office. It involved a Welsh officer, Tim, who seemed to have a particular hatred for all inmates, and a young lad recently transferred from a northern jail. We accepted large intakes from jails around the country in an attempt to ease the growing overcrowding in Britain's prisons at the time, even though it meant we had to allocate three inmates to each cell.

Tim took an instant dislike to this northern inmate, as he asked if he could make a phone call when he arrived on the wing at about eight o'clock one evening. This request was perfectly reasonable, as he was transferred without notice and his wife and small child were due to visit him the following morning at his old prison. He just wanted a minute to tell them not to waste their time and money, as well as to advise them about his new location. Tim made it clear that he was not going to allow this phone call, despite the fact that inmates on other landings were being given access to phones, which obviously upset the new prisoner. Although he expressed his frustration, he did not 'kick off' and he returned to his cell with no further argument.

However, although he had not caused any trouble, his card had been marked by Tim who, for the next few days, shadowed his every move in an attempt to wind him up enough to have a go. The inmate showed remarkable self-restraint until he made a request to see a governor on application-one morning and handed it to Tim, who happened to be the officer on duty. It was general practice at the Scrubs at that time to rip up the majority of prisoners' applications, as they generally meant more work for the staff. Tim, however, did not tear up his request, as he saw another opportunity to use it.

Tim summoned me to the office and told me he was "going to have that cunt" and that I just had to back up his story. The inmate came in and Tim immediately started to shout and scream at him, telling him he had a bad attitude. He got up from behind the desk and walked round the front to physically push the inmate. Finally, having had enough and in an attempt to protect himself, the inmate grabbed Tim. They grappled each other to the floor and both fell against the office door, effectively locking the three of us in the office. I pressed the alarm bell and attempted to separate Tim and the inmate, but they had got themselves wedged between the door and the desk, both being quite big lads. Eventually I managed to pull them apart and had to stand between them to prevent Tim from launching at the inmate again, as he was now going mad.

The next problem I had was that, with the door now free to open, there was a horde of staff tearing down the landing to get a piece of the action in true Scrubs style. The first officers through the door were staff from the adjacent seg unit, who dived straight in. As soon as Tim said he had been assaulted, one of them smacked the inmate in the face and they both dragged him back down to the floor. I will give the lad his due: he did not go down easy, but he did not physically strike any of the officers concerned.

He just kept saying that he was the one that had been assaulted. Eventually he was dragged screaming and under restraint to the seg where he was greeted by the reception committee, who would have given him a few digs to teach him that you cannot assault an officer in the Scrubs and get away with it.

Tim and I, in the meantime, had to fill out our reports of the incident. He had already sorted out what he was going to say, and it was useless for me to try to say anything different, as he had three or four other officers willing to put on paper that they had witnessed the incident and confirm that he was attacked by the inmate without provocation. He also covered his back by claiming to have received injuries, such as muscle strain in his back, and entering this in the accident book. This was to ensure that the prisoner would receive maximum punishment on adjudication and that Tim could take a week or two off on the sick. On the adjudication, Tim produced a report from his doctor. He had taken three weeks off work and possessed paperwork from other staff confirming his version of events, so the inmate never stood a chance.

This kind of cover-up was typical of the prison adjudication system, but at the Scrubs it was even more finely tuned. It was expected that an officer could call on another officer to confirm their version of an incident, and this practice was well known even by the governors. Prison adjudications have been likened to kangaroo courts, and this is certainly true in my experience, especially at the Scrubs.

By Christmas I was beginning to get used to the regime on B-Wing and I had also sussed out which members of staff I could talk to. About a week before Christmas, I heard from my old mate Charlie when he sent me a letter and a card to the wing. He had been doing well on house block four until some Iraqis who had hijacked a plane arrived. Charlie is very patriotic and hates bullies and terrorism, so when these Iraqi terrorists began strutting about on the wing Charlie felt he had to step in. In typical Charlie style, he hijacked the

hijackers and taught them a lesson while holding them hostage in his cell. Classic! Once again, Chaz, I've got to hand it to you.

The arrival of this card and letter, plus a letter from Mr Outram regarding his recommendation that I should be put forward for a Kostler award for my work with Charlie, stirred up some unrest among certain other members of B-Wing staff. One or two of them showed their disgust that I had received correspondence from a prisoner, not least Charlie, who received such a brutal reception when he arrived at the Scrubs.

My personal life had taken a dramatic turn at around this time, as I had recently been reunited with my childhood sweetheart, Natasha. I was at this stage living in my own flat near Uxbridge, and Natasha would drive over from Greenwich, where she was working two or three times a week. We enjoyed good times both in the flat and down the Heath Tavern, the local pub on the Uxbridge Road. I was really happy, but was growing to hate working as a prison officer more and more each day. I think meeting Natasha again reminded me who I was and how my personality did not suit the way I was being pressured to behave in the Prison Service.

I still enjoyed a drink and had a funny night on the piss whilst on nights the week before Christmas. I had gone sick for a couple of nights because Natasha had come to stay, and when I returned on the Saturday I was told that I would be taking care of the lifers' hostel just outside the gates next to the officers' club - oh dear! My senior officer, himself a self-confessed pisshead, briefed me on what to do: "Just go and have a drink in the club until about half twelve, then go and count the lads and report the numbers to the control room, and then if it's still open go back to the club."

I, of course, followed his instructions to the letter and fell out of the club at about three o'clock in the morning barely able to walk let alone count. I bounced through the hostel, going from one room to the other counting the inmates, who were cursing me from their beds. I reported sixteen inmates secure in the hostel to the control room - not bad seeing as there were only twelve housed there at the time; still, better too many than too few!

I sat on the chair in the office and spilt a two-litre bottle of water, with which I was trying to sober myself up, all over the chair and myself. I decided that I had to attempt to dry the chair, so I took the base off it, together with the wooden frame, and found that it luckily fitted into the industrial drying machine in the hostel's laundry. For some reason the din of the wood-framed base banging around the metal drum of the dryer was the last straw for the already pissed-off inmates. Let's just say that three of the biggest and meanest-looking ex-murderers housed in the hostel were recruited by the others to 'persuade' me to take the chair out of the dryer.

After about an hour or so's drunken sleep, I awoke and wandered into the kitchen to make a coffee. Strangely enough, the sudden lull in conversation by the tired-looking inmates and the look of 'we are going to kill you' in their eyes made me lose my appetite for coffee and I slipped away quickly and quietly. Instead, I went home to catch up on some sleep, checking I wasn't being followed and locking the flat door firmly behind me. I woke some hours later at around dinnertime and remembered I had to drop an application form for a transfer back to Belmarsh into the personnel department.

Once I had done this, I called into the club only to be greeted by the words "That's him" as someone pointed me out to the hostel senior officer, who didn't look very happy. After hearing how he had spent the morning listening to complaints by a string of inmates who greeted him in the form of a queue outside his office that morning, I decided to leave and return to the neutral ground of the Heath Tavern. I spent a few hours in there sitting at the bar alone with my thoughts about how I was becoming tired of the routine at the Scrubs. The lack of time I could spend with Natasha was getting to me and I hoped I would get my transfer approved as soon as possible. In fact this simple request once again proved too difficult for the 'brains' behind the Prison Service to action without problems.

Depressing is the only way to describe my day-to-day working life at that stage as I waited for news of my transfer request. I was constantly battling to swim against the tide in terms of the attitude of the majority of staff towards their treatment of all inmates. It was clear to me that the Scrubs was too set in its way to accept change or an officer with different work ethics. Perhaps they were scared what might come out. At times it became so difficult that even I thought it might be easier just to fall in line with everyone else and act as they did, but my conscience would never allow it.

However, on Valentine's Day 1998 something happened that confirmed to me that it was worth persevering with my methods of working. I had arranged to meet Natasha after work to take her to the Valentine disco at the staff club. This was a bit of a private joke between us, as many years previously I had taken her to a country and western evening at Bexley mental home with my old army mate, Kia, as his sister and mum both worked there as psychiatric nurses. Natasha has never let me forget this romantic gesture, especially the bit when John Wayne chased her down the corridor in a wheelchair fully equipped with the Stetson and pair of six-guns whilst returning from the toilet!

Anyway, back to the Scrubs. I had just walked from B-Wing to the gate to deposit my keys when one of the gate staff informed me in their usually jolly style that I was to return to the wing immediately. My protests that I had prior engagements were ignored, as whatever was going on had caused a lockdown, meaning that no one could either leave or enter the prison anyway. I therefore had no choice but to return to the wing and see what was happening. On my arrival I was told to report to the threes landing office where I found the duty governor and senior wing management, who cut their conversation dead as soon as they saw me in the doorway.

I was informed that an inmate on the threes landing had barricaded himself in his cell and was threatening to harm himself and smash up the cell, and that he was refusing to come out until he had spoken to me. I walked down the landing to the area outside the cell to find about a dozen staff fully kitted out in riot gear, goading and tormenting the inmate through the door with threats of what was going to happen to him when they got hold of him for fucking up the wing routine - nice one boys! My first request was that they retreated to the landing office to remove the intimidation factor from an already tense situation. After some hesitation and protests from many of the squad's members, the governor reluctantly ordered them to retire to the office and I began talking to the inmate.

He had only been in the prison for about three or four days, and I noticed immediately a nervous fear in his voice. After ten minutes or so of my persuading him that the riot teams, which he described as 'the pack of wolves', were out of earshot and no one was taping or listening to our conversation, he began to calm down slightly. He agreed to take down enough of the barricade to allow me to gain entry and talk to him face to face, so long as I guaranteed that the riot teams would not storm the cell. I relayed this to the duty governor, who reluctantly allowed me to carry on. I must admit that I still could not guarantee that they would not storm the cell over me as soon as I gained entry, but it was a risk I had to take - not least because I was now keeping Natasha waiting and that was something I feared more than any riot team trampling over my head.

I knew the inmate in question was no threat, and as soon as enough of the barricade was removed I gained entry. I spent approximately half an hour talking to him about why he felt this course of action was necessary rather than talking to an officer. I should have known the answer to that one. He stated that he had been told by one of the cleaners that I was the only officer he could trust and that he was in fear of his life so he could not go to anyone else. It turned out that he had received threats of serious injury and persecution from a group of staff on the wing via a message from an inmate employed on the hotplate. Basically, he was told that the staff didn't like him and would make his life hell by victimizing him. He seemed genuinely in fear of his life and felt the action he had taken was the only way to avoid reprisals.

After he had told me this, I informed him that all I could do was transfer him to the rule 43 unit for his own protection, albeit against the staff rather than other inmates. Most inmates do not like this option, as rule 43 also houses the sex offenders and there is a danger that you could be mistaken for one of them, but this lad was so convinced that if he stayed on the wing he would be seriously injured or killed that he felt he had no other option. The problem was, he would not name the inmate messenger or the staff involved, if indeed he knew who they were at that stage. I knew that this would impede any subsequent investigation that I could initiate into these allegations; in short, the intimidation factor of these bully squads would prove enough, once again, to avert justice being done.

All I could do at that stage was promise him safe passage off the wing and onto the 43 unit and a guarantee that I would submit a report of what he had told me to the governor on that unit the following morning. I knew, however, that it would be taken no further and that any follow-up on my part would fall on deaf ears, and that by the morning the whole incident would be forgotten and the staff involved would be triumphant in the fact that they had got the inmate removed from their wing and would be free to move on to their next victim. All I had to do was persuade the duty governor to allow us safe passage from B-wing to the 43 unit without the overzealous riot teams jumping us halfway down the landing.

Permission was granted and I escorted the lad to the unit without incident, albeit with the riot teams close on our heels spouting threatening remarks in an attempt to keep the intimidation going. Once he had been delivered safely to the unit, I was able to leave and attend the Valentine disco, albeit a couple of hours late. We did not stay long, however, as word had obviously spread quickly about the incident. Let's just say that my ears were burning slightly and I could feel eyes glaring at me from various groups of officers around the club.

This incident confirmed two things to me: one, that I must be doing something right in the way I carried out my duties to gain that sort of trust from a very scared young man; and two, that I was never going to be accepted by the staff at the Scrubs and would always be an outsider. Thankfully, I did not have to suffer the backstabbing and dirty looks for much longer, as not long after that particular incident I received an official letter from Belmarsh's personnel department, giving me a transfer date that was about six weeks away.

I therefore decided that I needed to act swiftly and approach a letting agency about the flat. I found a tenant quickly and within two weeks I had moved into Natasha's house in Wildfell Close, Kent. I struggled with the two-hour commute to and from the Scrubs for the next few weeks, my imminent transfer date being the only thing that kept me from ending up like Michael Douglas in that film Falling Down. However, only days before my anticipated return to Belmarsh I was notified that once again there had been a fuck-up and I didn't have a place at all.

While waiting for news of my transfer, a further incident took place that was to be the final straw that broke the camel's back for me. As previously mentioned, an ongoing investigation was under way at that time into brutality against inmates by certain members of the segregation staff. Despite various attempts to exonerate the staff members involved, the net was closing in and this time, I am thankful to say, the outcome did not look good for them.

I came into work one morning to find the gate had been 'frozen' and all staff were to report to the officers' club. When I entered the club, I found that someone had opened the bar and it was packed with one hundred or so officers, many of whom were drinking pints of ale even though it was still only about seven in the morning. I asked one of the B-Wing officers what was going on, to which he replied that the POA (Prison Officers Association) had called a strike in support of the 'Scrubs Four', as the accused officers had been labelled.

I had not become a member of the POA, as I did not feel that the subscription fees each month validated the job they were supposed to do, so really I had no right to be there. I had not actually told anyone that I was not a member, as the Scrubs at the time was a staunch union prison, but I knew I would get no support if I decided to stay and, besides, I did not agree with what they were doing. I felt sure that the accused staff members were guilty and I did not feel they should be allowed to get away with their actions any longer.

I had to leave quietly and explain to the staff on the gate that I did not wish to join the action, and so I requested that they let me through to my place of work. As you can imagine, this blacklisted me even more than I was already, but I stood by my principles and I believe that made me a better man than most of those outside the gate. The strike went on for the whole of that day, and there were in fact about half a dozen of us non-union members who had reported for duty that day.

Despite our initial fears of reprisals from the inmates for being on lock-up most of the day, apart from feeding times, the majority of them respected the fact that if it had not been for we few and the governors drafted in from other London prisons, they would not even have received any meals that day. Needless to say, I was not flavour of the month when the rest of the staff returned to work, and I thought it best to take a few days off sick while the dust settled. Incidentally, the Scrubs at that time had one of the worst staff sickness records. I recall a funny thing I noticed when reporting back for duty: once so many staff were having time off and putting it down to sickness and diarrhoea, but they could not spell the latter on their self-certificated sick note, that they had written it in big letters on the noticeboard in the orderly room for all to copy.   .

Rather than bore you with the details of the problems I encountered trying to solve yet another red-tape fuck-up by the Prison Service, I will just say that this time my experience helped me to resolve the matter a lot quicker than the previous Scrubs transfer. It only took about a month of persistence on my part before I received concrete confirmation of my transfer to Belmarsh, and before I knew it I found myself back in the familiar surroundings of house block three's staff room.

16
BACK IN BELMARSH - AND OUT AGAIN

I felt relieved and happy to be back initially - relieved that I would no longer have to endure the rat race of commuting through London and happy that Natasha and I were together again. For the first time in my life, I felt everything was going right and we would be happy forever. Nothing had changed at 'the Marsh' apart from the fact that most of the young officers I had served with previously were now senior officers on the wings. The routine was still the same and house block three was still the induction wing.

I was soon reunited with my old mate Bosley who, I was pleased to see, had retained his dry sense of humour and 'don't give a fuck' attitude, and he quickly had me in fits of laughter once again. It didn't take long for me to fall back into the regime of the wing and begin to build my own unique rapport with the inmates on the house block. I had hoped to meet up with my old pal Charlie, who I thought might pass through at some stage, but unfortunately I was not to see him again until after I left the Prison Service. I learned that the Service had built a new 'super-max' unit at Woodhill Prison to house the prisoners considered to be the most dangerous in the system, and this was where Charlie had been sent.

I spent the next few weeks getting back into the prison's regime, or at least trying to as I had other more important things on my mind. Natasha was pregnant with Morgan and was not having a particularly easy time of it.

I was growing increasingly tired of the politics involved within the Prison Service and was becoming worried that, in order to comply with the way some of my colleagues thought a prison officer should behave, I would have to let them change who I was. This, of course, would go against the advice I had been given years earlier by my old mate Simon's dad, Jim, and I knew I didn't want to do that. I was now in a bit of a predicament: I knew

I had to get out of the Prison Service, but I still had a family to support and it was a well-paid secure job if nothing else.

The numbers of assaults were on the increase as well as the numbers of suicides, or attempted ones, by inmates. Many members of staff treated these attempts as a bit of a joke and would even ignore the routine of keeping an eye on inmates on suicide watch in the sick hope that they would actually do themselves harm. I had witnessed such attempts before and had seen inmates who had cut themselves, overdosed and hung themselves using their bed sheets - some unsuccessfully, and some who had actually achieved their aim.

One particular suicide attempt I witnessed was probably the final straw so far as my decision to leave the Service was concerned. It was not the most gruesome suicide attempt I had seen. It was more the way in which it was handled that finally pushed me to the decision that enough was enough. It involved a young inmate on the threes landing, who was obviously finding prison life difficult and who had already fallen foul of the stronger inmates and bully element of officers. As a result, he was on suicide watch.

On that particular day, I came on duty after lunch and began to unlock the threes landing. That was when I discovered the inmate lying on his bed, which was partially covered in blood. He had cut both his wrists with the razor blade I could see lying in a pool of blood on the floor, although he was still very much alive, indicating that he had only just carried out the attempt. I immediately put on a pair of surgical gloves, which I always carried with me, and began to wrap his wrists in towels. Whilst doing so, I sent another inmate to alert the staff so they could arrange for medical assistance. Some ten minutes later no one had arrived, so I decided to take the inmate to the house block's treatment room. I told him to keep his hands raised in order to stem some of the flow of blood from his wrists, and helped him along the landing.

When I arrived, I discovered that the nurse had not even been notified, so I left him in her hands and went in search of 'Niff Naff', the name given to the house block governor, to get some answers. My first point was that the inmate had been placed in a single cell, which is strictly against the rules of suicide watch, and also the razor he had been issued with should have been taken off him. I then tackled the issue of the lack of assistance and staff attitude towards suicide attempts in general. He offered no answers to my questions and neither did he at any time ask whether I had been affected by what I had just witnessed or whether I wanted to see a post-incident counsellor, which should be normal practice. Instead, he said that the inmate was just seeking attention, as, if he had really wanted to kill himself, he would have done so. Of course this was possibly true, but it was not the sort of comment you would expect from a trained prison governor.

The inmate did eventually receive treatment and subsequently made a full recovery. I, on the other hand, now had to endure the typical backstabbing behaviour from certain members of staff. Because I had effectively saved a prisoner's life, I was considered a soft touch - apparently I should have left him to carry out his wish. The stress of dealing with such attitudes was beginning to take its toll on me, coupled with the fact that Natasha was coming to the end of her pregnancy.

No more than two weeks later I fell foul of the bad element of staff once again. I came on duty at one o'clock for a late shift and began unlocking the landing for association as normal. However, when I opened cell 28, which housed three inmates with whom I usually got on well, one of the inmates came flying out of the door at me, brandishing a table leg. Luckily I managed to dodge the piece of wood as he tried to hit me with it and I instinctively grabbed the inmate and wrestled him to the floor. He was not a small man, but when the others in the cell realised it was me they helped calm the situation down. This was one of the advantages of building a good working relationship with the inmates and treating them fairly, whereas another lone officer faced with the same situation would almost certainly have been seriously injured. The inmate was, of course, escorted to the segregation unit and charged with assault on an officer.

It turned out that a certain officer called Geoff had taken a dislike to this inmate and had spent the whole morning and lunchtime winding him up.

Obviously he had been 'stewing' behind his door for an hour and a half and just flew at the first uniform he saw, which unfortunately happened to me. I had seen this happen before when an innocent member of staff had been hurt due to another's unprofessional bully-boy tactics. The incident left me shook up and annoyed. I carried out the rest of my shift, but in my mind I had finally reached the decision that I could no longer work in such an environment.

When I returned home that night I was still shaking with anger and Natasha noticed and asked what was up. I told her what had happened and that I felt that if I returned to work I would end up assaulting another member of staff before being put in the same situation again. She was fully supportive and told me that if I felt so strongly I shouldn't go back. The next morning she rang 'Niff Naff' and explained that I was stressed out and wouldn't be going back for some time.

In fact I spent nearly the whole of the following year on sick leave due to stress and received no visits or help from the Service at all. The only correspondence I got was when I had to go to see a Home Office approved doctor after six months, who signed me off for a further six months. I was, of course, still being paid: full pay for six months and half pay thereafter. This gave me a chance to think about what I was going to do with my life. The truth was, I didn't no; all I knew was that I couldn't return to the Prison Service.

It was nice to spend time at home with Natasha during the latter days of her pregnancy. She took paid maternity leave, which meant we were not losing any money. This would not last, however, as the Prison Service would soon stop paying me and I would then go onto statutory sick pay. I had to decide to resign officially from the Prison Service and seek other employment.

Altogether I had spent almost seven years as a prison officer. However, had it not been for certain financial commitments and my need for job security at that time in my life, my service would have been considerably shorter. I had enjoyed some good times, such as my work with Charlie, and I had met some interesting people, but the ignorant, violent, cowardly, bully-type people I came across far outnumbered the good. These people really are a cancer that is eating away at the Service from the inside out and destroying what should or could be a highly respectable and rewarding career. Unfortunately it is, as many of you will no doubt agree or have experienced for yourselves, much easier sometimes just to go with the flow rather than constantly attempt to battle against it. Many like me have no doubt tried, but inevitably we all find the constant struggle far too stressful and eventually have no more fight to give, so we end up either being swept away with the majority or simply resigning to try to forget the whole experience. Some simply get caught up in the web of lies, deceit and bullying tactics just by being in the wrong place at the wrong time, and like me find themselves hitting a brick wall of ignorance and mistrust when they try to report any unprofessional conduct by fellow officers. Alternatively, they just feel too intimidated by senior staff and management to pursue the matter further.

Trying to avoid being sucked into this conspiracy of false accusations and victimization took its toll on my mental state of mind after a while - so much so that I would go home on occasions with so much anger and frustration bottled up inside, usually as a result of unnecessary confrontations caused by unprofessional members of staff, that I would often feel as if I could totally lose control and have an overwhelming urge to smash up the house. I felt many times that my personal safety and indeed my own liberty were constantly being put at risk due to the uncontrollable antics of many of my colleagues. To put it bluntly, in 'Jim speak' their behaviour boiled down to nothing less than ignorant arseholes with piss-poor training and management by men who themselves had cut their teeth in the violent, bullying world of a penal or borstal system, which involved the 'short sharp shock' treatment that has long since been proved to be ineffective.

The problem as I see it is that it is quite the opposite to short and sharp these days, and the shock is in fact meted out as a constant battering of an individual's emotions over many months. In my old mate Charlie's case, he has endured non-stop sensory deprivation and both mental and physical pain for over thirty years. I finally cracked under the pressure after just seven years, and I was supposed to be on the side of the instigators. I had the benefit of being able to walk out of the gates at the end of my shift and go for a walk or a drive, have a few beers, or confide in a loving family to help me unwind when I got home. Charlie and countless others like him don't have this luxury and so just get buried deeper and deeper into the belly of the system. They get no relief from the pressure, or the chance to talk to a loved one or anyone who cares about their position. In the dead of night they are left feeling totally alone, having had all traces of human emotion knocked out of them through either physical or mental aggression.

In the end, for the sake of my sanity and the well-being of my family, I had to admit that I could no longer subject myself to working in that type of hostile environment. I felt powerless to change the way the Prison Service had been conducting its clandestine methods of running its business for so many years, and felt I had no choice but to get out of there.

Since leaving, I have felt it necessary to write to the Home Office on a couple of occasions in search of answers to points I felt needed explaining - the first being the reasons behind the decision to twice refuse me clearance to visit Charlie. I expressed how I could not understand how I was able to work in three high-security prisons but was not able to visit a prisoner as a civilian and I was intrigued as to how this decision had been reached. I was in contact with Charlie via letters, I had a permanent residency in the UK, and I did not have a criminal record - all these I knew were key factors if you wanted to be passed to visit a Category A prisoner. As you might expect, the reply from the Home Office was a typically vague excuse to the effect that it was not common practice to divulge the reasons for refusing someone's visiting status, and as an ex-employee I should know the process involved in vetting all potential visitors. Well, yes I do know, and I feel that I fit their criteria perfectly. I can only assume that someone in their ivory tower could possibly harvest a grudge against me, feeling embarrassed by the fact that I have broken ranks and spoken out against staff misconduct, and they are scared of what my honesty might uncover. In true Home Office style, they have chosen just to ignore me and hope I will eventually grow tired and go away in much the same way that they bury Charlie and others like him deeper and deeper inside the system in the hope that their failings in the treatment of these prisoners in their care will be buried with them: the classic 'out of sight out of mind' tactics.

On another occasion I wrote to my old boss in the Green Jackets, Sir David Ramsbotham, a man for whom I have the greatest respect and who was at the time employed as the Chief Inspector of Prisons, to voice my opinion and concern about Charlie's treatment and the behaviour of some prison officers I had encountered. He wrote a very good letter back to me, dated 7 April 2000, saying he would pass my comments and concerns on to the Director General of the Prison Service and ask him to respond. To this date I have never received a reply from the Director or his staff, other than to acknowledge receipt of the letter I sent to Ramsbotham. In his reply to me, Sir David Ramsbotham did comment, and I quote: "The behaviour of staff in some of the prisons beggars belief and the verbal evidence I hear from other places confirms it is not confined to those prisons on which we have been reporting most recently. This is a sad state of affairs and one of which the Service should be ASHAMED."

Strangely enough, Sir David resigned from the post after a relatively short term in office, Perhaps, like me, he too realized he would get no support in implementing any procedures to stamp out this unacceptable behaviour, or maybe he was pushed out because he came too close to exposing the truth about the corrupt and violent staff in the employ of the Prison Service, not to mention the inadequate conditions of many of our prisons.

All I can say about my resignation is that it felt as if a great weight had been lifted off my shoulders. It has taken a long time to readjust and I hope that by sharing my knowledge with you it will lighten the burden of shame I carry from what I have witnessed or been involved in whilst working for the Prison Service. At the time, I was fortunate to have something wonderful to look forward to and to help me forget the Prison Service, for a short while anyway - the impending birth of Natasha's and my baby.

Morgan Jennifer Dawkins was born on 19 February 1999 at Chatham's All Saints Hospital. This was a great day for me and Natasha as well as for her older sister, Lauren, who thought that her arrival had been specially arranged for her own birthday the following day. It had not been an easy pregnancy, but thankfully Morgan was born a bouncy, healthy baby. Her arrival meant that I now had to motivate myself to find work. The truth is, however, I had no idea what I wanted to do, except something that I would enjoy and would support the family at the same time.

I got a sales job selling CCTV and security systems, which I gave my best shot but at the same time discovered I am not a salesman. So I moved to the printing firm where Natasha worked and became their warehouse manager. This suited our situation, as we could travel to work together and drop Morgan off with Natasha's friend Donna or her sister Sam, who had agreed to look after her. Initially I was happy at the printers, but after a few months I had not been offered the opportunities I had been promised and, when my current position looked threatened due to the loss of a large contract, Natasha and I decided I should leave.

Natasha was earning a fairly good wage, so we thought it would be a good idea for me to sign on and stay at home to look after Morgan. In reality this seemingly sensible move was to destroy our relationship due to my feeling depressed the longer I was out of work. At this time I also made contact with Charlie, who had just published his own book Silent Scream, and I became involved with many of his friends and supporters. Suffice to say for the present, the details of my life since leaving the Service have been eventful and emotional and would be best told as a separate story.

I reached an all-time low in my life for a period, as I didn't even no where I was going to live let alone get a secure job to build a new life for me and my girls. I worked for a time as a labourer with my old mate Simon and then, when made redundant, I took another printing job that Natasha helped me find. Nothing I did, however, really appealed to me or struck me as something on which I could build a career.

However, just when I was beginning to wonder if I would ever get my life back on track, a friend I had made, who was a director in his own family's tanker business, came to my rescue and offered me a job in his firm. I have worked for them for the past year and really enjoy it. They also put me through my heavy goods licence training, which is something I had wanted to do but could not afford to pay for myself. Once again, the full details of my new job are best kept for another day, just like my involvement with Charlie since leaving the Prison Service.

My life is not fully back on track, but for the first time in almost two years the future looks brighter than ever. Who knows what it will hold, but I just hope that I am able to continue to enjoy life and provide for my family as best I can. I am sure I will continue to help Charlie in any way possible and will let you know how I get on, but for now I have said all I can. I will leave you with the favourite phrase of my old pal, which everyone should remember throughout their lives:

"ITS NICE TO BE NICE."

17
EPILOGUE

As I have already mentioned, this book has taken almost six years for me to complete for various reasons. As a result of this, some of the events that have occurred over the last couple of years have not been recorded. The main one in the recent past to have affected me personally is the sad passing away of my grandparents. Due to the rift in my relations with my immediate family, I felt unable to attend the funerals, and this is something that has tormented my conscience ever since. I did, however, manage to send flowers, and my thoughts are always filled with memories of the wonderful contribution they made to my life.

My own life collapsed around me four or five years ago when, after a period of unemployment that left me growing increasingly depressed and introverted, Natasha and I split up. Not for the first time in my life, I once again felt all alone and rejected: Jim against the world. How did I deal with this sudden isolation? Yes, you guessed it, my old nemesis - lager. With nowhere to live and no family to fall back on, I took shelter in my local pub, The Crispin, and began a two-year mission of self-destruction by drinking to block out the reality of my situation. The landlord and landlady, Peter and Alli put me up in the recently converted cellar in a room with no windows and just enough space for a single bed. It was my own prison cell, although smaller than your average cell and with less furniture and no ventilation, and with access via the men's toilets.

It was as if the previous 15 years or so of my life had been eradicated, as once again I found myself alone in my box with nothing more than a small bag of clothes and alcohol-soaked memories of the life I once had with Natasha, Lauren and Morgan. I felt anger and frustration at not being able to deal with my situation, and so I shut out everything that was too painful to deal with. I found it difficult to socialize with anyone unless I had had a drink, after which I felt people accepted me and thought I was hilarious.

Consequently, I drank more and more, and the more I became accepted by my new social circle of 'friends' in the pub, the more I turned my back on Natasha, Lauren and Morgan and Natasha's family. I wasn't eating, sleeping or even bothering too much about personal hygiene. Instead, I was drinking heavily every day and becoming even more bitter and resentful. I now believe I was slipping into a period of mental illness.

Looking back at that period of my life now, I can see some distinct similarities between my own position and that of Charlie and other prisoners within the prison system. I rarely left the pub, apart from when I had to drag myself to work to pay my rent and bar tab. When I could drink no more, or Peter insisted on shutting the bar, I returned to my 'cell' through the men's toilet, where I was locked until the bar opened again. The pub became my prison and the bar my period of association. I was again becoming institutionalized, as I had to a certain extent been in the Army and Prison Service, and in much the same way that the prison system has institutionalized Charlie. I even received the odd 'visit' when Geoff, my father-in-law, came in for a pint. He would try to tell me how I was destroying my life but, of course, I didn't listen, and instead just joined the other 'inmates', i.e. drinkers in the pub, in slagging him off for trying to tell me how to live my life. I was slipping further and further from reality, and I was becoming more and more paranoid, angry, bitter and aggressive.

I soon began to feel I was invincible, and after a few months I started to venture out with one or two of the lads to some of the other pubs in town. It wasn't long before I became accepted in most of them. People would recognize me when I entered, and this gave me a certain feeling of status that I lacked in my sober life. I began to feel like I was becoming quite a 'face' around the town's social scene. It felt like I was being given respect and admiration - something I thought I had never received before. In my mental state I had forgotten all my early lessons in life from Max Bygraves and others like him. I felt like the hardest man in town and had totally turned my back on Natasha and the girls. However, after living this life for a year or so, those early lessons would come back to me rather abruptly and painfully only too soon, on one cold early Sunday evening in

November 2000.

I had been drinking all day as usual, and had already visited one or two pubs when I went into a pub with a notorious reputation for violence. I went to the bar to order my second pint, and while I waited for it to be poured one of a group of lads sitting at the bar said to me, "You're that gobby cunt that knocks about with that lot from The Crispin, ain't you?" I looked at him and in typical drunken arrogance replied with a smirk, "No, not me mate. You must have the wrong bloke, you muppet". I collected my pint and returned to my table feeling good about how I had dealt with the wanker at the bar. I finished my pint and left the pub alone to walk back to The Crispin, but as I walked past the pub car park I received a heavy blow to the back of my head, which sent me crashing to the floor in a semi-conscious state. For the next few minutes, I was aware of three or four sets of boots raining shattering blows on my head and body. I tasted blood in my mouth after one or two blows got past my arms, which I had wrapped around my face and head. I felt nauseous as other blows connected with my ribs and abdomen. I could do nothing but adopt a foetal position and hope my attackers would soon get bored or someone would intervene and distract them long enough for me to get up and try to defend myself. Unfortunately this didn't happen, and I lay there for what seemed like an eternity thinking I was going to be kicked to death. I remember an extra vicious blow to the side of my head and then the lights went out. I woke up still lying on the pavement in extreme pain and spitting out blood, with somebody asking me if I was okay. I felt like saying, "Do I look fucking okay?", but remembered how opening my mouth without thinking had got me into this mess, so I replied, "Yes, I think so".

I then staggered back to The Crispin and ordered a pint. However, the look on Peter's face told me I was more seriously injured than I thought. He told me I needed to go to hospital and advised me to go and look at myself in the mirror. What I saw staring back at me nearly made me fall on the floor again. I looked like the Elephant Man: my head had swollen to almost twice its size, my eyes were blood red and my face was covered in bright red marks from the boots and trainers that had connected with it. I could see my left eye and cheekbone were closing up, and my left forearm had swollen to the size of my thigh as this had obviously blocked many of the kicks. "Remember, there is always someone harder than you around the corner", I said in my head as Max Bygraves' words of wisdom came back to me after 15 years.

No one in the pub was obviously going to volunteer to take me to hospital. In fact none of my so-called mates even offered to call me a cab. So, as if the blows to my head had flicked a switch in my memory circuit, I went to a place I knew I could get help: I went home, where Natasha still lived with Morgan. By rights she didn't even have to open the door to me after the way I had treated her and ignored her and Morgan over the past year, let alone take me to hospital, but take me she did. After a few hours of waiting for treatment and X-rays, I was amazed to find that I hadn't suffered any broken bones as the doctor had first suspected, and I was allowed to leave with some painkillers.

This was the wake-up call I needed, albeit it a painful one. I realized that I had to sort myself out and get my life back before I ended up dead in a gutter somewhere. Over the following year, I faced one of the hardest uphill struggles of my life. I began by securing myself a job with a local waste-tanker firm. The money was good, but the hours were very long and sometimes I wouldn't get home all week. This benefited me for two reasons: one, it kept me out of the pub and so aided my battle away from the drink that was making me so ill; and two, it provided me with a good enough wage to be able to start taking Natasha out for nice meals and treat Morgan to days out at the weekend.

At around this time, I felt ready to try to make contact with Lauren again, whom I had not seen for the best part of a year due to my state of mind and personal predicament. Quite understandably this took some time to arrange, as Jackie obviously had concerns about Lauren's welfare following my lack of commitment. Slowly but surely, however, everything began to fall back into place, as I clawed my way out of the seemingly bottomless black hole that had been my life.

I threw myself into work and, after a few months had passed, my HGV training was starting to earn me some good money. I had begun to see Lauren again and was spending more time with Natasha and Morgan. It was not long before we began to have Lauren to stay again at the weekends. We have come a long way in the last three years or so and, even though we have had a number of setbacks, we are still together and our future now looks good.

I have kept in touch with Charlie over the period since leaving the Prison Service, and attended his hostage trial at Luton Crown Court and his subsequent appeal at the Old Bailey. I was happy to provide evidence about his treatment and also a character reference based on my dealings with him, but I was not allowed to present them on either occasion. I really feel that had I been given the opportunity to speak I might have been able to help change the jury's opinion of the man. I have been privileged to be involved in a number of social and media events concerning Charlie, and as a result I have met many interesting characters along the way. I have finally, after some five years and three or four attempts, been cleared by the Home Office to visit Charlie in prison. The enquiries I made with the local police as to the reasons for my previous applications being refused were non-conclusive, as they said there was no problem at their end. It would appear that it was the Home Office that was blocking my application, although when I wrote to query the reasons for this I was given the standard reply: "It is not Home Office policy to discuss the reasons why a person is refused Category A visiting rights". I have made a few visits since finally being cleared in the early part of 2006, but it still saddens me to see the conditions in which the Prison Service still insists on keeping my old friend. Charlie is now 55 years old and is still being subjected to closed visits even with his own mother, to whom he cannot even give a hug when she goes to see him. This is in a prison that holds some of the most infamous convicted sex-crime perpetrators and child murderers. Even that rat Ian Huntley can be seen in the main visiting hall on occasions, cuddling and laughing and joking with teenage kids, as you are escorted through to where Charlie is still being held in solitary confinement. How can that be allowed when Charlie, who has NEVER killed anyone, can't even give his own mother a kiss? Charlie knows that he will always have my support and that I will always be available if he ever needs my help, and I am sure it will not be very long before the Prison Service has to admit its failings and release Charlie - and let me tell you, that will be some party, so I hope to see you all there soon.

As for the other people mentioned in the book, I have lost touch with most of them over the years. I still see Harry, who is currently working as a mechanic for Vauxhall, and Gary Thompson, who is still in the Army but will come to the end of his 20 years' service in the next couple of years. He is currently training to become a paramedic in preparation for his release. I see Simon every now and again, who is still happy with Sharon and they now have two lovely little girls, Rachel and Courtney. Occasionally I am in touch with Tim Marsh, Wayne Smith and a few other lads from the Green Jackets via the phone or email.

So what does the future hold for me? Well, Natasha gave birth to our beautiful new baby boy Thomas on 12 November 2006, so with Lauren, Morgan and now Thomas our lives will be pretty much occupied with the joys of trying to provide for their needs and enjoying watching them grow up; that precious time does not last very long, as I am sure all you parents will agree. I have a few ideas, but my main ambition now is never to fall back into the mental hell I found myself in when I was drinking, not least for Natasha and the children's sake, as they deserve much more from me. We have recently moved into a nice house, which we are slowly transforming to our taste. I have also recently started my own business in locksmithing, as I was growing tired of working for other people and decided to have a go at working for myself. I just want to continue to support my family as best I can, give them a good life and never let them down as I have in the past, as it is them I have to thank for supporting me through all the bad times when most people would have just left me to destroy myself.

I have been fortunate enough to have made some very good friends both through writing this book and as a result of my support for Charlie, not least Dave Courtney, who has very kindly offered to include me in a number of his projects. We are planning to do a joint tour, which will include book signings for various charities for which Dave is a patron, and he also wants to involve me in his very unique 'An Audience With' shows, which he performs at venues throughout the UK. For anyone reading this who has not been to one of these shows, I would urge you to look out for one and go along, as Dave's unique brand of humour and very open and honest views on his past experiences of the London underworld make it a highly enjoyable and entertaining evening. I never tire of listening to Dave's stories when he is on stage and thoroughly enjoy being part of the show. A line that always raises a laugh when I join Dave on stage during the show is when Dave says: "Hello, the last time I saw you you were hitting me on the head with your truncheon". If someone had said to me ten years ago that I would be enjoying games of pool at Camelot Castle (Dave's home) or joining him and people like Roy 'Pretty Boy' Shaw at book signings or other such events, I would have told them they were mad. But that is exactly what I do now, and it just goes to show that it does not matter what you do or did for a living so long as you treat people with a bit of respect and carry out the job you do conscientiously; then people will treat you the same in return. Dave tells me he has great plans for the future in relation to my joining him in various media and social events, so watch this space.

Life hasn't always been easy, not least because I believe I was institution-alized at an early stage in the Army. It has taken me a long time to realize that you don't get anything for nothing in this life and the only way to get where or what you want is to work for it or at it. Natasha and I are very happy, and I have two great girls and a new baby boy who are all growing up fast. At the time of writing this, it has been 21 years to the day since I first joined the Army, even though it seems like only yesterday. I am looking forward to the next 20 years, as I feel confident that life will continue to get better. I am now living for the long-term future and am fully aware of my responsibilities as a father. This is something I had struggled with over the years when trying to overcome my own insecurities, problems with alcohol, depression and feelings of low self-esteem. I hope you have enjoyed the read and are now a little wiser as to what can, and indeed does, go on behind the closed doors of our prisons. I also hope that there is someone reading this who is in a position to make the difference I felt I could not during my time in the Prison Service. So, with that in mind, I will leave you with this thought and urge you to remember to enjoy life to the full and be nice to each other, as only you can make a difference in your life. To quote a great saying from my pal Dave Courtney :

"IT'S NICE TO BE IMPORTANT, BUT IT'S IMPORTANT TO BE NICE"

THE AUTHOR - JIM DAWKINS

Harlow-born Jim Dawkins left home in Eltham at the age of sixteen to pursue a career in the army and served with the Royal Green Jackets from 1985 to 1991, including tours of Canada and Northern Ireland. Upon leaving the army, he joined the Prison Service and spent the next seven years training and working in Wandsworth, Wormwood Scrubs and Belmarsh prisons. In 1999, Jim left the Prison Service, ill with stress and disillusioned by the abuse levelled out to inmates by many of the staff. Jim eventually settled down with his childhood sweetheart, Natasha, and has two daughters, Lauren and Morgan and a son, Thomas. One of Jim's goals in life is to fight for the rights of long-term high-security inmate, Charlie Bronson, with whom he has struck up a remarkable friendship. He wants the prison service to pull itself out of the Victorian mentality and give Charlie the chance he deserves to work towards his release and lead the normal life he yearns for.

"I'm not known for admiring prison officers but Jim is very different. It takes a hell of a lot of courage to turn your back on a mob when you are on your own but that's exactly what Jim did. He earned the respect of prisoners by treating them with respect. Some of them make life hard for themselves by treating the chaps like shit. If you show my mate Charlie Bronson respect he will show you it back, treat him like shit and he will destroy you! I admire Jim for taking a stand for what's right no matter what the others say. Lets hope we see Charlie out here soon ... I know Jim will be invited to the coming home party!"

- Roy Shaw

"The courage it took to write this book should not be underestimated. The will to turn your back on the sheep of corruption and join the lions to hunt only for the truth and what's right is inspiring. This book slashes through the anti Bronson propaganda to bring you the real man... Not the media made myth. Many of you I'm sure will have swallowed the bait and the hook and decided that Charles Bronson is a violent lunatic who kills people for fun (He has NEVER killed!), Jim will tell you Charlie is none of those things... And he's right. You see, Jim has one big advantage over those who believe all the hype... He actually KNOWS the man! Here's the true story from the inside out... NOT the outside in." - **Tel Currie**

"As a former high risk double category A prisoner who served a decade in the British Prisons during the tumultuous mid-1980s to 1990s, and also a recent spell on remand in the High Security Unit at Belmarsh prison. There is very little anyone can tell me about our disgraceful prison system. Like the author, I have witnessed the persecution, brutalization, alienation and even suicide of fellow prisoners. I have met remarkably humanitarian and truly evil screws. Nonetheless, I have never met a screw like Jim Dawkins who was prepared to "unlock" and let us stroll down the landings of his mind and experience the daily moral conflict of being a good man in an uncomfortable blue tunic. One can only admire and respect the strength and courage it took to write this book. It was so easy for Jim to have gone with the grain and become another tea-room cynic and pocketed his pay slip at the end of the month; it was so easy for Jim to have got blood on his boots while no one was looking. This is more than a book about a disgruntled prison officer; this is a book that should become essential reading for everyone who has an interest in crime and the criminal justice system. This book that will be read in a thousand years time." - **Terry Smith**

"I enjoyed reading the book as it brought back a lot of memories and incidents that I was involved in." - **Nosher Powell**

"Generally I would never read a book written by a screw or an ex-screw, but Jim Dawkins is a very down to earth and truthful man. He believes in Charlie Bronson like a brother, and is doing his very best to help his appeal. This book is very good and unveils a lot of prison secrets, told by a man who saw the wrong doings. I spent a long time myself on the Category A unit in HMP Belmarsh so I know it is the truth. If you want to know the truth behind our prisons then you must read this book!" - **Joe Pyle**

A GEM OF A SCREW AND A DIAMOND GEEZER! "On a personal level and having been privileged to have met Jim Dawkins on many occasions over the years, it must be said that he has most certainly earned respect in and amongst some of Britain's most hardened inner circles for having been prepared to rightfully slag off and blow the lid on an always politically protected Home Office Prison establishment hierarchy and secret society. All Jim has done with his book and his revelations is to expose the shocking truth of what regularly happens on a daily basis behind closed doors. He has always and rightfully so, stood firm and can still be relied upon 200% as a fearless key witness in support of the release of disgracefully treated and shamefully incarcerated great man himself – Charlie Bronson. I was there at the Old Bailey High Court hearing in London at Charlie's appeal. Jim Dawkins was there ready to stand in the dock and give evidence in support of Charlie's case against the 'seemingly always unblemished prison establishment'. Sadly the court would not allow him to give evidence against the Home Office – I wonder why? I wish him well with the book!"
- Andy Jones, Owner and Creator of 'The Crime Through Time Museum'

"I can remember the last time I read a book as powerful as Loose Screw. It was in 1992. It will probably be over a decade before I read another."
- Mike Hallowell, The Sheilds Gazette

"When I saw Razor Smith's write-up in 'Inside Time' on 'The Loose Screw' I thought this is a first! Ordered it straight away and posted a message on my website to let other prisoners wives and families know that at last a screw has spoken out and is telling the truth! As the wife of a man serving life, my knowledge of the REAL system is very limited, there has only been rumours of prison officers brutality, lies and corruption, until now.
The powers that be have always done a thorough job of papering over the cracks, brushing under the carpet and concealing any incriminating evidence against themselves. Jim Dawkins book is like a breath of fresh air, he has opened my eyes to many injustices that are everyday occurances in our prison system. I commend him for his honesty and bravery in being the screw to unlock this box of secrets. Well done Jim."
- www.prisonchatuk.com